A comparative study
of referendums

Manchester University Press

[G]overnment of the people, by the people, for the people shall not perish from the earth.   (Abraham Lincoln, Gettysburg Address)

[T]he referendum raises many problems about the nature and form of democratic government. Here we enter a field of political theory that has been much debated and where many issues still remain unsolved.   (Jan-Erik Lane, *Constitutions and Political Theory*, p. 131)

A comparative study of referendums

Government by the people
second edition

MATT QVORTRUP

MANCHESTER UNIVERSITY PRESS
Manchester and New York

distributed exclusively in the USA by Palgrave

First edition published 2002 by Manchester University Press

This edition published 2005 by
Manchester University Press
Oxford Road, Manchester M13 9NR, UK
and Room 400, 175 Fifth Avenue, New York, NY 10010, USA
www.manchesteruniversitypress.co.uk

Distributed exclusively in the USA by
Palgrave, 175 Fifth Avenue, New York,
NY 10010, USA

Distributed exclusively in Canada by
UBC Press, University of British Columbia, 2029 West Mall,
Vancouver, BC, Canada V6T 1Z2

British Library Cataloguing-in-Publication Data
A catalogue record for this book is available from the British Library

Library of Congress Cataloging-in-Publication Data applied for

ISBN   0 7190 7180 1 *hardback*
EAN   978 0 7190 7180 5
ISBN   0 7190 7181 X *paperback*
EAN   978 0 7190 7181 2

This edition first published 2005

14 13 12 11 10 09 08 07 06 05   10 9 8 7 6 5 4 3 2 1

Typeset in Palatino with Frutiger
by Servis Filmsetting Ltd, Manchester, UK
Printed in Great Britain
by Bell & Bain Ltd, Glasgow

Contents

List of figures, tables and boxes

Figures

Tables

Boxes

Acknowledgements

This book would not have been written without the help of numerous others, foremost among whom are: Ted Becker, Vernon Bogdanor, David Butler, Oonagh Gay, Alex Hickman, Bruno Kaufman, Bill Kissane, Arend Lijphart, Yasmin Mayohas, Laurence Morel, Brendan O'Leary, Quintin Oliver, Rick Ridder, Nigel Smith, Gary Sussman, Dane Waters and members of my family. Errors are my own.

I dedicate this book to Anne, Rome and ice cream.

Introduction to the first edition: should we have more referendums?

> In the last resort, the arguments against the referendum are also arguments against democracy, while acceptance of the referendum is but the logical consequence of accepting the democratic form of government. (Bogdanor 1981, 93)

Democracy means government by the people. Yet in all countries the role of the citizen is limited to periodic general elections and occasional referendums, especially in the UK where until recently *parliamentary sovereignty* was an article of faith.[1] This perception has changed in recent years, with the Labour Government holding several referendums on issues ranging from devolution to the European constitution. This use of referendums is not, however, unique to the UK: at the time of writing, the Netherlands, a country that has hitherto *never* held a nationwide referendum, is to hold one on the European Constitution.

Indeed, almost all European countries are moving towards a greater use of referendums (Belgium seems to be the only exception). Should we endorse this trend or should we condemn it as populism? Should the role of the citizen be increased, and, if so, how should it be increased? This book seeks to provide answers to these questions, using the methods of comparative political science.

Approximately 70 per cent of the world's countries have provisions for the holding of referendums, provisions that are not mere relics of long-forgotten commitments to the ideals of participatory democracy known from Athens. More than 98 per cent of the world's countries have held referendums, and provisions for referendums have in different forms been included in *all* the new constitutions in the new democracies in Eastern and Central Europe. Countries which previously have not held referendums have resorted to this device in recent years, the UK being a case in point. Until the 1970s referendums were considered to be unconstitutional as they were inconsistent with the dogma of the sovereignty of Parliament. This debate has completely vanished; the question is no longer whether referendums are constitutional, but rather whether some issues rather than others should he submitted to referendums.

Referendums are rare (except in Switzerland, Italy and half of the USA), and only very few countries hold more than one referendum per electoral cycle. Despite their infrequency, in terms of their implications and the publicity they generate referendums are important. Consider, for example, the Danish Euro referendum in June 1992. Following a national debate (and more than 1,300 newspaper articles), a narrow majority of 50.1 per cent of the Danish voters rejected the Maastricht Treaty, which was endorsed by all the major political parties in Denmark. The rejection forced European governments to rethink the project of European federalisation, arguably altering the course of the process of European integration. The question is should we endorse the use of an institutional device which allows the citizenry to undercut its elected representatives?

Answers to these questions require us to test the device's processes against a set of criteria which all democratic systems must meet. Moreover, outline why it is necessary to submit issues to referendums, and we must show how and when these criteria can be made workable in practical politics.

This book is based on the assumption that, as a minimum, all democratic institutions must meet three criteria:

- *equal participation*: all groups and classes must have an equal influence on the result;
- *enlightened participation*: all individuals must have a basic understanding of the issues;
- *minority protection*: no referendum may threaten recognised civil and political rights. (Dahl 1982, 6)

The extent, to which a democratic process, as defined by these criteria, is a good polity, or even the best political system, is a question I touch on only briefly in the book.[2] I simply assume that an institution that is consistent with these criteria is democratically acceptable.

Another and far greater problem is whether it is possible on the basis of comparisons to draw conclusions as to the desirability of referendums. John Stuart Mill noted that if the findings in one country are 'not adequately compared with other instances nothing is more probable than a wrong empirical law will emerge instead of a right one' (Mill 1973, 917). A study that purports to identify recurrent effects of referendums must take as its point of departure the acknowledgement that some polities are comparable. Or, as Morsei Ostrogorski once wrote,

> the variety of national characters and historical accidents ought not to be ignored, but the traits common to different countries predominate in existing civilisations, where political institutions are nearly everywhere framed on the same model, where social conditions produced by economic evolution are the same, and where men and women are subject to similar influences and move on parallel lines. (Ostrogorski quoted in Barker and Howard-Johnson 1975, 427)

It is these latter conditions that are important in comparative political science. It is difficult to draw conclusions regarding the consequences and effects of institutions if the background variables differ. 'Comparative politics', argues B. Guy Peters, involves the development of theories 'explaining behaviour within groups of countries which are essentially similar' (Peters 1998, 37) This *most similar systems approach* cannot guarantee that a discerned pattern is indisputable: politics is not an exact science. We have to accept that 'the status of statements about the impact of institutions is not causally determinative (A causes B), but probabilistic (A tends to be associated with B)' (Stepan and Skach 1994, 128). We cannot *prove* that referendums in, say, Britain would be consistent with the normative ideals just because referendums in comparable countries have proved to be compatible with those ideals, but that consistency does seem probable if we can identify common effects of referendums in the latter polities. These findings will enable us to decide whether or not the use of referendums should be advocated. The comparative method is not foolproof panacea, but it is the best available method of evaluating the effects of institutions.

This book answers a normative question: when, if at all, should citizens be allowed to vote on public policies?

In chapter 1, case studies are used to determine when the referendum is compatible with the ideals of minority protection and enlightened and equal participation. That referendums (under certain conditions) can be compatible with the criteria of democracy (as defined above) does not, however, imply that we ought to have more referendums. To draw that conclusion we must first develop a case for the referendum, i.e. a justification of why we should depart from the (relatively) efficient system of representative government.

Chapter 2 outlines the political theory of the referendum as developed by the constitutional lawyer A. V. Dicey (perhaps the only theoretician to develop a theory of the referendum). According to Dicey, the referendum is to be seen as an alternative to other democratic checks on the executive, a people's safeguard against encroachments by the elected representatives. Dicey argued that the introduction of the referendum would strengthen representative government, as the elected politicians would be more susceptible to the views of the citizens if the fate of controversial laws ultimately depended on the consent of the majority of the voters. Dicey therefore made a case for obligatory referendums on constitutional issues.

One drawback of this theory is, however, the possibility that the electorate will vote indiscriminately against all measures proposed by Parliament. As Sir Henry Sumner Maine wrote in 1890, 'The prejudices of the people are far stronger than those of the privileged classes; they are far more vulgar; and they are far more dangerous because they are apt to run counter to scientific conclusion' (1976, 87). Chapter 3 tests this theory of the *reactionary electorate* through case studies of referendums in different categories in a number of countries.

Chapter 4 considers whether Dicey's theory is a sufficient constitutional safeguard or whether the introduction of obligatory referendums is necessary. I survey the effects of Diceyan referendums in selected countries, as well as briefly considering the recent British debates on the use of referendums; additionally, a case study of the Irish referendum is added to the second edition. In the latter part of the chapter, the British political parties' motives for resorting to referendums are considered.

Chapter 5 considers two alternative referendum models: respectively, the *minority veto* (which allows a minority in Parliament to demand a referendum on a law passed by the Government) and the *popular referendum* (which allows a specified number of citizens to demand a referendum on a law already enacted). Using the previous findings I discuss whether these provisions are more likely to be consistent with the Diceyan ideal of the referendum than is his own proposal.

Chapter 6 concludes the book and presents a number of proposals for practical reforms.

Note

1 Interested readers can consult my book *The Political Philosophy of Jean-Jacques Rousseau: The Impossibility of Reason* (Manchester: Manchester University Press, 2003).

Introduction to the second edition: Bruno and the army

Here's a true story – and an odd one at that. Bruno, like so many of his generation, was a pacifist. He could not see the reason for military spending and found the very idea of learning to kill positively nauseating. But Bruno was Swiss – and, therefore, he had no choice but to serve in the army. Now, Bruno could run away or opt for a prison sentence. Neither option appealed to him, so he decided to get the army abolished.

Was his decision an act of lunacy? Was he ready to retire to Bedlam? Not at all – at least, not in Switzerland. For in the small alpine republic the citizens enjoy the privilege of proposing amendments and changes to the constitution provided that they can gather signatures from 100,000 people. Being a man of initiative, Bruno did not procrastinate, and a year later, in 1987, the Swiss voters were asked in a referendum if they wanted to abolish the army. Bruno's proposed constitutional change was voted for by 40.6 per cent of the electorate. Bruno, it would seem, was unsuccessful. But the story does not end here. The Swiss Government, being comprised, on this occasion, of a sensible lot, got the message: enthusiasm for conscription was waning, and so the Government introduced the option of a *Zivildienst* (non-military conscription for conscientious objectors).

The story of Bruno is a unique one. Not many people have the tenacity of purpose of Bruno Kaufmann – and not many countries have provisions for direct democracy as radical as does Switzerland (New Zealand and California being other examples). But for all its uniqueness, the tale of Bruno shows that referendums can have real policy effects, effects indeed that encourage and facilitate moderation and consensus politics.

There are, it is true, other examples that point in a different direction, i.e. referendums which have had unfortunate consequences for minority groups, proposition 189, a Californian ballot initiative aimed at the withdrawal of all non-emergency health care from illegal immigrants, being a case in point.

This book is neither an apologia nor a critique. Its aim is to review the consequences of the use of the referendum in modern democracies. More often than not, discussions about referendums are simplistic, lacking in nuances, and tend to be based on insufficient evidence. Proponents of referendums – and other kinds of direct democracy – tend to regard increased citizen participation as a goal in itself and, occasionally, as a panacea capable of resolving all the ills of society. On the other hand opponents of referendums, no less simplistic in their outlook, tend to regard referendums as undemocratic – a 'fact' which they 'prove' by reference to Hitler and Napoleon's enthusiasm for letting voters support decisions already made by their dictators.

Certainly the referendum can be abused in countries not based on the principles of the *rechtsstaat*, though it is to be doubted that any practices are worthy of the adjective 'democratic' if they are not conducted in accordance with the principles of the rule of law. To determine if, or when, referendums are desirable the record must be analysed dispassionately. We have to determine whether the voters are capable of deciding on the complex issues presented, whether a referendum leads to minority oppression and whether all sections of a society are offered a chance to participate. This will be done below.

As is perhaps inevitable for a book on a controversial topic, this one has received its fair share of criticism – and occasional praise. It is an honour to have one's work criticised: it shows that people take it seriously. It is, however, beyond the scope of this brief introduction to offer a reply to my critics. Suffice it to say that preparing the second edition I have sought to learn from them and improve on my argument. To that end, I have added appendices on the regulation of referendums, the effect of campaign spending and qualified majority requirements. In addition I have up-dated the tables, some of the case studies, and in many places rewritten the text. Substantially, however, the argument and the conclusions are the same.

The distinguished writer Simon Hug has criticised my approach for being too qualitative. I have no intention of countering his claim. While he and others seek to present theoretical arguments in mathematical clothing, I maintain that political science is best understood as a *moral* science, and that, while not discarding quantitative approaches, political phenomena are best studied using the methods of the humanities – in particular, those of history. Interested readers might consult my article 'In Search of Lost Time' (Qvortrup 2004), in which I present a manifesto-like defence for my approach to the science of politics.

I am conscious that no book can resolve all of the pertinent issues. I fundamentally agree with the late Robert Nozick's dictum that 'there are other words on subjects than last words'.

July 2004

1

The referendum and the ideal of consensus government

We are democrats, not because the majority is always right, but
because democratic traditions are the least evil we know. If the majority (or 'public opinion') decides in favour of tyranny, a democrat need
not therefore suppose that some fatal inconsistency in his views has
been revealed. He will realise, rather, that the democratic tradition in
his country was not strong enough. (Popper 1963, 351)

'Most objections to direct democracy are, when you look closely,
objections to democracy' (*Economist*, December 1996). This view has
led to the conclusion that referendums, and hence democracy, can
justify enactments even if they discriminate against minorities. US
Supreme Court Justice Harlan expressed this view in *Hunter* v.
Ericson, asserting that the referendum is 'grounded in neutral principles [although it] might occasionally operate to disadvantage negro
political interests' (Bell 1978, 7). This position is as untenable as the
argument is compelling. It can be sustained only if we accept the view
that democracy is a method for deciding issues by majority voting.

In his famous Funeral Oration, as recalled by Thucydides (1954,
102), Pericles noted that Athens' system of government 'favours the
many instead of the few; this is why it is called a democracy' Given
our veneration of the ancient Greeks, it is perhaps not surprising that
it has been the view of much Anglo-American political thinking that
a system of majority voting is the hallmark of a democratic system
of government (Riker 1982). True, James Madison did acknowledge
the dangers inherent in this system of government, and he developed ingenious solutions to prevent majority rule from degenerat-
ing into an oppression of minorities (Madison, Hamilton and Jay
1987, 122).

Yet neither of these solutions has provided democracies with a tool against the perplexities which nationalism and religious intolerance pose. This definition of democracy does not provide us with an argument against the plebiscites organised by Adolf Hitler (Zucher 1935, 91); indeed, the definition implies that the Hitler plebiscites were democratic!

There is, however, another definition of democracy which emphasises that democracy is more than plain majority rule. 'What is democracy?' asked the great Czech statesman and philosopher Thomas Masaryk. He provided the answer himself by saying that 'democracy is discussion' (quoted in Warren 1941, 34). This simple definition was subsequently elaborated by the Danish theorist Hal Koch in *Hvad Er Demokrati?* (1992, 22).

> The essence of democracy is not the vote but the discussion. The vote is assuredly an integral part of democratic decision-making. When the matter has been fully discussed, then a vote must be taken. For it is the vote which shows if the discussion has been fruitful. What is undemocratic is the fruitless debate where neither side listens with an open mind.

Therefore, democracy is rather an attitude towards other people, which is based on a mutual respect for the views of others; an attitude which is based on a willingness to test the strength of our ideological and political convictions in a free debate. The precondition of democracy is ultimately a willingness to engage in discussion, because we acknowledge that our own views offer only a part of a solution. As Masaryk put it, 'Democracy is a *Weltanschaung* and a way of life', one which hinges on respect for the rights of other individuals, as well as a recognition of their views (quoted in Szporluk 1981, 72). It was perhaps this *Weltanschaung* that John Stuart Mill had in mind when he noted that 'one of the most indispensable requisites in the practical conduct of politics is conciliation: a readiness to compromise; a willingness to concede something to opponents, and to shape good measures so as to be as little offensive as possible to persons of opposite views' (1991, 385).

This understanding of democracy has usually led theoreticians and practitioners to the conclusion that representative democracy must be the norm and that referendums are to be avoided as a pure direct democracy, a system that allows voters to vote only 'yes' or 'no', would institutionalise majoritarianism and consequently be inimical to the ideal of democracy as discussion.

Yet referendums cannot be likened to direct democracy as this was practised in ancient Athens, the New England town meetings or in the Swiss *Landesgemeinden* (local referendums). Referendums, initiatives (votes initiated by the citizenry) and recalls (public votes of confidence in an elected politician) are not necessarily alternatives to representative government. The referendum is rather a supplement to indirect democracy (Malberg 1931, 256), 'a mechanism which allow the voters to bypass the political parties without necessarily undermining the system of representative government' *(ibid.)*.

A proponent of referendums can easily accommodate his or her view to Mill's argument against a complete direct participatory democracy, namely that 'since all cannot participate personally in any but some very minor portions of public business it follows that the ideal type of a perfect government must be representative' (Mill 1991, 385); indeed it might even be argued that a referendum is a necessary complement to representative democracy which fails to recognise the advent of party government and the influence of organised interest groups. Much has changed in the way that representative government works. Burke had told his electors: 'Your representative owes you not his industry alone but his judgement; and he betrays, instead of serving, you if he sacrifices it to your opinion' (1902, 447).

This description is no longer accurate – if, indeed, it ever was; moreover, it is open to question whether this elitist conception of democracy prohibits the use of referendums as a *supplement* to or a *corrective* of representative democracy. This argument carries little weight if the legislator falls prey to organised interest groups, big business or a three-line whip. Buchanan and Tullock (1962, 283) summed up the latter danger in a paragraph which still seems to be accurate:

> In the face of observable pressure-group activity with its demonstrable results on the outcome of specific issues presented and debated in legislative assemblies, that behavioural premise that calls the legislator to follow a selfless pursuit of the 'public interest' or the 'general welfare' as something independent of and apart from private economic interest is severely threatened.

It was in recognition of the unanticipated influence of interest groups, big business and the 'party machine' on the process of representative government that the US populists propagated the introduction of the referendum and the initiative in order to check the party machine and organised interest groups. The populists introduced the referendum not as an alternative to representative government, but as a means of improving indirect democracy and, indeed, as a conservative check on the legislatures (Cree 1892). The reformers were not intent on radical change; nor did they intend to undermine representative government. They supported the referendum simply because the legislatures had not lived up to the ideal described by the founding fathers of the republic. The referendum was not linked to the ideals of ancient Athens, the New England town meetings, the Swiss *Landesgemeinden* or radical theories of participatory democracy of the kind which (many years later) have been championed by radicals (Pateman 1970). Referendums were not seen as alternatives to representative government, but are rather supplements to indirect democracy. Woodrow Wilson emphasised:

> It must be remembered that we are contrasting the operation of the initiative and the referendum, not with the representative government which we possess in theory and which we have long persuaded ourselves that we possess in fact, but with the actual state of affairs, with legislative processes which are carried out in secret, responding to the impulse of subsidised machines, and carried through by men whose unhappiness it is to realise that they are not their own masters, but puppets in the game. (Quoted in Munro 1912, 134).

This defence of direct democracy does not imply that all populists were blind to possible defects of referendums. The dangers of direct democracy *were* perceived: J. Holman thus warned that low participation would permit a small percentage of citizens to pass legislation through initiatives' (Holman in *ibid.*, 14). Yet most populists believed that the referendum was a panacea which would encourage political interest and improve the quality of government (Cree 1892).

These views were recognised by such early twentieth-century European scholars as Dicey, Lecky and Hobson, to name but three. Most theorists, however, rejected the idea of the referendum for the simple reason that it was incompatible with the notion of consensus government, incompatible, that is, with the ideal that democracy is a *Weltanschaung* based on a willingness to seek compromise solutions through a process of discursive deliberation. Max Weber thus argued that 'the referendum knows nothing of the compromise on which the majority of all laws depend in a polity with strong regional, political, confessional and social cleavages' (quoted in Möckli 1994, 356). This view was shared by his socialist compatriot Karl Kautsky, who criticised the referendum because it violated the principle that 'all laws ought to be the result of a compromise between different groups in a society' (1911, 78). The referendum was also criticised by the British authority James Bryce, who complained that it 'gives no opportunity for amending a measure or arriving at a compromise upon it; it is the bill, the whole bill, and nothing but the bill' (1921, 159).

All of the above writers, moreover questioned whether the voters were capable of deciding complicated issues. US political scientist David Magleby has recently restated the view that referendums exacerbate conflicts. In his study of US referendums, Magleby asserts that 'direct legislation serves to intensify conflict and lead to a politics of confrontation. In contrast, indirect democracy is generally structured to facilitate compromise, moderation and a degree of access of all segments of the community' (1984, 181).

These assertions are, if they can be empirically substantiated, devastating for the populists' arguments, as they asserted that more referendums would facilitate government by discussion and provide the voters with a check on their elected representatives. Nathan Cree, the leading theoretician behind the populists' support of direct democracy, had made a case for the referendum because it would facilitate 'government by discussion ... which would giver freer play to the political ideas, aspirations, opinions and feelings of the people' (1892, 16). The question is, which of the hypotheses are we to believe. Do referendums entrench positions or is the reverse true? It would seem that Magleby's assertion is based on the belief that referendums inevitably are a centrepiece of a political system. Yet there are, as Butler and Ranney have noted, *two* worlds of the referendum: One where the referendum (and the initiative) is central to the political process; and a second world, where the referendum is used rarely, mainly to solve intricate and often constitutional issues. There is, consequently, reason to question the universal accuracy of Magleby's findings.

There are several empirical examples of referendums outside of the USA which have served the function of facilitating compromises and perhaps even stimulated discussion. The UK referendum in 1975 provides an example of one which facilitated discussion between groups that previously had been hostile towards each other. As one campaigner concluded after the poll, 'most of us found the political truce refreshing and some wish it to continue' (Butler and Kitzinger 1976, 132).

Groups on the Left co-operated with groups on the Right with the common aim of taking Britain out of the European Community (EC). One Conservative opponent of British membership noted after the campaign: 'I, for one, am more sympathetic now to the Labour Party and to organised trade unionism than I was before. Only someone as blinkered as Edward Heath could provoke into opposition people who are a good deal more loyal and patriotic than he is' (*ibid.*, 137). A lady from Norfolk noted: 'I have learnt one thing myself – that is that not all trade unionists are selfish left-wing extremists but are in many cases more patriotic than many a Tory and certainly as hard-working as many employers' (*ibid.*). These sentiments may not be representative of the UK electorate as a whole, yet they indicate that the referendum in 1975 provided the voters with an opportunity to form alliances which transcended the traditional party-political cleavages. Butler and Kitzinger commented that almost every group seemed to have come to 'the realisation how easy it was, with a little effort, to find common ground on a whole range of issues', that the other side was 'human (almost)', or that, as in Sussex, they could no longer 'regard each other as people with horns and tails' (*ibid.*, 131).

In this way the referendum gave rise to discussion, which perhaps moved the UK closer to the notion of a democracy of discussion. It is perhaps fair to say that the 1975 referendum yielded the result predicted by the populists. As Bogdanor (1981, 84) has commented:

> The EEC referendum ... encouraged a sense of social unity by ena-
> bling some political activists to reach out across party lines and estab-
> lish contact with those holding similar opinions on the EEC but
> widely differing opinions on other political issues ... The EEC refe-
> rendum seemed to bring out a sense of public spirit which had barely
> been tapped by the political parties.

This view challenges the crudely simplified and empirically disput-able conception of direct democracy In short the empirical evidence does not support the claim that direct democracy is inimical to a system of government which facilitates compromises. Moreover, as party discipline rather than free-spirited discussion is the order of the day in most modern parliaments, one might even argue that a system of referendum democracy is closer to the ideal of government by dis-cussion than is representative government, as parliamentarians' views are determined by the whips rather than by their own deliberations.

Moreover, it could be argued that the positions would be even more entrenched if no referendum were held. An example of the latter is provided by the continued debate on abortion in Arkansas, where the courts struck down proposals for referendums on abortion, with the result that the two camps' positions became even more entrenched (Cronin 1989, 214).

Thus, there are empirical examples which show that the referendum can have exactly the same effects as those attributed to representative democracy. Examples of referendums which facilitated compromise solutions and which reached beyond the initial antagonism are provided by the polls in Denmark on the Maastricht Treaty in 1992 and 1993. Those referendums are instances which in the end resulted in a compromise solution that transcended the initial dichotomy. A majority of the Danish voters were opposed to a single European currency, the Western European Union (WEU) and the introduction of European citizenship. Yet the majority of Danes were in favour of the 'Social Chapter' and the strengthening of the powers of the European Economic Community (EEC) over environmental policies. Following the rejection of the Maastricht Treaty, in June 1992, the politicians were forced to arrive at a compromise solution.

In October 1992 the parties reached an agreement on the 'national compromise' which stipulated that Denmark should seek four opt-outs from the Maastricht Treaty. Among the significant aspects was a refusal to allow Danish participation in the third phase of the European Monetary Union (EMU), a refusal to support a joint European defence policy, including joint military forces under the WEU, and a refusal of joint citizenship and common legal policies. This compromise was presented to the other governments of the EEC countries at the summit in Edinburgh in December 1992. The other governments accepted the Danish compromise, but stressed that the Edinburgh agreement was an *ad hoc* solution, which would have no effect on the other countries which applied for membership of the European Union (EU). This agreement was supported by a majority of 56.8 per cent of the voters on an 86.5 per cent turnout (the turnout in the second referendum was thus 3.5 per cent higher than in the first Maastricht referendum).

One cannot conclude that the Maastricht referendums remedied the shortcoming that some referendums have led to discrimination against minorities. What the referendums show is merely that the

initial rejection of the Maastricht Treaty spurred the elected representatives to negotiate a solution, which transcended the simplified
choice of the 1992 poll. Through the referendum they could force the
politicians to reach a more acceptable solution or at least *a* solution
acceptable to the majority of the voters. The referendum performed
the function of a constitutional safety-valve which ensured that the
decision reached by the Government was supported by the majority
of voters.

One of the reasons for adopting consensus democracy is concern
for minority rights. It is, as already noted, often argued that referendums are likely to violate minority rights. Madison believed that the
problem of the tyranny of the majority was especially acute in referendums because a 'common passion or interest will, in almost every
case, be felt by a majority as a whole', without much regard for the
minority (quoted in Sunstein 1985, 40).

There has been no shortage of writers who have criticised referendums on the same grounds. Magleby points out that several citizen-
initiated referendums have been 'targeted at various minority groups
such as establishing English as an official language of the State [of
California] or quarantining AIDS' victims' (1988, 608). The most frequently quoted argument based on this view is perhaps that of
Derrick Bell (1978, 18–19), who wrote that the

> emotionally charged atmosphere often surrounding referenda and
> initiatives can reduce the care with which the voters consider the
> matters submitted to them. Tumultuous, media-oriented campaigns,
> such as the ones successfully used to repeal ordinances recognising
> the rights of homosexuals in Dade Country, Florida, St. Paul,
> Minnesota, and Eugene, Oregon, are not conducive to careful think-
> ing and voting. Appeals to prejudice, oversimplification of the issues,
> and exploitation of legitimate concerns by promising simplistic solu-
> tions to complex problems often characterise referendum and initia-
> tive campaigns.

That such campaigns can result in the passage of laws which violate
the rights of minorities is a tendency intensified by the consideration
that the rational voter spends very little time considering the various
initiatives on the ballot, especially if the law is unlikely to have a significant influence upon him or her. He or she may, therefore, be more
susceptible to simplistic rhetoric. A similar conclusion was reached
some years earlier in a study by Hamilton (1970) of 'open housing'. In
the 1960s the Californian legislature had passed a law prohibiting

racial discrimination by estate agents and owners of 'apartment houses'. The estate agents, who had opposed the legislation, sought to repeal the law with an initiative in 1964. In an emotional and heavily financed campaign, the opponents of the law won a two-to-one victory (*ibid.*, 124).

Bell's diatribe against the referendum seems, however, somewhat one-sided, and the fact that he cites few concrete examples gives rise to doubts about his thesis. Ronald Allan (1979, 1026) has criticised Bell, arguing that

> apart from open housing referendums and low income housing referendums, all he [Bell] cites in support of his proposition are two pre-civil war referenda. Moreover ballots that lose are not much of an argument against initiatives. Thus the only state-wide measures that Prof. Bell cites (apart from open housing measures) to demonstrate the seriousness of the 'growing threat' that direct democracy poses for individual rights are Washington's attempt to control obscenity, Maine's desire to perpetuate its traditional method of financing schools, and California's tax reduction proposition. Those measures collectively do not constitute much of an assault on individual rights.

Moreover, Bell does not attempt to compare the work product of direct democracy with that of representative democracy. Shaun Bowler and Todd Donovan's more recent critique found that practically all polls on issues concerning discriminations were held locally (Bowler and Donovan 1998a, 41). It is, therefore, impossible to conclude that referendums are more likely to result in oppression of minorities' rights than is representative government. There are examples of legislatures which have adopted measures threatening the civil liberties of minority groups. Historian Henry Steele Commager, not an unqualified supporter of referendums, has pointed out that representatives in the USA have often enacted measures which threatened civil liberties and minority rights: 'New York purged itself of socialists … the Oregon legislature outlawed private schools and the Nebraska legislature forbade teaching in German, the Tennessee legislature prohibited the teaching of evolution … The list could be extended indefinitely' (1958, 65). Moreover, the US Congress enacted anti-Communist laws, whereas the Australian Parliament's similar attempt to restrict the freedom of some of its citizens was rejected by the voters. (Australians rejected a government-sponsored proposal for a constitutional amendment that banned the Communist Party in the 1951.)

The latter case indicates that the voters have occasionally used the referendum to protect civil liberties, rather than to undermine minority rights (Cronin 1989, 92). Allen's critique of Bell is certainly an important contribution because it disposes of some simplistic arguments against referendums, although Allen's unreserved support of referendums does need to be qualified. His defence of direct democracy cannot disguise the fact that some state-wide referendums have produced results which were at odds with the civil liberties of minorities. Proposition 189, a Californian proposal which sought to deny 'non-emergency health care, schooling, and social services to illegal immigrants', passed comfortably in 1994, as did an anti-gay measure in Colorado in 1992; these, and a growing number of similar measures, have often been struck down by the courts (Miller 1999). Yet it is undeniable that referendums, like systems with purely representative democracies, can be used to discriminate against minorities. A balanced conclusion seems to be that the referendum is neither better nor worse than representative democracy. The sad fact is that both direct and representative institutions of democracy can be used to enact legislation which discriminates against minorities, which is why we need constitutional courts and bills of rights: minorities are always vulnerable and in need of special protection.

It is perhaps curious that referendums affecting civil liberties and minority rights have been relatively rare – and thus far unsuccessful – in Switzerland (Möckli 1994, 45). One would, all other things being equal, expect similar tendencies in Switzerland as in the American states, as the frequency of referendums in this polity rivals that of California.

A possible explanation of the significantly low incidence of referendums directed against the interest of minority groups in Switzerland can be explained by the so-called 'double majority' required in referendums on international treaties, constitutional amendments, parliamentary counter-proposals to initiatives and initiatives for partial revisions of the constitution. The double-majority requirement is that the proposal must receive the majority of all the votes cast, as well as majorities in more than half of the twenty-three cantons. The result is that it has been impossible for the German-speaking majority of the population to enact legislation that impairs the rights of the minorities. This double-majority requirement, which is also a prominent feature of the Australian constitution, proved to be efficient as early as 1866 when the Catholic and conservative opposition groups (which mainly represented the non-German cantons) succeeded in blocking radical legislation put forward by the majority. That these mechanisms for minority protection have prevented the majority from passing legislation against the interests of the minorities does not, however, mean that the Swiss have avoided discriminatory referendums altogether. Referendums as far back as that of 1874 show that even the Swiss have discriminated against minorities, as was the case when the majority approved the infamous Anti-Jewish Slaughter House Law (Hobson 1909, 63).

Yet the Swiss have not endorsed anti-immigration measures (they have rejected five such measures since 1970). These tendencies seem to falsify Bell's thesis, namely that citizen-initiated referendums tend to precipitate ill-considered, often knee-jerk, decisions by voters on complex issues. Indeed, the outcome of the referendum in September 2000, in which 66 per cent rejected a constitutional initiative that would have limited immigration, speaks for itself.

While the Swiss referendums might indicate that a plebiscitary democracy can be compatible with minority protection, the US initiatives and referendums have occasionally yielded results which disfavoured minorities, like the gay marriage ban in several states in 2004. This is not because the referendum produces simplistic choices, but because American voters and politicians have been more prone to enact legislation which discriminates against minorities. However, most of these referendums have been challenged in the courts. Five out of eight initiatives affecting minorities have been invalidated in part or in entirety, and all initiatives concerning campaign finance reform have been invalidated (Miller 1999).

Apart from the unsuccessful Australian referendum on a ban on membership of the Communist Party in 1951, there are no examples of referendums targeted at minority rights in polities with relatively few referendums. Yet there have been referendums which, due to a combination of circumstances, have led to confrontations between majority and minority groups and have exacerbated ethnic and religious tensions, and thus had adverse consequences from the point of view of consensus government. Two referendums stand out: the Belgian referendum on the return of King Leopold in 1950 and the border poll in Northern Ireland in 1973.

The Belgian referendum exposed the deep-seated divisions between the Flemings and the Walloons, the former voting massively in favour of the return of the king, the latter vehemently opposing his return. The result, the majority in favour of the return of the king, led to riots, which forced the monarch to abdicate. It was these divisions which some years later led the Tripartite Commission on Constitutional Reform to the conclusion that the referendum in Belgium 'risquerait de provoquer et d'ancer de graves oppositions entre les communautés' (quoted in Morel 1992, 858).

The border poll is another example of a referendum that exacerbated a political conflict. A referendum held in the whole of Ireland, as a single unit, could not solve the problem, let alone change the wish of the Unionist majority in the province to maintain the status quo. The referendum served only to entrench already existing hostilities: the referendum cannot, as Bogdanor has noted, do much to 'unite a fundamentally divided society' (1981, 149).

These outcomes might be taken to suggest that emotive issues, such as religion and nationalism, are ill-suited for referendums. Yet there are, as so often is the case in political science, several exceptions to what at first sight might appear to be a general rule. Some ethnic and nationalistic issues have, in fact, been resolved by referendum in an amicable way The devolution referendums in the UK (Scotland and Wales – 1979 and 1997), Denmark (Greenland, 1979) and Spain (Andalusia, 1981, the Basque Country, 1979, Catalonia, 1979, and Galicia, 1980) were all characterised by the fact that prior negotiations had taken the issue out of the hands of the extremists. The same can be said of the Northern Ireland referendum in 1998. Although it would be erroneous to conclude that in each case the referendum solved the problem, it was certainly an important factor, because it gave the seal of legitimacy to a compromise decision reached by the various elites. The issue in each case was resolved by a combination of prior discussion and a subsequent referendum, i.e. elite accommodation followed by public approval.

It is not only devolution referendums that have been instrumental in solving nationalist tensions. The 1920 Danish–German dispute over Schleswig-Holstein, an area over which two wars had been fought in the nineteenth century, is an illustrative example. A generation earlier Lord Palmerstone is said to have quipped that 'only three people knew how to solve the conflict, one who was dead, another was in a lunatic asylum, and the last, Palmerstone himself, had forgotten it' (quoted in Kissinger 1994, 112). In 1920 the conflict was resolved through a referendum. The German majority in the south voted to remain within Germany (despite massive campaigning by the Danes), while the Danish majority in the north voted to rejoin Denmark. The literature on the Danish–German referendum in 1920 indicates that it is possible to use the referendum as a conciliatory device, in this instance because the two areas were ethnically homogeneous and especially because nationalism was a cross-cutting issue, i.e. nationalistic sympathies transcended class-based sympathies (Beigbeder 1994). It is tempting to interpret these findings in the light of the theory developed by Madison *et al.* in *The Federalist Papers* (1978). He argued that minority rights are protected by enlarging the jurisdiction, so that 'society itself will be broken into so many parts, interests, and classes of citizens that the rights of individuals, or of the minority will be in little danger from interested combinations of the majority' (quoted in Bowler and Donovan 1998b 1021). Cross-cutting cleavages – majorities that cancel each other out – are more likely in larger polities than in smaller ones. Figures from the USA indicate that this theory is supported by statistical data. Bowler and Donovan found that only 27 per cent of anti-minority measures (dealing with AIDS, language, gay rights and desegregation) passed at the state level, whereas 75 per cent of the same measures passed at the local level. In short, cross-cutting cleavages in larger areas prevented minority oppression, while the reverse was true at the local level. The same tendency has been observed in Switzerland where local referendums occasionally have been directed against minorities (*ibid.*, 1020).

These cross-cutting cleavages helped to create coalitions between otherwise antagonistic groups of workers and employees, which in turn led to embryonic schemes of co-operation. Moreover, the referendum was held after the elites in the two communities had ironed out their differences. It seems possible that it was the lack of these cross-cutting cleavages which in part explains the consequences of the Belgian and Northern Ireland/Ulster polls, both polities being characterised by what Yves Meny calls 'overlapping cleavages' (1993, 20).

The ethnic divide in Belgium coincides with an economic divide (the Flemings are the more affluent) and a secular – religious divide (the Walloons are the more secular). The same overlapping cleavages are present in Northern Ireland where the religious – nationalist divide is exacerbated by a class cleavage (the Catholics are predominantly working class). Such overlapping cleavages need not result in social and political tensions: Lijphart (1977) has famously shown how consociational mechanisms can overcome even fundamentally divided societies.

Yet it appears that referendums are likely to jeopardise the social preconditions for unity in divided societies, as happened in Belgium in 1950 and in Northern Ireland in 1973. What is interesting in this connection is that some of the same features have been found in California and Oregon (the American states where referendums have been used to discriminate against minority groups, especially Spanish-speaking immigrants). It is characteristic that linguistic, ethnic, religious and racial cleavages in the two states are 'overlapping', which may, perhaps, explain why referendums have produced outcomes that have threatened minority rights in either state.

One might, on the basis of these two cases, hypothesise that referendums on ethnic, linguistic or religious issues are likely to result only in social tensions and possibly discrimination against minority groups in polities characterised by 'overlapping' as opposed to cross-cutting cleavages, and that referendums ought, therefore, to be avoided in these polities; or that it should at least be stipulated that such polls should be held only in large (state-wide or nationwide) areas, where the majorities, in a Madisonian fashion, can cancel each other out. However, the fact that it was possible to hold a referendum in Northern Ireland (in 1998) which established cross-community alliances indicates that this conclusion is too stark; a less stringent conclusion might be that issues concerning nationalism and religion should be submitted to the voters only when prior agreement has been reached at the elite level.

Henry Sumner Maine noted: 'Democracies are quite paralysed by the plea of Nationality. There is no more effective way of attacking them than admitting a majority to govern but denying that a majority so entitled is the particular majority which claims this right' (Maine 1976, 51). The cases of Belgium and Northern Ireland show that not only nationality, but also religion and language, are capable of 'paralysing democracies'. Yet we need not accept the definition of democracy as simply a system that admits a majority to govern. Democracy is also, perhaps even predominantly, about 'finding ways in which majorities and minorities can live together, discuss their differences, and build on what they have in common', as a Member of Parliament (MP) put it in a Commons debate about Northern Ireland in 1987 (*House of Commons Debates* – HCD – 12 February 1987, 446). It is because issues of religion, language and nationality, especially when combined, arouse emotions which make compromises impossible that referendums on them should be avoided, at least if we maintain that consensus government and the protection of minorities are goals in themselves.

The fact is, however, that relatively few referendums in Western democracies have been held on these issues. Most referendums, at least in the 'second world', are called to endorse well-matured constitutional changes or else are on matters which split political parties and are not concerned with ethnic, linguistic or religious issues.

That referendums in the main perhaps have only adverse consequences in polities with overlapping cleavages (such as Belgium, Northern Ireland and possibly California) leads to the tentative conclusion that the referendum is compatible with minority protection, as long as governments refrain from holding them in small, divided societies (although they can, of course, be acceptable when they are held after an agreement has been reached by the elites, as in Northern Ireland in 1998).

The principle of participation and the referendum

That they rarely threaten the rights of minority groups does not, of course, imply that referendums are desirable. Some might still regard referendums as wrong in principle: as Sir Patrick Nairne (the civil servant who organised the British referendum on the EEC in 1975) observed, 'if Members of Parliament are elected to settle national issues of major policy brought before them by the Government, is it right to throw such issues back to the voters to settle' (Nairne 1998, 1). Others believe that referendums would enhance the citizens' interest in politics, increase participation and perhaps lead even to an improvement in legislation.

The latter view has influenced even political practitioners – as well as theoreticians. In *Representative Government*, John Stuart Mill sought to show that 'the only government, which can fully satisfy all the exigencies of the social state, is one in which the whole people participate' (quoted in Thompson 1976, 13). For democratic theorists what was advocated by Mill is known as 'the principle of participation' (*ibid.*, 1976, 14). The same view has been proposed by career politicians such as Dick Gephardt, who once, in the early 1980s, urged the adoption of a national advisory referendum, stressing that there is a growing feeling among American people that their votes no longer count, that politicians fail to respond to legitimate concerns, and that they have little or no impact on policy decisions. People are frustrated. Voters stay at home on election day and yearn for a clear choice on issues. When given clear choices the evidence points to increased participation in the democratic process. (Quoted in Cronin 1989, 173)

This belief in the edifying consequences of direct democracy not only points toward a greater use of referendums, but even suggests that we should introduce a system of direct participation through electronic devices. It is beyond the scope of this study to consider these proposals. Yet the thrust of Benjamin Barber's argument (1984) still goes to the core of the debate over the desirability of referendums.

The questions empirical political scientists and sociologists must ask themselves are whether these assertions about the consequences of the referendum can be empirically sustained and are the consequences of direct democracy as laudable as the theorists tend to assume? I attempt to answer those questions by considering whether the referendum is compatible with the *principle of participation*, which requires that each citizen be as involved as is possible and that the voters become as knowledgeable about the issues as they are able. To determine whether the referendum is instrumental in reaching those goals, we ask: does the referendum enhance participation and does it improve the citizens' knowledge about the important questions put before them?

The past thirty years have witnessed an increased belief in the virtues of direct democracy: a deluge of books and pamphlets both advocate the increased use of referendums and initiatives, and support the idea of new ways of direct participation. US political scientist Benjamin Barber, sums up the core belief of the trend thus:

Only direct participation, activity that is explicitly public, is a completely successful form of civic education for democracy The politically edifying influence of participation has been noted a thousand times since first Rousseau and then Mill and de Tocqueville suggested that democracy was best being taught by practising it. (Barber 1984, 235–6).

Yet Barber, for all his enthusiasm, was well aware of the limitations of radical democracy: as he conceded, when participation is 'separated from power, then civic action will only be a game and its rewards will

Table 1.1   Relationship between voter turnout and initiatives on the ballot (%), 1978–84

Turnout of eligible voters	1978	1980	1982	1984
States with initiatives on the ballot	44.7	59.9	46.8	54.5
States without initiatives on the ballot	39.0	55.0	39.8	51.5

Sources: Schmidt (1989); Cronin (1989).

seem childish to women and men of the world; they will prefer to spend their time in the "real" pursuit of private interests' (*ibid*.). The experiments with deliberative democracy and 'teledemocracy' have been thus far but games, and that might explain the low level of interest. The real test of direct democracy is therefore whether people vote in referendums and participate in other forms of direct democracy when they actually have the opportunity to influence major political decisions. Following Barber, one would expect to find a higher turnout in polities which employ the referendum. At least one empirical study supports this hypothesis: David Schmidt (1989) found that the turnout in American states with initiatives on the ballot had turnout rates on average about 5 percent above the turnout rate in states with no initiatives on the ballot (see table 1.1).

There has been considerable debate about these findings. It has been claimed that Schmidt failed to consider systemic factors like the historically low turnout in southern states (which rarely have provisions for direct democracy), where the relatively recent enfranchisement of African-American voters has meant that a large section of the electorate is still in the process of learning to use its newly won freedom. David Everson has challenged a conclusion similar to that put forward by Schmidt. Corrected for systemic differences, by excluding the south, Everson found that the average turnout in '[northern] states with initiatives declined by .06 while non-initiative states dropped by .04', during a period when turnout dropped relentlessly in all elections and referendums.

Thus it seems that the initiatives have, if anything, lowered turnout. But is this tendency invariably true for referendums in general? Do opportunities for participating in referendums result in political apathy? Findings by comparative political scientists seem to support Everson's findings. Butler and Ranney have in fact found that 'turnout in referendums has been consistently lower than in general elections, and sometimes much lower' (1994, 6). The same conclusion has more recently been reached by Yannis Papadopoulos, who concluded that 'the more we multiply to the opportunities to participate, the more we multiply the exclusions [because of a lower turnout]' (1994, 26).

Yet to dismiss Barber's hypothesis on this basis would be premature. It has been asserted that 'democracy is best taught by practising it', that is a more frequent use of referendums would lead to a higher turnout as more voters become interested in political issues. It is, however, curious that the theoreticians of direct democracy have thus far failed to test this proposition empirically, especially as it can be tested relatively easily by calculating what statisticians call a 'correlation coefficient'.

It is, of course, true that statistical analysis can oversimplify complex and complicated relationships, although this ever-present danger should not discourage the use of statistical techniques (as long as one acknowledges the limitations to quantitative methods). A calculation of the correlation between turnout and the frequency of referendum may not answer all questions as to what determines the turnout rate, but it can indicate whether there is statistical evidence to support Barber's thesis (table 1.2).

A calculation of the correlation coefficient between the average turnout and the number of referendums held in selected Organization for Economic Co-operation and Development (OECD) countries does not point towards a corroboration of Barber's thesis; there is a negative correlation of $r = -0.70$. This fact sits uneasily with the predictions made by proponents of direct democracy in general and of referendums in particular. It is, of course, true that their frequency is but one of the factors affecting the turnout rates in referendums; registration laws, the salience of the issues and the political culture (an elusive concept) are all factors that are to be taken into account. Yet on empirical grounds it is undeniable that a frequent use of referendums generally results in a drop in the turnout rate. In short, a frequent use of referendums seems to be associated with a lessened interest in voting (see table 1.3).

Yet the trouble with this model is, as is often the case with models based on quantitative data, that it misses the exceptions to the rule, the residual cases that are inexplicable, and we must therefore consider other factors that might explain the residuals. An often men-

Table 1.2 Registration and average turnout for referendums in Western democracies, 1970–92

Polity	Number of referendums	Average turnout (%)	Registration[a]
Switzerland	158	41.4	1
California	78	35.0	0
France	2	48.8	0
Italy	18	70.2	1
Denmark	4	78.7	1
Ireland	9	78.7	0
Austria	1	64.1	0
Britain	1	64.0	0
Norway	1	77.6	1
Sweden	1	84.8	1
New Zealand	3	64.3	0
Finland	1	70.8	1
Canada	1	75.7	0
Belgium[b]	1	92.4	1
Australia[b]	16	93.4	0

Notes: Average turnout $= 67.71 + 9.68 \times$ Rolling Register Dummy $- 0.24 \times$ number of referendums; $r = -0.78$, $r^2 = 0.61$; Sign F $= 0.0089$, standard error $= 9.78$.
[a] Registration dummy: 1 = rolling register; 0 = no rolling register.
[b] Australia and Belgium are not relevant to the calculations because of the compulsory voting requirements.
Sources: Based on Möckli (1994); Crewe (1981); and Butler and Ranney (1994).

tioned factor is that the electoral registration laws may have an influence on the turnout in elections and referendums. G. Bingham Powell has hypothesised that 'when citizens must make a double effort to register and to vote, voting becomes a significantly more difficult act, and turnout is likely to be lower' (1982, 5). The fact that turnout is high in Scandinavia (where voters are automatically added to the electoral register whenever they move to a new constituency) might explain why the turnout there has been higher than in countries without a 'rolling register', for example, the UK (until 2000), New Zealand and Ireland.

We might, thus, expect that a more efficient system of electoral registration will result in an increasing turnout, or that it will at least reverse some of the negative effects of an increasing number of referendums. Powell's hypothesis can be tested by incorporating a dummy variable (which assumes the value 1 if the country in question has a rolling register and the value 0 if it does not have a rolling register) into a regression equation. The calculation suggests that the registration laws play a significant part. The multiple R for the model is -0.78, while the r^2 of the model increases from 0.49 to 0.61 when we invoke the registration dummy. The existence of a rolling register evidently does have an impact on the turnout, yet a calculation of the beta-weights still shows that the number of referendums is the most important factor statistically, with a beta-weight of -0.77, somewhat higher than that for the registration dummy (beta-weight: 0.33). These regression model results indicate that the turnout in referendums is depressed as the number of referendums increases. Yet neither the apathy model nor the 'registration model' can explain why turnout in the 1993 Italian referendums on the abolition of proportional representation (PR) in Senate elections and state funding of political parties was 12 per cent higher than the average turnout for referendums after 1970.

Nor, it seems, can the apathy theory explain why turnout increased, by 9 percentage points in California's controversial Proposition 13 referendum in 1978, or for that matter why the turnout rose from the 'normal' 40 per cent turnout level in Swiss referendums to a stunning 78.3 per cent in the Swiss referendum on membership of the European Economic Area in December 1992.

In other words, we must find yet another factor that occasionally affects turnout and reverses the downward trend. One possible explanation is provided by the theory of a 'civic reserve' developed in *The Civic Culture* (Almond and Verba 1963). The authors speculate that citizens, while generally uninterested in politics, are able to mobilise resources if (or rather when) their interests are threatened. The general tendency towards a lower turnout in referendums may momentarily be reversed in exceptional cases. Almond and Verba write that the 'citizen has ... a reserve of influence. He is not constantly involved in politics, nor does he actively oversee the behaviour of political decision-makers. But he does have the potential to act if there is a need' (*ibid.*, 418). Following this theory, we might attribute the results in these residual cases to the existence of a civic reserve which is triggered when the voters, for a variety of reasons, are concerned about an issue.

This hypothesis seems to go a long way in explaining why Italian voters, at least, momentarily reversed the downward trend of lower participation in 1993. The 1993 referendums provided the voters with an opportunity to change the political system by annulling the state funding of parties. That is to say, the referendum on the, in all seven laws, allowed the voters to take 'a decision that the parties and the political elites were unable, and above all, unwilling to take' (Uleri 1996, 122). The citizens' momentary increase in political interest was not driven by a sudden enthusiasm for participatory democracy but was rather the result of the voters' growing impatience with the ineffectual and even corrupt political elite.

This pattern is perhaps even clearer in the Swiss referendums, in which the turnout has occasionally plummeted below an average of 37 per cent. Yet the Swiss voters showed an ability to draw on civic reserves when they were asked to give their assent to far-reaching proposals such as the membership of the European Economic Area – a free trade area comprising the members of the European Free Trade Association (EFTA) and the EU – in 1992, and the abolition of the army in 1989.

The perception that the Swiss political elites were gradually approaching membership of the EU gave rise to suspicion among a citizenry notoriously sceptical of international organisation, and it resulted in a massive political debate. The sudden increase in the turnout rate has thus been attributed to the fact that 'a significant number of Swiss citizens fear losing an important part of their popular rights if the country were to join the process of European integration' (Kobach 1997, 195). The turnout in the 1992 referendum might thus be interpreted as an instance that triggered the citizens to call on their civic reserves.

This interpretation is supported by a study by Marques de Bastos (1993), who found that Swiss voters engaged in 'selective participation'. According to de Bastos, participation (the turnout) is a function of the perceived importance of the issue on the ballot. The ordinary voter sees no reason for wasting his or her energy on relatively uncontroversial issues; citizens do, however, react when there is a risk that the result will be determined by an unrepresentative minority, as was the case when they turned out to vote against anti-immigration measures in the early 1970s.

This theory of civic reserves thus paints a relatively bright picture of the experience with referendums. That many citizens fail to vote in referendums might even be interpreted as a commendable tendency, in line with the apparent conditions which pluralists have identified as requisite for maintaining a stable democracy. To quote from Albert

O. Hirschman's theoretical study, 'the ordinary failure, on the part of most citizens to use their potential political resources to the full makes it possible for them to react with unexpected vigour, by using normally unused reserves of political power and influence, whenever their vital interests are threatened' (1970, 32).

The civic reserve interpretation indicates that provisions for referendums that allow the citizens to react when their interests are threatened are preferable to a system in which the number of referendums is considerably smaller. The Swiss and Californian systems provide citizens with an efficient means of preventing the legislature from passing unpopular laws, as they can initiate referendums. The same is not true for countries without this provision for 'voter vetoes'.

That over 30 per cent of the citizens vote on issues which otherwise would be decided behind closed doors in committee rooms is in itself a remarkable achievement, which, along with the significantly higher turnout rates on controversial issues, seems to suggest that polities within what – following Butler and Ranney (1978) – we might call the 'first world' of referendums are considerably closer to the ideal of democracy which underlies Mill's principle of participation (Thompson 1976, 15).

This conclusion does, however, ignore one important fact: that turnout in the controversial referendums in Switzerland, California and, to a certain extent, Italy is as a general rule lower than the turnout in the uncontroversial referendums in polities like the Scandinavian countries and New Zealand. Danish commentators have noted that the turnout in the 1986 referendum on the Single European Act was 'disappointingly low' (75.4 per cent). Yet the turnout in this referendum was nevertheless higher than those in controversial Swiss referendums such as that to abolish the army in 1989 and indeed higher than the record turnout in the 1956 lottery referendum (proposition 37) in California in 1984.

The civic reserve interpretation cannot disguise the fact that frequent referendums depress the turnout significantly. The conclusion that there is a negative correlation between turnout rates and the frequency of referendums leaves us with the apparently contradictory conclusion that referendums on the one hand increase responsiveness, as they *potentially* provide each citizen with opportunities for expressing his or her preferences as to the final outcome, but on the other hand decrease public responsiveness because the provisions for referendums apparently lead to lower turnouts, even when corrected for those in which the citizens use their civic reserves. The question is whether this tendency necessarily undermines the democratic case for more referendums. That the overall turnout rate generally is low does *not* prove that the voters are becoming apathetic; the low turnout might simply reflect the phenomenon of *selective participation*, that is, the voters, so to speak, take turns at the polls by voting when they have a particular interest in the given issue.

The selective participation thesis thus states that the turnout in a referendum is a function of political interests rather than of sociological factors such as education or of socio-economic variables. The low turnout poses a problem only if it can be shown that the 'selective participation' thesis is incorrect – if particular groups and classes are consistently over-represented, while the reverse is true for other groups.

The proposition that voters engage in selective participation can be tested statistically using a measure called the 'ratio of representation' (RR) (Dahl 1956). The RR measures whether a group's representation is disproportionately high or low: RR = 0 indicates that the group is neither under- nor over-represented; a negative value of RR indicates that the group is under-represented and it is over-represented if the RR is higher than 1. Using this measure, we can conclude that the selective participation thesis is falsified if the discrepancies in the turnout rates are significant, whereas the opposite would be true if the discrepancies between the groups were insignificant. It would have been desirable to conduct a wide-ranging comparative study including all selected countries, yet lack of empirical material and space limitations force me to restrict the study to two countries, one from each of the 'worlds' of referendums, namely Denmark and Switzerland (see table 1.3), although I also consider data from California and New Zealand.

A calculation of the RRs in the sixteen Swiss referendums held between 1988 and 1990 shows that senior managers and graduates are somewhat over-represented (RRs of, respectively, 20 and 18), whereas unskilled workers and citizens with less than 9–11 years of education are somewhat under-represented (RRs of, respectively, −12 and −19). Yet these groups account for less than 30 per cent of the respondents. What is more interesting are the representativeness of the larger groups, the more junior managers and non-manual workers. A look at the data for these groups tells a different story: junior managers and non-manual workers are closer to the ideal of RR = 0 (RRs of 2 and −1, respectively). What the Swiss figures show is that education is somewhat correlated with participation, whereas the same tendency is less

Table 1.3   RRs in referendums in Denmark and Switzerland

	Denmark	Switzerland
Occupation		
Senior manager	8	20
Junior manager	−1	2
Junior non-manual	−1	−1
Unskilled manual	−7	−12
Education (years)		
0–8	−2	−19
9–11	−1	−19
Graduate	2	18

Source: Figures for Denmark kindly supplied by Jorgen Goul Andersen, University of Alborg, from Switzerland by *Vox-Analysen* 1988–90.

obvious when testing the data on occupational groups. This finding does not falsify the 'selective participation' thesis, but it does indicate that socio-economic and educational factors rather than political interest determine the turnout, a finding that some might see as an argument against referendums altogether. Yet one cannot in fairness say that the Swiss referendums are representative examples. To determine whether referendums generally strengthen the rule of the elite requires us to consider the data from a country in the 'second world of referendums', such as Denmark.

It is evident that the richer and better-educated citizens of Denmark were slightly over-represented in the three referendums in 1986, 1992 and 1993 (all of which concerned European integration). Yet it is striking that the differences in participation rates between the groups were markedly less pronounced than in Switzerland. This fact could perhaps be explained by an exceptional level of interest in European integration. A calculation of the RRs in Denmark shows that graduates and senior managers were only slightly over-represented (RR of, respectively, 8 and 2), whereas unskilled workers and the least educated were only slightly under-represented (RRs of, respectively, −7 and −3). These findings seem to suggest that the negative consequences of the referendums in Switzerland are less significant in a country with fewer referendums, although it might be argued that the RR for more junior managers and non-manual workers (who comprise more than half of the sample population) have RRs converting towards $RR = 0$.

Table 1.4   RRs in candidate elections

	Denmark	Switzerland
Occupation		
Senior manager	6	15
Junior Manager	−1	0
Junior non-manual	−1	−5
Education (years)		
0–8	−3	−6
9–11	0	−7
Graduates	3	2

Sources: Worre (1987) for Denmark and *Vox-Analysen* 1988–90 for Switzerland.

The question is whether these findings prove that frequent referendums *ipso facto* decrease representativeness of the voters in a way which favours the rich and the well educated. It is possible that the RR discrepancies are simply slightly greater in Switzerland, while they are smaller in Denmark. It is, in other words, equally possible that the richer and better educated simply participate more than other groups, irrespective of whether they are voting in referendums or candidate elections. The hypothesis that the RR discrepancies in Swiss referendums reflect a general tendency towards over-representation for particular groups in polities with frequent referendums can be tested only by comparing the RRs in referendums with the RRs in candidate elections. What is required is a comparison between candidate elections, and table 1.4 shows the RRs in candidate elections in Denmark and Switzerland.

The Swiss electorate is in fact less representative than the Danish electorate. Senior managers and graduates participate more than other groups (RRs of, respectively, 13 and 2), and unskilled workers and citizens with less formal education are still under-represented (RRs of, respectively, −5 and −7). Yet the differences are less significant than they are in referendums. The Swiss findings do in fact resemble those of the Danish general election.

This difference in the RRs suggests that representative democracy in Switzerland leads to greater equality in participation than do referendums, although the differences are relatively small. This conclusion cannot be drawn from the Danish results. It is in fact noteworthy that the discrepancies in the RRs in the Danish referendums were slightly *smaller* than in the general elections, i.e. referendums

Table 1.5   RRs in California and New Zealand

	California	New Zealand
Occupation		
Senior manager	2	2
Junior manager	3	−1
Junior non-manual worker	−3	−1
Unskilled manual worker	−5	−7
Education (years)		
0–8	−12	NA
9–11	3	NA
Graduate	5	NA

Sources: Magleby (1984); Simpson (1992), 'Introduction'.

are in this case more representative than are candidate elections. Yet the overall results do not point towards any marked differences in the RRs between the two worlds of the referendum. It is in fact difficult to prove that 'the less educated [and] poorer voters are underrepresented' (Magleby 1984, 110).

It has been suggested that the flaw in the Swiss referendum heaven is that the choir sings with a strongly upper-class accent. The low turnout does indicate that a referendum democracy is hardly a viable, let alone a democratically legitimate, alternative to representative democracy; yet even sceptics will note that the RR discrepancies are pronounced only if one focuses exclusively on the marginal groups. The fact is that the RRs of the junior non-manual and junior management workers (who comprise more than 70 per cent of the respondents) approximate to the ideal of RR = 0.

This suggests rather that the most negative worries about Swiss direct democracy have been exaggerated. It might, however, be argued that these figures are unrepresentative: because Denmark and Switzerland are small European consensus democracies, there is no guarantee that the same findings would emerge if we instead study other polities like the two majoritarian democracies, California and New Zealand.

Table 1.5 shows the RRs for California and New Zealand. The figures give us no reason to alter the interpretation that the RR discrepancies are relatively unaffected by the frequency of referendums. The discrepancies between the groups' RRs are in fact smaller in

California (a country in the 'first world' of the referendum) than they are in New Zealand ('second world').

These figures do not amount to a proof of Barber's thesis that democracy is best learned by practising it, yet the findings challenge the elitist objection against referendums, namely that 'the under-representation of some groups in deciding propositions is a problem across states' (Magleby 1984, 110).

Referendums and voter knowledge: some empirical findings

It has been one of the most persistent arguments for the introduction and use of the referendum that it would allow the citizen to 'develop a lively interest in the public affairs in part under his own management' (Sullivan 1893, 93). Or, as Barber has argued, if voters

> sometimes seem unfit to legislate, it may be because they have for so long been passive observers of government. The remedy is not to continue to exclude them from governing, but to provide practical and active forms of civic education that will make them more fit than they were. Initiative and referendum processes are ideal instruments of civic education. (Quoted in Rouke, Hiskes and Ziràkzadeh 1992, 19)

One would, following Barber, expect that the voters' political interest and engagement would increase as a function of a more frequent use of the referendum. This optimistic assessment has been attacked by others, most strongly by Nelson Polsby and Aaron Wildavsky who, writing about Californian referendums, assert that a frequent use of referendums will lead to a decline in voters' knowledge about the issues. As they put it: 'To learn what is involved in a seemingly innocuous proposal to raise somebody's salary or issue bonds takes hours of study To understand twenty or more is unduly onerous' (1984, 279).

Thus the introduction of a Swiss-style referendum democracy would merely create a system in which the voters would be unable to form an opinion about the issues as a result of time constraints. Polsby and Wildavsky's conclusion is an intuitively powerful one, not least when one considers the growing body of theoretical literature concluding that it is irrational for citizens to participate as their influence on the outcome is infinitely small. Polsby and Wildavsky's assertion is vividly illustrated in the following outcry by a new Californian voter:

Sometime in mid-October a massive booklet arrived in my mailbox. At first I thought it was the local phone directory. Closer examination revealed it to be a 'ballot pamphlet' from California's Secretary of State. Its contents included a staggering array of bond acts, proposed constitutional amendments and statutory initiatives. The pamphlet contained the complete text of each measure ... summaries prepared by the State's Attorney General, analyses by someone identified as the Legislative Analyst ... just as I was struggling through the state ballot pamphlet and beginning to wonder how I had graduated law school ... the postal service delivered another ballot pamphlet. This one was compiled by the Los Angeles City Clerk and contained text, summaries, arguments, pro and con, and rebuttals for approximately half-a-dozen city ballot measures ... By the time a third pamphlet arrived, a gift from the County Registrar–Recorder with information concerning the county measures, earthquakes were starting to look appealing. (Eule 1990, 1508–9)

Yet we cannot, simply on the basis of circumstantial evidence, draw the conclusion that the Californian and the Swiss use of referendums leads to voter ignorance. A truly scholarly study must offer substantial empirical proof of the assertion that the voters in the 'first world' of referendums have insufficient time to consider the issues on the ballot and that, as a consequence, they have a limited knowledge of the issues.

Two scholars who have attempted to test this hypothesis are the Swiss political scientists Erich Gruner and Hans Peter Hertig, who studied Swiss voters' actual knowledge in the forty-one issues submitted to the voters between 1977 and 1980. They initially asked voters the following question: 'What were the reasons that you voted for/against (title of the referendum)?' About four-fifths of the voters were able to give reasons for their decisions (see table 1.6).

That he or she is able to give reasons for a decision to vote either for or against a proposal does not demonstrate that the voter understands the issues. Over 90 per cent of the voters in New Zealand's referendum on electoral reform could, for instance, give reasons for their decision to vote for or against the introduction of PR (most mentioned dissatisfaction with the Government). Yet it is unlikely that the same proportion of the voters had a commanding knowledge of the different electoral systems involved. Such reasons for voting are, of course, legitimate; yet they tell us very little about the voters' actual knowledge. It is for this reason that it is necessary to supplement the ques-

Table 1.6 Could/could not give reasons for voting intention

Category	Total N	%
Could give reason for decision	12.150	78.4
Could not give reason for decision	3.343	21.6

Source: Hertig and Gruner (1983).

Table 1.7 Extent of Swiss voters' knowledge of the political issues

Categories	N	%
Adequate	2,674	24.1
Reasonable	7,619	56.5
Poor	5,200	19.4

Source: Hertig and Gruner (1983).

tions about voting behaviour with questions about the actual issues. Hertig and Gruner (1983, 19) consequently asked the respondents a second question, 'On (date of the referendum) there was a referendum on (title of the referendum). Could you, briefly, explain the intended effect of this proposal?'

Voters who 'could mention at least one central feature of the proposal' were categorised as having 'an adequate (*gute*) knowledge of the issue'; those who could mention an issue which was related to the proposal were categorised as having 'a reasonable (*mittelere*) knowledge of the issue'; and voters who were unable to relate the proposal to any political issues were categorised as 'having a poor (*schlechte*) knowledge of the issues'. The findings are reported in table 1.7.

There has been considerable debate about the interpretation of these findings. Some scholars have taken heart from the fact that 56.5 per cent of the voters were able to mention an issue related to the proposal. Others have suggested that the fact that referendums in the late 1970s concerned exceptionally complex technical matters explains the low level of understanding of the issues among the voters, i.e. the findings are artificially low.

These findings sharply contrast with anecdotal evidence from the recent Danish referendums, especially the Maastricht referendums in 1992 and 1993. In the wake of the first referendum on the Maastricht Treaty the Danish news magazine *Maanedsbladet Press* conducted a survey in which it asked a representative sample of voters about the

Table 1.8   Extent of Danish voters' knowledge of the political issues

Categories	N	%
Adequate	436	39.1
Reasonable	561	51.1
Poor	102	9.2

Notes: Adequate: knew a great deal/fair amount; reasonable: know just a little;
poor: heard nothing about.
Source: *Eurobarometer* (1993).

Maastricht Treaty. The same questions were subsequently put to a random sample of the members of *Folketinget*, the Danish Parliament. The surprising result was that the voters' knowledge on average surpassed that of the non-specialist MPs. Yet it is difficult to compare these results with the Swiss data. What is needed is a comparison between the Hertig–Gruner data and similar questions put to a sample of respondents in a country from the 'second world' of referendums.

The questions in the *Eurobarometer* survey of 1993 enable us to reconstruct a set of figures which can be made comparable with Hertig and Gruner's results. On the basis of these figures, we can conclude that only 10 per cent of the Danish respondents were unable to give reasons for their voting intentions (the comparable Swiss figure was 21.8 per cent), and that 39 per cent had an adequate knowledge, whereas only 24.1 per cent of the Swiss respondents fell into this category. Slightly fewer Danish voters had a 'reasonable' knowledge about the issues, 51.1 per cent against 56.5 for the Swiss (see table 1.8).

The Danish Maastricht voters were certainly better informed than their Swiss counterparts: only 9.2 per cent of the Danes had a poor knowledge of the issues (19.4 per cent of the Swiss fell into this undistinguished category). It would appear therefore that the Danes' knowledge of the issues was marginally better than that of the Swiss, possibly because the media coverage of the Maastricht Treaty was significantly more intense than the media coverage of the Swiss referendums.

Yet there is a more substantial reason why the Danes appear to have been better informed than the Swiss: the Danish voters were asked to categorise the extent of their knowledge *themselves*, whereas the Swiss were categorised according to objective criteria. This difference is likely to have biased the result: respondents are often reluctant to concede their lack of knowledge about current issues. It is therefore likely that the Danish figures exaggerate the respondents' actual knowledge of the issues (see table 1.8).

If there was a small difference in the *extent* of the Danish and Swiss voters' knowledge of the Maastricht issues, there was little to differentiate their understanding in *qualitative* terms. The relatively small differences between the two peoples' level of knowledge is not conclusive proof that frequent referendums are consistent with a high degree of voter understanding, i.e. the ideal of enlightened participation. The figures rather indicate another tendency, namely that frequent referendums can be consistent with the ideal of the (relatively) knowledgeable citizen. The Swiss voters in the referendums studied by Hertig and Gruner (1983) might not have acquired the same degree of specialist knowledge which one finds among MPs. That more than 80 per cent of the respondents (which included voters and non-voters alike) had a reasonable knowledge about the proposals hardly falsifies Barber's thesis about the edifying consequences of referendums. This is a potentially revolutionary finding, which challenges the elitist assumptions to which many political scientists subscribe.

It has been the prevailing view that the frequent holding of referendums is inimical to the ideal of 'enlightened understanding', because frequent referendums are incompatible with the democratic ideal that the voter is denied the time for reflection necessary to arrive at his or her considered judgements. Polsby and Wildavsky asked: 'Is the citizen better off guessing or following the advice of the local newspaper rather than trying to choose a legislator or a party to represent her interests?' (1984, 279).

The findings detailed above show that very few voters are 'guessing': the majority of both the Danish and the Swiss voters had a fair idea about the issues on which they were called to decide, whereas the Californian data suggests that it can be difficult for voters to identify a representative who shares their ideological outlook. It thus seems that even relatively frequent referendums are compatible with the ideal of 'enlightened participation'.

Box 1.1   Voter knowledge in a representative democracy

In order to arrive at a fair assessment of the consequences of direct democracy we are required to contrast all aspects of referendums with representative democracy – and the level of citizen knowledge is no exception. It is the classical argument for representative government that the voters delegate power to representatives who share their political and ideological convictions (see Burke). Their identification of suitable representatives presupposes that the voters are indeed able to distinguish between the ideological positions of the politicians. A recent US study tested this assumption by asking the voters to identify their own ideological positions, and to subsequently identify the local representatives' ideological positions. Of the respondents, 61 per cent were able to identify the representatives' ideological positions correctly, while 39 per cent had voted for candidates with ideological preferences different from their own (*California Journal*, 3 March 1991, 138):These figures are consistent with similar findings from the 1970s. The Michigan study of the 1978 congressional elections showed that less than one-fifth of all adults knew how their congressman had voted on any issue (Wolfinger in Ranney 1981, 54). This figure may seem relatively depressing to supporters of representative government, yet it is perhaps explicable when one acknowledges that another study from the same period showed that only 30 per cent of the respondents were able to identify their local representative (Field Institute poll, 3 March 1988). These figures do not support uncritical arguments for representative democracy. The low level of voter knowledge may indicate that Californian voters find it easier to make a decision on an issue than to decide on which candidate to support.

A preliminary conclusion

These findings do not, of course, allow us to conclude that the referendum can be an alternative to representative democracy. Even Jean-Jacques Rousseau, the great champion of direct participatory democracy, acknowledged that 'each man should not be at liberty to propose new laws at pleasure; but that this right should belong exclusively to the magistrates' (1993, 35). The empirical evidence presented above gives us no reason to question this assertion. Even the referendum in Switzerland is used as a supplement to representative democracy (only 4 per cent of the bills are decided by popular referendums). Referendums in the 'first world' often result in a lower turnout, yet the statistical evidence does not reveal differences in the RR significant enough to call in question the democratic legitimacy of the results. The middle classes in Denmark and Switzerland are neither under- nor over-represented and the differences in RR in referendums and candidate elections are relatively minimal (if one disregards the over-representation of the senior managers).

The differences between the RRs of the two worlds of the referendum are relatively insignificant (indeed the discrepancies were smaller in California than in either Denmark or New Zealand). Moreover, the level of public understanding of the uncontroversial referendum issues in Switzerland approximates to the level of understanding of the controversial issues in the Danish Maastricht referendums.

These findings do not allow us to conclude that referendums have the effects identified by Barber (1984). Yet the empirical evidence clearly shows that the elite theorists' denunciations of referendums have been generally premature. The analysis shows that referendums in *both* 'worlds' are consistent with the criteria of equal and enlightened participation. The referendum might not be the panacea that some have suggested, yet it does provide 'a genuine adjustment to modern constitutionalism' (Friedrich 1950, 571).

'In theory and in practice modern democracy has been haunted by the spectre of direct popular action as an alternative to all kinds of representative schemes', wrote Friedrich (*ibid.*, 570). Some – like Barber and Becker – have claimed that referendums would enhance political interest and increase political participation. Others have claimed that referendums would lead to the tyranny of the majority. The foregoing analysis falsifies and vindicates both propositions, depending on the circumstances.

Referendums in the 'first world' of the referendum, where 'initiatives and referendums are prominent strands in the fabric of political life' (Butler and Ranney 1978, 221), generally lead to a lower turnout, though not to significantly less enlightened voters. This finding does not mean that referendums are alternatives to representative democracy: the experiments with deliberative democracy, as well as theoretical considerations, clearly indicate that referendums can serve only as supplements to representative democracy, although the voters' knowledge is sometimes higher in referendums than in candidate elections. Referendums in polities with 'overlapping cleavages' *can* have outcomes that are detrimental to the ideal of minority protection (though this happens rarely). Yet a referendum on ethnic issues can 'take the heat out of the conflict' if it follows an agreement reached between the elites representing the communities. These findings both show that the referendum can be compatible with our normative criteria and they suggest that the referendum can be conducive to the ideal of 'democracy by discussion'.

Referendums on issues that divide political parties often lead to cross-party alliances, i.e. the emergence of hitherto unthinkable coalitions. This tendency is in itself an indication that occasional referendums can strengthen a system of politics by mutual understanding and may contribute, at least indirectly, to the emergence of Masaryk's ideal of 'democracy as a *Weltanschaung* and a way of life based upon the respect for the rights of other individuals, as well as a recognition of their views' (quoted in Szporluk 1981, 72).

Appendix: The reasoning voter

Some political scientists have developed an alternative approach which, in its different way, reaches similarly optimistic results about the voters' ability to make considered decisions in the voting booth. They emphasise that voters cope with information demands by using information shortcuts (Sniderman, Brody and Tetlock 1991, 18) The voters do not need in-depth (encyclopaedic) knowledge of the issues in order to make informed decisions. Reasoning voters are approximately rational, trying to come to terms with decisions about which they are vaguely informed; that is, they seek to decide rationally 'with limited information and processing capacity' (*ibid.*). The 'reasoning voter' is thus a description of 'voters [who] actually do reason about parties, candidates and issues' by investing their votes in collective goods on the basis of 'costly and imperfect information under conditions of uncertainty' (Popkin 1991, 7). In contrast to private investors, these 'public' investors have 'less incentive to gather costly information' (Downs 1957, 119). They therefore look for shortcuts – ways in which they can make optimal decisions on the basis of information inexpensively acquired.

These insights have recently entered the sub-area of initiative and referendum studies through the seminal work of Arthur Lupia. He wrote: 'As an alternative to the costly acquisition of encyclopaedic information, voters may choose to employ information shortcuts. For example voters can acquire information about preferences or opinions of friends, co-workers, political parties or groups, which they may then use to infer how a proposition will affect them' (1994, 71). In this study of the 1990 insurance initiatives, Lupia demonstrated that apparently ill-informed voters, with knowledge of the insurance industry's preference on insurance regulation initiatives, had opinions which were nearly identical (within 3 per cent) to those of well-informed voters. These findings have been corroborated in a recent study by Bowler and Donovan, in which the authors show that 'voters can and do think about and decide upon propositions in ways that make sense and in ways that take advantage of readily available information' (1998c, 165).

One of the paradoxical findings of these studies is that voters make use of information from advertisements. Campaign spending does not, according to these findings, induce the voters to vote for the richer side; rather, advertisements provide the voters with cues which enable them to make up their minds. One of the most frequently cited cues is the elite endorsement. The voters do not study the proposals in detail, but they base their decisions on elite cues. The voters in Washington's term-limit initiatives in 1991 thus took their cues from Speaker Tom Foley's position on the issue. Foley's stance had a dramatic effect on the 'probability of supporting the initiative, depending on feelings toward Foley. Those with negative feelings toward Foley [were] almost twice as likely to vote for the initiative [which he opposed]' (Karp 1998, 161). These findings prove neither that voters deliberate nor that they evaluate policies from an objective perspective. They do, however, indicate that the voters have the cognitive ability to respond to the steep information demands presented to them, and that they are likely to reason and vote in accordance with their preferences.

2

A. V. Dicey's theory: the referendum as the people's veto

If a Controversie arise betwixt a Prince and some of the People, in a matter where the Law is silent, or doubtful, and the thing be of great Consequence, I think the proper *Umpire* in such a case should be the Body of the *People*. (Second Treatise, article 242: Locke 1988, 427)

Representative government is the norm in liberal democracies. The referendum cannot, as I argued in the previous chapter, replace indirect democracy. This view has often forced proponents of representative democracy to renounce all possible forms of direct democracy; thus, in an editorial in 1911 (the year when California adopted the initiative and the referendum), the *Los Angeles Times* commented that the 'ignorance, and caprice, and irresponsibility of the multitudes' would henceforth substitute for the 'learning and judgement of the legislature' as a result of the introduction of the referendum device (quoted in Key and Crouch 1939, 437).

This position, though in accord with constitutional principles since Blackstone, is not in harmony with the principles of liberal constitutionalism. Classical liberal constitutionalists, like John Locke, did indeed defend representative government. Yet Locke did not regard Parliament as omnipotent. The power given to Parliament was but a *concessio imperil*, that is, a temporary and limited delegation of power. The establishment of a representative democracy did not therefore mean that the people had given up their rights; they had merely transferred the execution of those rights. As Locke explained, the 'power of the legislature being derived from the people by positive voluntary grant and institution, can be no other than what this positive grant conveyed, which is being only to make laws' (1988, 363). It followed from this that a check on Parliament was needed. The check envisaged was a strong second chamber. Yet liberal constitutionalists did not anticipate that both chambers of the legislature would fall prey to the influence of interest groups and lobbyists, let alone that the entire system could be captured by the party machine. Trust in a purely representative democracy therefore gradually declined, as legislatures were unwilling to consider legislation supported by the vast majority of the voters while enacting laws that favoured the organised interest groups and the party machine. This problem was particularly acute in California where the Southern Pacific Railroad enjoyed a monopoly of political influence, as well as controlling the party system. The situation was perhaps most accurately summed up by Delos F. Wilcox who noted that 'the citizen of every state has seen legislature after legislature enact laws for the advantage of a few and refuse to enact laws for the welfare of the many' (1912, 50–1). The same view was expressed by one of the most prominent supporters of direct democracy, Theodore Roosevelt, who argued that the 'special interests which would be powerless in a general election may be all powerful in a legislature if they enlist the services of a few skilled technicians' (quoted in Munro 1912, 60). This system could not be remedied through a Madisonian form of indirect democracy; indeed, representative democracy was a part of the problem. The only solution to the problem, it seemed to the populists, was the introduction of direct democracy. It was generally believed that the introduction of the referendum and the initiative would lead to the result that 'the fraudulent claims bills that slide through our legislature will be vetoed by the people, and legislative extravagance will be checked' (Magleby 1984, 21).

The populists thus generally considered the introduction of the initiative and the referendum as a comprehensive means of bypassing legislatures. Some of the populists even went so far as to demand that representative democracy be replaced by the initiative, the referendum and the recall. J. Allen Smith, a radical politician, argued that the introduction of the referendum and the initiative was an attempt to 'get back to the basic idea of the old town meeting, where local measures [were] directly proposed and adopted or rejected by the people' (quoted in Magleby 1984, 22). Lars A. Ueland, a Dakota farmer and assemblyman, was equally convinced that the initiative and the referendum would 'furnish the missing link, the means needed, to make popular self-government do its best. Programs and reforms will then come as fast as people need them ... I would rather have the complete initiative and referendum adopted in state and nation than the most ideal political party that could be made' (quoted in Anderson 1962, 38).

These hopes did not materialise when the referendum and the initiative were implemented in the USA. The referendum in fact proved to be more than simply a check on the excesses of legislatures: the outcome was rather that the people 'took into their own hands duties which are the object of a representative government' (Ostrogorski 1902, 551). This was not of, course, wholly intentional, as not all the populists sought to replace representative democracy with the referendum and the initiative. Prominent proponents of direct democracy, like Woodrow Wilson, Theodore Roosevelt and, among the theoreticians, Nathan Cree, indicated that the referendum was to be seen as a corrective rather than an alternative to indirect government, but they failed to spell out where to draw the line between representative and direct democracy and, indeed, why a line needed to be drawn at all.

The populists' demands for the introduction of referendums resulted in yet another unchecked power, the people. One theoretician in particular addressed himself to this problem, for which reason the contribution of Albert Venn Dicey (1835–1922) to the political theory of the referendum is an important area of study.

Dicey has never been given full credit for what he was, one of the greatest liberal theorists. 'History buries most men, and then exaggerates the height of those left standing', wrote the novelist John Updike (1992, 228), an observation that seems to be particularly true of Dicey's status as a political theorist. This is regrettable, as Dicey, perhaps alone among liberal theorists, sought to develop a political theory of the referendum which combined elements of both representative and direct democracy. Dicey's main reason for the introduction of the referendum was a profound dissatisfaction and frustration with the practical implementation of the principle of representative government, which he thought and hoped could be remedied by elements of direct democracy.

Dicey did not, however, restrict his argument to a *defence* of the referendum: he also pointed to the potential dangers of an extensive use of the device, as well as making a case for the superiority of parliamentary government. The referendum for Dicey was not therefore an alternative to indirect democracy, but an addendum[1] to representative government, which would facilitate the political education of the voters as well as creating an incentive for Parliament to address the concerns of the electorate.

Dicey was not the only British writer to advocate the referendum:

William E. H. Lecky had advocated the referendum in 1899, and Henry Sidgewick (one of Dicey's friends) had supported the introduction of referendums 'to avoid a deadlock resulting from a disagreement between the two chambers [of Parliament]' (Sidgewick 1891, 559). Yet Dicey was the only theorist to incorporate the theory of the referendum within a comprehensive liberal theory of representative democracy. It is this accomplishment which gives Dicey a special status among supporters of the referendum.

Dicey was initially opposed to the introduction of the referendum, which in 1884 he had described as 'one of the most dubious devices of Swiss Democracy' (quoted in Rait 1925, 122). He gradually changed his view as he realised that the House of Lords, the traditional check on the powers of House of Commons, was gradually losing its legitimacy, a problem that was intensified by the erosion of the informal checks which traditionally had prevented Parliament from legislating beyond its mandate. He therefore concluded that the time had come for the British to borrow 'from America the constitutional provisions which, by delaying alterations in the Constitution, protect the sovereignty of the people', i.e. the referendum (1890, 506).

The lack of checks and balances in the British constitution was, in Dicey's view, epitomised by the Liberal Party's conversion to Irish home rule (a policy which he personally detested and deemed to be unpopular with the voters). He argued that the lack of a constitutional check on the powers of the House of Commons increased the 'possibility ... of a fundamental change passing into Law which the mass of the nation do not desire' (Dicey to Bryce, 23 March 1911, in Dicey 1982). Dicey therefore made a case for the introduction of the referendum as a 'people's veto' which would prevent 'the passing of any important Act which does not command the sanction of the electors' (*ibid.*, cix).

It was Dicey's big idea that the referendum was 'the only check on the predominance of party which is at the same time democratic and conservative' (1890, 507). The attraction of the referendum was that it would make 'democracy itself a check on party tyranny' (quoted in Cosgrove 1981, 107) without undermining the system of representative government which 'appears to be an essential characteristic of a civilised or progressive state' (Dicey 1899–1900, 70).

Dicey saw it as the main deficiency of the system of representative government that a small majority in the House of Commons could change the constitution. The system, as it existed at the beginning of the twentieth century, was in Dicey's estimation vulnerable to the 'excesses of a party which has obtained a parliamentary majority out of proportion to its real power' (quoted in Cosgrove 1981, 109). The problem was, in other words, that a democratically elected majority of Parliament could enact legislation which was opposed by its electors. Although of little concern in matters of ordinary legislation, this would be a fundamental problem in matters of irreversible constitutional change which, argued Dicey, 'ought not to be made by a body of men who do not clearly represent the final will of the nation' (quoted in *ibid.*, 161).

The general election of 1885 was a case in point. In 1885, W. F. Gladstone, the Liberal prime minister, had not included home rule in his election addresses and had generally sought to avoid any reference to Ireland during the campaign. The election was instead fought on rival programmes of social amelioration (Emden 1962, 219). Yet after the election Gladstone claimed a mandate for the policies of home rule. A similar situation emerged, in Dicey's view, after the general election of 1906. Writing to J. St Loe Strachey in May 1908, Dicey, complained that Asquith's Liberal Government had 'played an iniquitous trick. They came into power as zealots of free trade. They are retaining office as socialists' (Dicey to Strachey, 20 May 1908, quoted in Cosgrove 1981, 107).

The fundamental problem was that, although the majority of voters favoured the Liberal Party over the Tories, it seemed that an even larger majority was opposed to Gladstone's policy for home rule. The problems surrounding the 1885 general election showed, in Dicey's view, why the referendum would have a beneficial effect. As he wrote to Strachey:

> I value the referendum first because it is doing away with the strictly speaking absurd system which at present exists, of acting on the presumption that electors can best answer the question raised, e.g. by Home Rule, when it is put together with such a totally different question of prohibition, and generally that it is wise to mix up systematically, questions of persons with questions of principle, & secondly though in a certain sense mainly because the referendum is an emphatic assertion of the principle that nation stands above parties. (Quoted in *ibid.*, 108)

The problem displayed in the 1885 general election was not unique. It was in fact a recurrent pattern of all general elections that the citizen was 'placed upon the horns of a dilemma, from which there is no practical escape. They must either banish from office men whose policy they in many respects approve, or else sanction the passing of a law which they believe to be impolitic' (Dicey 1890, 495). Dicey, himself a Liberal opponent of home rule, saw this as yet another example of the usefulness of the referendum, at least as it was practised in Switzerland. For the Swiss electors could 'send to Parliament members, say the Radicals, with whose policy they on the whole agree, even though these representatives have carried through Parliament Bills to which the Swiss voters refuse their assent' (*ibid.*, 496).

Political developments in the following years reinforced this conviction, especially when the Unionists almost split following Joseph Chamberlain's conversion to tariff reform in 1903. Chamberlain suggested that a higher tariff should be put on goods imported from non-empire countries in order that the revenue raised could be used for social reforms. This policy, which eventually became official Tory policy, was intolerable to many Unionist voters, not least the Free Traders who had left the Liberal Party in defiance of Gladstone's policy on the Irish question.

In the years following the Unionists' conversion to tariff reform, the Unionist Free Traders grew increasingly concerned that a vote for the Unionists would be a vote against free trade. (It should be noted that the referendum was used as a weapon by more than just the opponents of tariff reform: Joseph Chamberlain, confident that the public supported his cause, proposed that a referendum should be held on the issue). Dicey himself a Unionist Free Trader, lamented that the

> Unionist government has ceased to represent the belief in free trade which to all appearance commands the assent of the nation; the opposition does not represent the national and unshaken faith in the maintenance of the Union. Both government and opposition seem inclined to use their party machine to crush out of existence that small but vigorous body of Free Trade Unionists who share the beliefs that constitute the political creed of the nation. (1905, 311)

The Unionists' adoption of the policy of tariff reform had resulted in the absurd situation that neither they nor the liberals represented the nation. This was, in Dicey's view, yet another reason for the introduction of the referendum, for only a referendum could provide voters with the opportunity of supporting the party with which they were in general agreement, while at the same time allowing them to vote against proposals forwarded by that same party. This criticism was eventually recognised by Unionist leader Arthur Balfour. In the campaign prior to the second general election in 1910, Balfour promised that a future Unionist Government would hold a referendum before the introduction of tariff reform – a pledge abandoned by his successor, Bonar Law (Bogdanor 1981, 24).

By allowing the people to veto an unpopular law it would be possible for the electors to remedy the most visible dangers of party government, namely, that Parliament enacted laws that were opposed to the will of the majority of the voters (Dicey 1982, cxv). It was this insistence that the referendum was to have 'a purely negative effect' (*ibid.*, 1982, 382) which distinguished Dicey from the US populists and other radical proponents of direct democracy. Equally importantly, the insistence that the referendum was a purely conservative instrument also differentiated his view from the French tradition of *plebiscites* (Dicey 1890, 492) which had been used by Napoleon Bonaparte to acquire a mandate for his policies. Dicey was at pains to show that the intention as well the consequence of the referendum was purely conservative. He ceaselessly stressed that the referendum 'was the only mode available … (as far as a political mechanism can do anything) for proving an effective check on rash legislation as regards fundamental institutions' (quoted in Cosgrove 1981, 108).

This insistence on the conservative virtues of the referendum places Dicey solidly in the conservative tradition of limited government. Yet the fundamental difference between Dicey and the liberal theorists, from John Locke to Friedrich Hayek, was that he, like the radical US populists, saw the people themselves as the best possible check on the elected politicians, whereas other liberal theorists advocated elitist schemes. Henry Maine (1976, 87), (whose political views were close to Dicey's, believed that the political influence of the people would lead to 'confusion and dismay [because the] prejudices of the people are far stronger than those of the privileged classes'.

Dicey did not share Maine's belief that 'the gradual establishment of the masses in power [was] the blackest omen for all legislation' (*ibid.*, 112). Dicey, to be sure, was no radical democratic theorist. He merely emphasised that the referendum was 'at once a democratic institution, and, owing to its merely negative character, may be a strictly conservative institution' (1982, cxv). He had no sympathy for the initiative and other means of direct legislation, which would lead to the enactment of ill-considered legislation. He strongly refused to accept that 'the initiative [was] an essential part of the referendum' (1890, 496). The initiative was, or so he argued, 'neither in theory nor in fact … a necessary consequence of the maintenance of the referendum' (1982, 382). His position resembled that of his friend Strachey, who rejected the initiative on the following grounds: 'Under the initiative you do not get the committee stage for legislation. The stage under which trained advocates, critics, and lawyers debate the Clauses of the bill and render it workable in practice as well as sound in theory' (Strachey 1924, 29).

The system of deliberative representative government could be secured only by restricting direct democracy to referendums on controversial laws already passed by Parliament. The referendum as defended by Dicey to Lord Salisbury was 'nothing more nor less than a national veto' (quoted in Cosgrove 1981, 106), which would not facilitate 'any legislation which Parliamentary wisdom or caution disapproves' (Dicey 1890, 496); nor would it be a 'spur to … democratic innovation', but would rather be 'a check placed on popular impatience' (*ibid.*). This purely negative effect implied that the political system ultimately had to be based on some form of representative democracy. Dicey was consequently faced with the task of explaining why he ultimately placed his trust in an institution that he often attacked; that is to say, he had to draw a line between those issues to be decided by popular referendums and the class of issues that were to remain within the boundaries of the system of representative government.

Dicey did not view the referendum as an antidote to all the deficiencies of parliamentary government; nor did he believe that representative government could be replaced. He accepted that Parliament contained a far 'greater proportion of educated men endowed with "marked intellectual power"'; he conceded also that to substitute 'the authority of the electorate for the authority of the House of Commons and the House of Lords [would be] to transfer the government from the rule of the intelligence to the rule of ignorance' (1982, cx). Yet he did not accept that such concessions amounted to a valid objection against the referendum. As he put it, 'the referendum is a mere veto. It may indeed often stand in the way of salutary reforms, but it may on the other hand delay or forbid innovations condemned by the weight both of the uneducated and of the educated opinion' (*ibid.*, cxi). (Whether referendums in fact tend to stand in the way of salutary reforms is a question I take up in chapter 3).

Dicey maintained that legislation was to be a parliamentary pre-rogative, a stance based on his general views about representative democracy, which in large measure seem to have been influenced by John Stuart Mill's views as expressed in *Considerations on Representative Government*. Central to Mill's theory of representative government was the view that '[t]here is hardly any kind of intellectual work which so much needs to be done by experienced and exercised minds ... as the business of legislation. This is sufficient reason, were there no other, why [the laws] can never be made but by a committee of very few persons' (Mill 1991, 227).

Dicey, like Mill, found it 'difficult to imagine that legislation directed by the will of a popular assembly could reach the merit and continuity without the existence of some form of Parliamentary representation' (quoted in Cosgrove 1981, 11). He therefore maintained that the elected government 'of necessity [has to be] treated as the organ of the nation, otherwise the action of the nation is at every turn weakened' (*ibid.*, 161). Parliament was 'no mere debating society', but was rather 'entrusted with great though indirect executive authority ... [it] was or ... ought to be, concerned with the appointment and criticism of the Cabinet' (Dicey 1982, lxxxvii). These functions could not conceivably be carried out in a system of direct democracy, which instead would lead to 'spasmodic and irregular' legislation (Dicey 1900, 18). Parliament has to be given a legislative prerogative in the interest of political stability and efficiency.

While Dicey acknowledged that 'Parliament may be wiser than the citizens who elect it', however, he also acknowledged that a 'Parliament which does not represent its electors is not an assembly which illustrates the benefits of a representative system' (*ibid.*, 43). He agreed with Mill's conclusion that 'since all cannot, in a community exceeding a single small town, participate personally in any but some very minor portions of public business, it follows that the ideal type of a perfect government must be representative' (Mill 1991, 256). Dicey clearly favoured a system of representative government under which every member 'though elected by a particular constituency, was a person acting not for London, Middlesex, or Liverpool, but for the whole country' (Dicey 1900, 10).

Yet this Burkean ideal had become 'an absurdly false representation of the English House of Commons as it now exists', wrote Dicey, for 'the *closure* and the *guillotine* [had] destroyed that free and rational debate which was once supposed to be the soul of the representative system' (1910, 540). This view was strongly expressed in a letter to his friend Strachey:

> Personally I think that I should have preferred real Parliamentary government as it existed up to 1868. But I have not the remotest doubt that under the present condition Parliamentary government means a vicious form of government by party, and from this I believe the referendum may partially save us. It has the great merit of being the only check on party management which is in perfect harmony with democratic sentiment. (Quoted in Cosgrove 1981, 107)

This support for the referendum was strengthened by the English constitution's lack of formal checks on power. The system of representative government had the unfortunate consequence that it created 'a body of representatives with interests and wishes of their own' and gave 'undue authority to Parliamentary majorities' (Dicey 1900, 44). While Parliament for many purposes represented the nation, its majorities were not 'the same as the nation', argued Dicey, who found it 'repugnant … that a majority say, of twenty or thirty … should attempt revolutions and subvert the laws of the realm' (1895, 690).

Dicey accepted that the system of representative government increased 'the possibility of placing legislative power, indeed, the Government of the country, in the hands of persons who are supposed to be superior to the rest of community in education and intelligence' (1900, 44). Yet he did not agree that this was a sufficient answer to the remark that it is often well that electors confer wide powers on their parliamentary representatives and allow members that are better than themselves to determine the fundamental policies, and especially at a time when the system of party government had led almost to the extinction of the independent Burkean legislator. Dicey recognised that the growth of political parties increased the danger 'that representatives of the people may, consciously or unconsciously, place the interest of their party far above the welfare of the nation' (1910, 543). In the absence of appropriate constitutional safeguards, a majority in House of Commons could therefore 'arrogate to itself that legislative omnipotence which of right belongs to the nation' (Dicey 1912, 91).

Civic education and the limits of public participation

Dicey's primary aim was to develop a 'strong check on the … sentiment, or passion of the moment' (1910, 543), though it is crucial to note that he envisaged the referendum as more than a mere check on Parliament in general and the political parties in particular. Dicey in fact regarded direct political participation by the people as an 'end in itself' (1900, 1). He expressed principled support for the view that direct legislation, at least in theory, could have an educative effect. Mill had noted that 'any participation, even in the smallest public function, is useful', and 'that the participation should everywhere be as great as the general degree of the community will allow' (1991, 256). He consequently reached the conclusion that 'nothing less can be ultimately desirable than the admission of all to share in the sovereign power of the state' (*ibid.*).

Dicey shared that view: he clearly believed that an extension of public participation was desirable and lamented that the system of representative government diminished 'the part taken by the individual citizen [who received] little or no training in the conduct of public affairs' (1900, 25). Like Mill, he was convinced that a viable democracy required civic education for the individual, and this ideally could be gained through active political participation (*ibid.*). He expressed a principled support for Athenian democracy because 'the political education of Athens ... was ... better than that of an English member of Parliament', or at least 'incomparatively superior to the political education of the ordinary English elector' (*ibid.*). General elections had become contests between party leaders, not between rival political ideas, so that it had become 'idle to fancy that what the voters consider is simply, or mainly, the prudence, capacity or character of their representative' (1910, 547). The political education gained from a general election campaign was likely to be limited; the referendum, however, offered a possible solution to this problem, as the debate would be concluded by a decisive vote on the issue. As Dicey noted, 'Debates which are indecisive can never possess the full importance, or interest, attached to discussions which result in final decisions' (1890, 502). The referendum would therefore be a valuable supplement to representative democracy, which would facilitate political education, as it would allow citizens to distinguish 'between measures and men' (*ibid.*, 507). He continued:

> The referendum is, or may be, an education in the application of men's understandings to the weightiest of political concerns – namely, the passing of laws – such as is absolutely unobtainable by voters who have been trained to think, that their whole duty as citizens consists in supporting the Conservative or Radical party, and

that their blind acceptance of every proposed enactment, which happens to form a part of the party platform. (*Ibid.*, 508)

The referendum would, in other words, have a democratically edifying effect, simply because it allowed the voters to deliver the final verdict on a subject. This argument in favour of the educative consequences of participation is historically interesting, because it shows that Dicey based his case for the referendum (in part) on the same assumptions as the radical American theorist Nathan Cree, who, following Jean-Jacques Rousseau, had argued that the referendum would 'break the crushing and stifling of power of our great party machines … and have an elevating and educative influence upon voters' (1892, 16).

Yet Dicey, unlike Cree, believed that those beneficial effects required that referendums be kept to a minimum in order that the citizens had the opportunity and the incentive to discuss the issues. He based his qualified support for the referendum on a number of wider considerations concerning the likely effects of the use of direct democracy and concluded that the referendum was to be used only in exceptional circumstances. Not only did he consider it impossible that the affairs of a large nation were determinable by direct legislation, but he qualified his principled support of referendums by outlining a possible sociological consequence of direct legislation.

Dicey feared that an ever-increasing number of polls would result in lower turnout, which would be to the benefit of the educated elite. If referendums were 'frequent then it of necessity happens that a large number of the electorate will abstain from voting, and those who abstain in reality give up their share in political life' (1900, 28). This prediction was substantiated by empirical evidence produced by his friend James Bryce (1921, 463) and by A. Lawrence Lowell (1913, 183) who estimated that only an average of 30 per cent of the qualified voters participated in the referendums in American states. These considerations led Dicey to the theoretical conclusion that referendums could have a positive effect on civic political education, but that frequent use of the referendum would result in declining turnout. The referendum would have the desired effects only if the number of polls were restricted to a minimum.

The Referendum Act as an alternative to a second chamber

One of Dicey's main aims in his campaign for the introduction of the referendum was evidently to develop an alternative to the traditional check on the House of Commons – the House of Lords. The Lords had, in his view, been rendered obsolete by the advance of democracy, which he, following Tocqueville, saw as inevitable (Dicey 1893). It is perhaps surprising that he gave scant consideration to possible types of check on the Commons other than the referendum. An elected House of Lords would have been perfectly compatible with the over-riding principle that 'the will of the electors shall by regular and constitutional means always in the end assert itself as the predominant influence in the country' (Dicey 1982, 27). He did, in fact, consider the possibility of an elected Upper House (1895, 690), but abandoned it, seemingly because an elected House of Lords would be susceptible to the influences of the party machine, which had undermined his trust in the Commons (Cosgrove 1981, 158). He apparently came to a conclusion somewhat similar to the one reached by his friend James Bryce (1921, 462), who argued that the constitutions based on bicameralism merely created 'two rival Chambers, and ... they will be composed by the same kind of men. Why then have two?' Dicey's rejection of a reformed House of Lords was, however, also based on the view that the referendum provided a more efficient, and indeed a much more democratic solution to the problem of an unchecked legislature and that the referendum furthermore would be more consistent with the inevitable democratisation of society (Dicey 1893, 771).

Dicey did concede that a 'reformed Second Chamber might possess a veto more powerful than any check on legislation possessed by the present House of Lords', yet he found it undeniable 'that the authority of the best constituted Second Chamber would be far less potent than the authentic voice of the nation' (1910, 558), i.e. the referendum. He wrote:

> The referendum has one pre-eminent recommendation, not possessed by any of the artful, or ingenious, devices for strengthening the power of the Second Chamber, or of placing a veto in the hands of a minority Its application does not cause irritation. If the Lords reject a Bill people demand the reform of the peerage; if the French Senate (a popularly elected body) hesitates to approve a revision of the Constitution, the next scheme for revision contains a clause for the abolition of the Senate. Popular pride is roused, voters are asked

to make it a point of honour that a measure, which an aristocratic or select chamber has rejected, shall be carried. A Bill's rejection turns into a reason for its passing into law. Should a regular appeal to the electors result in the rejection of a Bill passed by Parliament, this childish irritation becomes an impossibility The people cannot be angered at the act of the people. (*Ibid.*, 507)

The possibility of reforming the House of Lords seemed not only unattractive but even undemocratic. Dicey therefore turned his full attention to the referendum, which 'would correct the defects' and 'check the further development of a party system' he believed to be 'working injury to the nation' (*ibid.*, 557). Yet it is important to acknowledge that Dicey's case for the referendum was anything but purely negative or conservative. There is, as he had noted in his 1886 study of the Swiss referendum, a long cherished tradition in Switzerland according to which the most efficient referendums (from the point of view of liberal constitutionalism) are those which are never held. This is because the voters are guaranteed the right to veto certain classes of legislation, thus reducing the politicians' enthusiasm for enacting grand-scale reforms on those issues for fear that their proposals might suffer embarrassing defeats at the polls (Neidhart 1970, 313).

The referendum would, in other words, be a mechanism to facilitate better and more responsive representative government:

> If it were certain that the ultimate fate of a measure ... would finally turn not upon the votes of members of Parliament, but on voters outside who never took part in the hollow and artificial warfare waged at Westminster, it is conceivable that speakers in Parliament might address themselves to the task of convincing an unseen audience [and] conceivable ... that the power of reasoning might become a force of some slight moment even in practical politics. (1890, 503)

Thus the introduction of the referendum would induce the legislators to be more accountable to the views of the electors. The mere possibility that its enactments could be vetoed by the people would spur Parliament to enact legislation that would be supported by the electorate. The referendum could, in this way, indirectly strengthen representative democracy. It might, therefore, be argued that Dicey anticipated that effect of direct democracy which many years later has found empirical support in a study by Kobach (1993, 67) of the effect of referendums in Switzerland:

Clearly the referendum reduces the discretion and powers of legislatures. However, it does not necessarily weaken their authority Arguably, people treat laws with more respect when they know that the statutes possess either the tacit or explicit support of a majority of the citizens. If an option to challenge a law via a referendum is available, then the fact that a law goes unchallenged implies that the people have tacitly given their consent.

Dicey's main concern was, in short, to introduce checks and balances to the British constitution which could exercise the role formerly performed by the House of Lords. Yet he remained opposed to the introduction of a written constitution, which in his view would destroy 'that kind of pliancy which has hitherto been the strength of the English State' (1886, 74). The seriousness of the political situation forced him, however, to find a compromise between his ideological commitment to a flexible unwritten constitution, on the one hand, and the dangers of party government, on the other. To maintain this flexibility required, paradoxically, that certain parts of the constitution be entrenched by a Referendum Act. 'Constitutional devices', he admitted in a letter to Lord Salisbury, 'can rarely do much good; they may however, I conceive, avert some evil from arising from unnoticed though very real alterations in the working of the Constitution' (quoted in Cosgrove 1981, 106).

An entrenchment of certain parts of the constitution through a Referendum Act, would, as he expressed it to Lord Salisbury, be the only efficient means of guarding 'the rights of the nation against the usurpation of national authority of any party which happens to have a Parliamentary majority' (ibid.). The contents of this Referendum Act were outlined in a letter to Leo Maxse in connection with the latter's forthcoming article in National Review (Dicey to Maxse 2 February 1894, quoted in ibid.). Dicey wrote: 'I should like for example to pass an Act enacting that … a referendum might be required by a resolution of either House, in respects of any Act e.g. affecting, 1) The rights of the Crown, 2) The constitution of Parliament, 3) The Acts of Union & other large constitutional topics which might easily be enumerated' (Dicey to Maxse 3 February 1894, quoted in ibid.).

It is obvious that this Referendum Act was heavily biased in favour of the Unionists. Dicey did not, however, anticipate difficulties in perceiving when a proposed bill was in conflict with one of the enumerated Acts; nor, it appears, was he concerned that a future Parliament might repeal the Referendum Act, without a referendum being held.

He did not believe that Parliament could simply pass a law in violation of the Referendum Act. Dicey acknowledged the existence of the problem, but he did not consider it a weighty objection. He wrote:

> It is true that an Act of Parliament might repeal or override the Referendum Act itself, but this though a plausible, is not a valid objection. The Referendum Act would practically be secured by the odium which any Ministry or party would incur by depriving the people of their right to be appealed to. I am quite certain that once established the Referendum would never be gotten rid of by anything short of a revolution. (*Ibid.*)

Another objection to the referendum was that it would hinder political progress – the standard complaint of socialists and radicals like Ramsay Macdonald (Meadowcroft and Taylor 1990, 51) and Clifford Sharp (1911).

Yet the same objection was raised by Conservatives like Lord Curzon (1894, 73) and, indeed, by Henry Sumner Maine. The latter had regarded it as the main deficiency of the referendum that the ordinary voter would reject even necessary reforms: 'Contrary to all expectations, to the bitter disappointment of the authors of the referendum, laws of the highest importance, some of them openly framed for popularity, has been vetoed by the people' (Maine 1976, 111). Dicey was not blind to these tendencies. Writing about women's suffrage, which he then supported (to his discredit, he later changed his mind), he noted that 'even those who, in common with the present writer, look with no disfavour on this reform, may gravely doubt whether it would, on a referendum, command the approval of the electorate' (Dicey 1890, 509). This may be the reason why Dicey did not favour the so-called 'popular referendum' which allowed Swiss voters to demand a referendum on *any* law enacted by Parliament. By granting the people this right, it was possible that they might reject progressive legislation. On the other hand, by restricting the referendum to the constitutional issues enumerated in the Referendum Act it would be impossible for the voters to repeal ordinary laws; they would be allowed to repeal only fundamental laws. The Referendum Act did not therefore allow the supposedly reactionary electorate to repeal ordinary laws. But, equally importantly, his proposal for a referendum would hinder the radical legislation which was likely to be one of the consequences of the populists' reforms. The referendum as advocated by Dicey could 'not hurry a single law', nor would it facilitate 'any legislation, which

Parliamentary wisdom or caution disapproves', simply because the referendum was restricted to a few fundamental issues (Dicey 1890, 496). The introduction of the Referendum Act would not be a 'spur to a democratic innovation'; it would rather be 'a check placed on popular impatience' (*ibid.*). It was for that very reason that Dicey recommended that the referendum be introduced into Britain. Dicey's case for the referendum was not 'due to any increased enthusiasm for the principles [allegedly] preached by Rousseau' (1910, 539), although he emphasised the politically edifying influence of participation, i.e. the view that democracy is best learned by practising it. His main reason for advocating the referendum was that it would give the people an effective veto against the continual encroachments of Parliament; the referendum was, for Dicey, consistent with the 'doctrine which lies at the basis of English democracy that the law depends at bottom for its enactment on the consent of the nation as represented by the electors' (1911, 19).

It was by outlining this theory of the referendum that he could propose an original solution to the age-old problem of *Quis custodiet ipsos custodes* – 'Who guards the guardians?' This alone should have been enough to secure Dicey a place among those considered the greatest liberal thinkers. Yet, questions remain. Was Dicey correct in thinking that the constitutional safeguard would give the voters a veto? Was he correct in considering it likely that the voters would have reactionary views? Was he correct in supposing that the voters would suffer from voter fatigue and that the more wealthy and better educated would benefit from low participation rates? Why did he fail to consider minority rights? It would seem that Dicey's theory while original, bites more off than it can chew. Answers to these questions require us to undertake an empirical study. We must therefore leave the field of political theory and return to that of political science.

Appendix: The 'initiative'

Although this book is concerned mainly – though not exclusively – with referendums proper, a study of the referendum would be incomplete without briefly considering the effects of its close relative, the *initiative* (a device which allows the citizenry to propose legislation). There are three kinds of initiatives:

- constitutional initiatives (which enable citizens to propose constitutional amendments);
- direct (legislative) initiatives (which enable citizens to propose laws);

- indirect (legislative) initiatives (which enable citizens to propose laws that will be voted on after the proposals have been debated by Parliament).

The constitutional initiative has been used frequently in Switzerland and California. The proposals have rarely been successful in the two polities: only 25 and 27 per cent, respectively, have been successful (Gobbi 1989, 157).

The legislative initiative, known in New Zealand and Uruguay, but not in Switzerland, is a predominately US phenomenon: 14 states have provisions for direct initiatives and 3 (Massachusetts, Maine and Wyoming) have provisions for indirect initiatives. There has been an increase in the use of initiatives in recent years. In 1992, 67 state-wide initiatives appeared on the ballots; in 1996 this figure rose to 92 (Gerber 1996, 191). This increase has been accompanied by a growth in the success rates: in the 23 American states that use initiatives, 42 per cent of 271 statewide initiatives considered by the voters passed. In previous decades the initiative passage rate in many states was considerably lower (*ibid.*).

The main objection against the initiative is arguably that it enables the voters to propose and pass populist legislation without the scrutiny of expert committees in the legislatures, an objection which supposes that legislatures and committees actually scrutinise legislation in ways that minimise the risk of populist legislation being enacted. While there is some evidence to indicate that this supposition has a basis in practice, the fact is that most initiatives, for better or worse, are sponsored by large interest groups (which can afford expensive legal and political advisors). This means that the quality of the legislation is generally as high as that of legislation initiated by the legislatures, although there are some instances of crude legislation which has proved unworkable because of lack of legal expertise among the initiators (Thomas 1990, 191). It is, however, difficult to conclude that this undermines the case for the indirect initiative, in respect of which legislative committees scrutinise the proposed bill and hold hearings prior to the proposal's submission to the voters. Such deliberation by legislators might indicate that Dicey's rejection of the initiative was premature. As Neal Peirce writes, 'the indirect initiative … strengthens rather than weakens representative democracy [by] forcing the legislators to come to grips with an idea they may have sought to avoid before. It brings into play forces of moderation, compromise and common sense so often lacking in direct initiatives' (1979, 15).

3

Do referendums stand in the way of 'salutary reform'?

It is possible, by agitation and exhortation, to produce in the mind of the average citizen a vague impression that he desires a particular change. But, when the agitation has settled down on the dregs, when the excitement has died away, when the subject has been threshed out, when the issue is before him in its detail, he is sure to find much in it that is likely to disturb his habits, his ideas, his prejudices, or his interests; and so in the long-run, he votes 'No' to every proposal. The referendum can only be considered thoroughly successful by those who wish that there should be as little legislation as possible. (Maine 1976, 111)

The diatribe of Sir Henry Sumner Maine (1822–88) is an instance of one of the most frequently used arguments against referendums, namely that they run counter to the people's so-called 'real' interests and result in political deadlocks and institutional inertia. Given Maine's concern, we might easily be persuaded that instead of considering ways in which power can be controlled, we should concern ourselves with devising a system for legislating that will efficiently and quickly respond to the demands of our economic and social conditions. Or, put differently, given this assessment of the voters' lack of competence, one might be tempted to conclude that an effective second chamber is preferable to a popular referendum, as the members of a second chamber are more likely to reach decisions informed by careful deliberation. Maine's prediction sits uneasily with the evidence of the extent of voters' knowledge, as presented in chapter 1. That chapter did not directly address Maine's concern, namely that voters would reach ill-considered conclusions and so would vote against necessary reforms. The question is, however, whether referendums inevitably lead to outcomes akin to those predicted by Maine. That question cannot, of course, be answered conclusively in a single chapter (and perhaps not even in a book). This chapter can offer only a tentative answer, one based on impressions gained from earlier studies by country specialists.

The thrust of Maine's argument was that the referendum would give power to the people in conditions in which they would be unable to exercise that power in accordance with their preferences and long-term interests. The referendum might, in a curious sense, be seen as an undemocratic device because it (allegedly) allows voters to vote against measures which, given adequate time and knowledge, they would have supported. This view was forcefully articulated by Ramsey MacDonald, who distinguished between what the people might *say* they wanted, for example in a referendum, and what a statesman *knew* was in the people's *real* interests (see Sharp 1911). The question is, however, whether the voters are in fact as conservative as is suggested by Maine and MacDonald, i.e. whether they do in fact 'vote "No" to every proposal'.

It remains the view of many that a growing use of referendums would legitimise mob rule. Many observers seem to agree that referendums would lead to the reintroduction of the death penalty and other populist measures. This assertion is not supported by empirical evidence: provisions for referendums have not led to the reintroduction of the death penalty in any of the countries studied (except the USA). Yet, the fundamental question remains: are voters likely to vote 'no' because their 'prejudices … are apt to run counter to scientific conclusions', as hypothesised by Maine (1976, 87)? To answer this question we must take a more detailed look at the voters' patterns of, *endorsement* and *rejection* of different categories of political issues.

We might get a rough answer by categorising the referendums in all the polities (Switzerland and the USA have been excluded due to lack of data) in five categories. The referendum categories are:

- transfer of sovereignty;
- constitutional issues;
- economic issues;
- moral issues and
- all the other miscellaneous issues such as adoption and driving on the right, which have been submitted to referendums.

Transfer of sovereignty referendums: support for integration

One frequently encounters the claim that electorates in European referendums on integration consistently reject changes to the status quo. There is, however, scant scholarly support for this assertion. A survey by the author found that 49 per cent of all referendums in Western Europe between 1945 and 1998 resulted in a 'no' vote (see chapter 4 below); 'Yes' votes in referendums on European integration generally occur when a government has recently taken office. This was the case in 1972 and in 1993, when the Danish Governments of Jens Otto Krag and Poul Rasmussen, respectively, had been in office for less than two years. The same was true in the UK's referendum in 1975, Harold Wilson having taken office less than a year before the referendum.

Most 'no' outcomes occur in cases of governments that have been in office for a good number of years. This was true for Danish Prime Minister Poul Schlüter's Government, which lost the Maastricht referendum in 1992, held ten years after Schluter came to power. (The same tendency can be discerned in other referendums, e.g. Charles de Gaulle's referendum on local government reform in France in 1969, Irish Prime Minister Eamon de Valera's referendum on the electoral system in 1958 and James Callaghan's referendum on devolution in 1979.) There are several reasons for this relationship. Governing is never cost-free: all governments break promises, fail to deliver and enact unpopular laws, and the number of sins of commission is often a positive function of the years in office. Looking at the Danish referendum in 2000, it is not surprising that the Danish 'no' side's most effective weapons were the Government's record of broken promises and the widely held perception that Prime Minister Rasmussen had failed to honour his election pledge not to tinker with Denmark's generous supplementary pension scheme (*Efterlonnen*). Utilising the perception that the Government was 'worn out' proved an effective means of cutting the 'yes' side's initial 15 per cent lead in the polls.

Another structural factor favouring the 'no' side was Denmark's prosperous economy. Voters often punish governments for their poor handling of the economy. A general election, it has been claimed, is a referendum on the government's macro-economic record (Lewis-Beck and Rice 1992). The reverse tends to be true for referendums on European integration in Scandinavian countries and possibly elsewhere. The Danes voted 'yes' in 1986 (on the Single European Act)

Table 3.1   Referendums on European integration in Western
Europe

Country (year)	Theme	'Yes' vote (%)
Austria (1994)	Membership	66.6
Denmark (1972	Membership	90.1
Denmark (1986)	Single Act	75.4
Denmark (1992)	Maastricht	83.1
Denmark (1993)	Edinburgh	86.5
Denmark (1998)	Amsterdam	76.2
Denmark (2000)	Euro	56.1
France (1972)	British entry	67.7
France (1992)	Maastricht	51.0
Finland (1994)	Membership	56.0
Ireland (1972)	Membership	83.1
Ireland (1987)	Single Act	69.1
Ireland (1992)	Maastricht	57.1
Ireland (1998)	Amsterdam	56.3
Norway (1972)	Membership	46.5
Norway (1994)	Membership	47.8
Sweden (1994)	Membership	52.2
Switzerland (1992)	EES	49.7
United Kingdom (1975)	Renegotiation	67.2

Sources: C2D, University of Geneva; Butler and Ranney 1994.

and 1993 (on the Edinburgh Agreement), with both referendums
being held during a recession. The Swedes and the Finns, both of
whom had taken a battering during the ERM debacle, voted 'yes' in
their accession referendums in 1994, while the Norwegians, who had
been unaffected by recession, voted against membership. The Danish
'no' side made the most of this tendency in 2000. The leader of the
Danish People's Party (a rightist Eurosceptic party), Mrs Pia
Kjærsgaard, campaigned on the slogan 'You know what you've got.
You don't know what you get.' This strategy wrong-footed the
Government, which was left in the awkward position of criticising its
own economic record in order to make a case for Danish membership.

The Danish referendum in 2000 is atypical. Most European referendums result in 'yes' outcomes (see table 3.1) and this one highlights why and under what conditions referendums on European
integration fail. There is nothing to suggest that the voters automatically vote 'no' to proposals for further integration; conversely, there is

nothing to suggest that the voters are enthusiastic about further European integration.

Not so Nice: the Irish referendum on EU enlargement

At a time when the British Government is pondering whether to hold a referendum on the Single European Currency – a time when pundits debate whether such a plebiscite is winnable – the Irish referendum on the 7 June 2001 provides food for thought. When the Irish people were asked to ratify the Nice Treaty, they declined: 53.87 per cent voted *nil* ('no'), albeit on a small turnout of just 34.79 per cent (despite the inclusion of two other ballots on the same day[1]), an outcome that broadened the perception that Euro-scepticism was increasing among the Irish voters (*Economist*, 14 August 2001).

Ireland was the only country to hold a referendum on the Nice Treaty. Following a court ruling in 1986 (*McKenna* v. *An Taoiseach*), the constitutional position in Ireland is that all amendments to the European treatises must be submitted to referendums (O'Mahony 1998). The prospect of yet another referendum in Ireland did not, however, send shivers down spines in Brussels. Previous plebiscites on European issues had been pro-hegemonic (Qvortrup 2000; see table 3.2), though there has been a slippage in the 'yes' vote in each campaign following the accession referendum in 1972. The referendum campaign on the Nice Treaty was not followed closely by the international media across the Continent. Few – if any – expected a 'no' vote. Having capitalised on substantial funds from the EU, the Irish have traditionally been among the most enthusiastic supporters of European integration.

Following the defeat, the *taoiseach* (prime minister), Bertie Ahern, and the foreign minister, Brian Cowen, were forced to attend the EU summit in Gothenburg with a less than desirable result. The other European governments were not exactly respectful of the Irish voters' rejection of the treaty. The response was, perhaps, predictable for observers mindful of European governments' reaction to the Danish voters' rejection of the Maastricht Treaty in 1992 (Svenson 1996,43). The summit effectively ignored the verdict of the Irish voters and declared that ratification and enlargement could not be halted, and that the Irish Government would have to solve the problem forthwith.

While the other European governments subsequently softened their approach, they showed little regard for the verdict of the voters,

Table 3.2 Referendums in Ireland, 1998–2004

Date	Yes (%)	Turnout (%)	Subject
12 June 2004	62.89	59.10	No automatic citizenship
19 Oct. 2002	62.89	49.47	Nice Treaty
6 March 2002	49.58	42.89	Equal rights for mother and child
7 June 2001	62.08	34. 79	Abolition of death penalty
7 June 2001	64.22	34.78	International Criminal Court
7 June 2001	46.13	34.79	Nice Treaty
11 June 1999	77.83	51.08	Recognition of local authorities
22 May 1998	61.72	56.26	Amsterdam Treaty
22 May 1998	94.39	56.26	Belfast Agreement
30 Oct. 1998	52.65	47.17	Confidentiality of government meetings
28 Nov. 1996	74.83	29.23	Bail to be more difficult

Sources: www.referendum.ie and www.ireland.com.

let alone the principle of democracy, as set out in the 1937 Irish constitution – which upholds the right of the people 'in final appeal, to decide all questions of national policy, according to the requirements of the common good' (article 6).

Could the Government have expected the 'no' outcome? Perhaps not, as the Government was riding high in the opinion polls. Moreover, the latest *Eurobarometer* poll (*Eurobarometer* 53) showed that support for EU membership in the Republic of Ireland stood at 75 per cent. While down from 83 per cent in the previous *Eurobarometer*, this was still a substantial percentage, bearing in mind that the EU average satisfaction rating (for all 15 states) stood at 49 per cent. Further, 86 per cent admitted that Ireland had benefited from EU membership. It would seem that the Government had little to fear, and that the referendum would be almost a formality, just as had the previous ones.

The 'yes' side was bolstered by the support of the main political parties, the business sector, the bulk of the trades union movement (with just one union dissenting), the farming organisations and the mainstream media. On paper, the combined electoral support for *Fianna Fail* (FF), *Fine Gael* (FG), the Labour Party and the Progressive Democratic Party (PDP) accounted for 85 per cent of the votes cast in the previous general election (1997). This augured well, if only the voters could be trusted to follow the cues and signals given by the parties. Even the Catholic bishops issued a statement seemingly in favour of a 'yes' vote.

The 'yes' side was challenged by a motley and determined set of 'no' groups, whose campaign out-performed the combined might of the proponents of the treaty. The 'no' campaign comprised such diverse groups as 'No to Nice' (drawn largely from Youth Defence, a pro-life group), the Green Party, *Sinn Fein*, the Irish Campaign for Nuclear Disarmament, the Justice and Anti-Poverty Body Action from Ireland (AFRI), the Peace and Neutrality Alliance, the National Platform, and Christian Solidarity. It did not help the 'yes' parties that they proved unable to work together with a general election looming in 2002; it seems that their lack of co-operatation was prompted by mutual mistrust and party-political rivalries. The 'no' side was, by contrast, unhampered by such rivalry.

It was not altogether surprising that the 'yes' parties failed to co-operate: they lacked an incentive to concentrate their endeavours. Opinion polls had predicted a relatively easy win, though alarm bells should have begun to ring on Saturday 2 June when an *Irish Times*–MRBI poll revealed that 45 per cent intended to vote 'yes', whereas the figure two weeks previously had been 52 per cent; some 28 per cent indicated that they would be voting 'no', an increase of 7 per cent on the earlier poll; while the number of those undecided remained the same at 27 per cent. Somewhat surprisingly, the political parties took little notice of the poll.

Past experience and present conditions should have dictated that the result would be favourable to the 'yes' campaign. What was the reason for the outcome? Elections and referendum outcomes are produced by many factors, and any attempt at an explanation will necessarily omit certain details and focus on a few major determinants. The evidence from the polls and the campaign, but not necessarily other campaigns, suggest – as argued above – that the following factors were responsible for the outcome:

- the booming economy;
- party-political in-fighting; and
- mixed and confusing messages.

The voters had deep and real fears to contend with, but in addition there were many matters of contention between and within the political parties. Referendums, as already noted, are generally won during recessions, when the voters are willing to experiment (as with the

Swedes and the Finns in 1994); whereas in times of economic growth, as the reverse is true (as with the Norwegians' 'no' vote to the EU in 1994).

This was also the situation in which the Irish referendum of 2001 was held: with a GDP growth of 11 per cent there was little incentive to experiment with changes, not least if these would lead to a reduction of Ireland's net gains of EU membership. Furthermore, the 'yes' campaign was lacklustre and ineffective: The political parties did not present a unified front, other than agreeing on the necessity for a 'yes' result; indeed, they seemed more concerned with party-political point-scoring, than with securing a 'yes' vote. The timing of the vote and the length of the campaign were severely criticised. Ruairi Quinn, leader of the Labour Party said that the decision to hold the referendum at that time was dictated by partisan electoral considerations: the *taoiseach*, he claimed, wanted to keep the autumn free for a general election, and gave this consideration priority over the treaty (*Irish Times*, 15 June 2001). Door-to-door canvassing, which normally distinguishes Irish elections, was used mainly, and to good effect, by the 'no' side.

Posters urging a 'no' vote appeared overnight throughout the country bearing succinct and stark messages. Those issued by the 'No to Nice' campaign were particularly effective – striking black-and-red posters with the message, 'You will lose! Power. Money. Freedom.' In contrast the few posters put up by the mainstream political parties barely merited a glance. 'No to Nice' spokesperson, Justin Barrett described the FF posters as 'basically background noise' (*Irish Independent*, 9 June 2001). 'Yes' posters proclaimed that 'Nice is good for Ireland, good for Europe' almost as if it were an unpleasant medicine which had to be taken for the health of all. FGs poster campaign was an exercise in cost effectiveness, with one eye on matters of domestic concern. Pictures of the candidates for the next general election appeared on the posters, each containing a personalised message to the effect that 'Joe Bloggs supports a "yes" vote'.

As a result of the McKenna judgment – the Government was constrained from using public funds to advocate partisan positions in referendums, so that the political parties had to dig into their own pockets to fund their campaigns, though none of the main political parties did so. FF admitted spending precisely (Irish) £40,612 on its campaign and affected surprise that the 'no' camp could be so well resourced and organised; Bertie Ahern even accused the 'no' side of accepting foreign cash, from Euro-sceptical Tories and American fundamentalist groups, though without offering any proof.

The response from the 'no' camp was to produce receipts and to seek a High Court injunction to prevent the *Taoiseach* spreading false information. The political parties judged it wise to exercise restraint in spending, with a by-election on 30 June in the South Tipperary constituency. The main parties feared that their allies would free-ride, and were hence unwilling to commit funds. In short, party-political considerations took centre stage. The three main parties were desperate for victory in the by-election: FF had lost five by-elections since taking power; FG's new leader, Michael Noonan, needed to win so as to consolidate his status as an effective party leader; and Labour had been humiliated in the same constituency a year previously when it lost the seat to an independent socialist and wanted to redress that defeat. In addition there was speculation that Ahern would call a general election in the autumn (the general election is due in 2002).

No party wanted to fight a general election with depleted funds, thereby conceding the advantage to the other parties. Further, the cash flow from corporate donations had been hit by tales of scandal and corruption emanating from the Moriarty Tribunal, and was set to suffer further depletion with the new electoral reform bill which would impose a maximum limit on the amount of money a party or politician could receive from companies or individuals. As a result of the McKenna judgment the Government set up the Referendum Commission, which was charged with presenting the arguments for and against in a balanced and impartial way; however, it had to struggle to simultaneously remain within the McKenna judgment, inform the electorate and stimulate debate.

There were more fundamental problems affecting the 'yes' campaign. The 'no' side had the advantage of being able to focus on one issue – to secure a 'no' to Nice. There is evidence of co-operation between the disparate anti-Nice groups, especially in terms of local canvassing and leaflet distribution: the prize was too great to be lost in ideological bickering. They were aided by the unease which had been gradually building up over the 'My vision of Europe' speeches by European leaders, by the anger over the reprimand issued by the Referendum Commission to Finance Minister Charlie McGreevy on his budgetary policies, and by the call for tax harmonisation by Lionel Jospin, the French prime minister, during the final stages of the referendum campaign.

The main political parties were distracted from their handling of the referendum campaign by the different games being played out in the political shadows, for instance, the Tipperary by-election. A robust, unified front would, it could be argued, have sent a powerful message to the electorate, but party-political considerations prevented this. Despite their commitment to the treaty, it was clear that the opposition parties believed that the onus was on the Government to play the main part. Michael Noonan, leader of the main opposition party, FG advised FF not to play the two ends of the market, speaking out of both sides of its mouth and using different people to make these speeches: 'I want them to be up, forthright, in front of this campaign as the Government with the responsibility' (*Irish Times*, 22 May 2001).

The three-week campaign was punctuated by criticisms of government strategy, and Labour and FG immediately absolved themselves of any share of the blame for the final outcome, despite the fact that their own efforts were hardly impressive. There were also different agendas within the Government itself, which was a coalition between FF and the PDP. It has been evident for some time that there are differences in approach to European integration between Bertie Ahern, the *taoiseach* and leader of FF, and Mary Harney, the *tánaiste* (deputy-prime minister) and leader of the PDP. Ahern's belief was that if we are in, then we must be fully in. The *tánaiste* had come out against further European integration, saying that it would be against the interests of Ireland which, she claimed, was spiritually 'a lot closer to Boston than [to] Berlin' (*Irish Times*, 21 July 2000). Speaking to a meeting of the American Bar Association, Ms Harney warned against a centralised Europe 'with key political economic decisions being taken at Brussels level', stressing that she 'believe[d] in a Europe of independent states, not a United States of Europe' (*ibid.*).

Remarkably there are cross-party links here. Finance Minister Charlie McGreevy (FF) and Harney tend to support the US model of free markets, low taxation and lower social provision. That there are different agendas being played out within FF is also clear. Ms Sile de Valera warned that EU directives and regulations 'can often seriously impinge on our identity, culture and traditions'. She did not favour closer integration within the EU, stating that Ireland's embrace of Europe had led the people at times 'to forget our close and very important ties with the United States of America' (*ibid.*, 19 September 2000). It was, therefore, hardly surprising that the coalition parties were unable to present a convincing case to the electorate.

In retrospect, to place all the blame for the 'no' vote on the political parties would be unfair: as Michael Gallagher pointed out, referendum issues rarely run along party lines (*Irish Independent*, 11 June 2001); and party supporters may show the same diversity of views on issues, just like their elected representatives, and vote accordingly. A pre-referendum poll (*Irish Times*–MRBI poll, 2 June 2001) showed that while support for the Nice Treaty among PDP supporters stood at 65 per cent, it was merely 51 per cent of FF supporters, 50 per cent of Labour voters, and 45 per cent of the strongly pro-European party FG.

The polls indicated that the Government was within close range of victory. The outcome perhaps would – or at least could – have been very different had the 'yes' parties been able (and willing) to co-operate, but that was not the case. The 'yes' side was split by internal rivalries between the parties, and the focus on the Tipperary by-election created tension within the camp. The proponents of the Nice Treaty were anxious not to carry the full cost of the campaign lest the other 'yes' parties gained an advantage in the by-election. Consequently, the parties of the 'yes' side failed to co-operate. The 'no' side, by contrast, succeeded in maintaining unity – ostensibly because the parties involved were too ideologically heterogeneous to pose an electoral threat to each other.

It is, however, possible that the treaty would have been rejected even had the pro-treaty parties managed to co-operate. Evidence from previous referendums on European integration suggests that voters tend to reject proposed treaty changes if the domestic economy is performing well. With a GDP growth in excess of 11 per cent, the Irish had little incentive to vote yes!

It is impossible to identify the determining factor – politics is not an exact science. Many distinct concerns combined to bring about the rejection of the Nice Treaty. Fear of a loss of independence – the neutral status of Ireland – added to loss of EU subsidies and people's anger at the Government for taking the electorate for granted disposed the majority of voters to vote 'no'. Further, the row with the EC over public spending, several ministers' Euro-critical remarks and general disagreement as the aim of Irish membership of the EU seem – with the benefit of hindsight – to explain the outcome. The referendum was another case of Murphy's Law: all that can go wrong will go wrong!

It seems that these factors combined in the 'no' side's favour in the next referendum on the Nice Treaty (held in 2002). It is, however, indisputable that the Irish can no longer be counted on as Euro-enthusiasts (*Kaufmann* 2004, 26). Proponents of further European integration are well advised to remember this, lest they suffer the same fate as the Irish 'yes' side.

Referendums on constitutional issues – with special reference to Australia

New constitutions, as distinct from new amendments, have generally been endorsed by electorates (though the Canadian voters' rejections of the Charlottetown Agreement and the French voters' rejection of the first proposal for a constitution for the Fourth Republic stand out as rather remarkable exceptions to the rule). The same is true of referendums on the relatively uncontroversial issue of voting age (held in Ireland and Denmark), of which all but one carried the day. The bulk of rejections in the category of constitutional referendums have been measures proposed by governments and were often drafted with a view to increasing the powers of the ruling party (examples are given below). Yet if we ignore Australia the success rate would have been considerably higher; for without Australia we would find that roughly 80 per cent had passed. The question is, therefore, whether anything can be forwarded to explain this. Australia stands out as the country with the poorest record on constitutional amendments: only 5 of the 26 referendums held there since 1945 have carried the day. This figure is even more striking if we consider that only 8 out of the 44 referendums held since 1902 have been carried.

This low success rate has been attributed to special institutional factors. It has been argued that 'the requirement of affirmative majorities in four states out of six, as well as a national majority, proves to be a stiff obstacle' to amendments of the Australian constitution. It is correct that this clause has occasionally prevented the adoption of measures supported by the majority of the voters: both the industrial relations and the marketing referendums in 1946 were supported by majorities (50.3 per cent 'yes' vote), but failed to win the support of majorities in more than half of the states; and the same was true of the simultaneous elections referendum in 1977 (62.3 per cent 'yes' vote).

These defeats, however, represent only 3 out of 24 of the total number of rejected proposals, so that the double majority requirement cannot be blamed for the spectacular failure of the remaining 21 constitutional amendments. Another hypothesis which may explain the

Australian reluctance to support the proposed measures is the general opposition to centralisation. The voters have, by and large, endorsed measures unrelated to the centre – periphery divide, i.e. rights for aborigines, judges' retirement and territory franchise for referendums; but they have consistently rejected attempts to strengthen the Federal Government. That 27 of the 35 rejected amendments would have increased the legislative powers of the Commonwealth Parliament seems to suggest that opposition to centralisation is the main reason for the voters' rejections of constitutional amendments. This tendency has been interpreted as evidence of a prevailing conservatism. The 'necessary progressive amendment' of the Commonwealth constitution has, according to one observer, been 'dashed by mindless partisanship, general apathy and ignorance' (Crisp 1978, 55).

It is undoubtedly correct that conservatism has played a role. The opposition parties have often been able to wage an effective campaign, raising fears of the consequences of the proposed measures in an attempt to embarrass the Government (even when the opposition agrees with the Government's proposals). This has often led to a situation in which 'many voters, puzzled by the wording, bemused by the complexity of the issue ... shrug their shoulders and vote no' (Aitkin 1978, 134). The most efficient tactic has been to highlight the (allegedly) unpopular prospects of further centralisation. Dean Jeansch (1992, 56) writes:

> In American style federalism such as Australia adopted, the powers of the central government are at the outset very limited, enumerated. Later suggested amendments are, therefore, almost inevitably proposals for citizens to transfer powers from the nearer to the more remote authority Such requests consequently tend to mobilise local pride and local interests against the changes ... abstract or complex constitutional issues are for most people hard to grasp and evaluate. Opponents of change paint the proposals as intended to give more of 'our' power to 'them', to let 'them' do things disadvantageous to us.

There are examples of referendums in which the opposition has sought to follow this strategy of appealing to the voters' sense of local pride and, indeed, opposition to centralisation. Yet we cannot in fairness conclude that opposition to centralisation is a conclusive proof of ignorance. As Geoffrey de Q. Walker (1987, 69) has argued, although 'respectable arguments can be put forward in favour of centralised national government as opposed to decentralisation of power through a federal system ... one can hardly say in fairness that a preference for decentralisation and federalism is conclusive proof of ignorance, stupidity and inertia'. A similar conclusion has been reached by Richard Miles who rebukes the traditional thesis that ignorance leads to 'no' voting: he writes that 'those who spend some time reviewing the cases for or against were more likely to vote "no"' (1998, 241).

Thus, while it is difficult to draw conclusions from this evidence, the poll suggests that the *correct* position, that which voters would have taken had they been fully informed, was a 'no' vote. The voters' reluctance to favour the proposals is, perhaps, rather a result of general uncertainty about the consequences of the proposed reforms. This interpretation seems especially plausible when applied to the referendum in 1988, when lawyers found that the 4 proposed questions would in reality result in 30 amendments to the constitution (*Australian Law Journal*, 1988, 977). This raised the suspicion that the Government had a hidden agenda and prompted cautious voters to vote against the proposals (De Q Walker 1987, 69).

Another tendency which may explain the low success rate in Australian referendums is the voters' reluctance to support measures interpreted as attempts to gerrymander the constitution. The proposal concerning democratic elections, which would have increased the Labour Party's share of the seats by requiring equality in the number of people in each constituency rather than equality in the number of votes, was rejected, apparently because the voters were unwilling to strengthen the position of the Labour Party *vis-à-vis* the bourgeois parties.[1] The 1967 Nexus proposal might be seen as another example of this fair-play tendency in Australian referendums. The proposed amendment would have altered the requirement in section 24 of the constitution that 'the number of members of the House of Representatives shall be, as nearly as practicable, twice the number of senators' (a section intended to safeguard the power and prestige of the senators). The smaller parties had gained seats in the Upper House since the introduction of the single transferable vote (STV) system for elections to the Senate in 1949, and they therefore had a strong interest in defending the system, as a reduction in the number of seats would reduce their influence. The danger of gerrymandering the constitution to the benefit of Labour and the Liberal–Country Party alliance seems to have convinced 59.7 per cent of the voters to say 'no' to the proposal (Coper 1987, 372).

This tendency may also account for the similar patterns in other polities' referendums on alterations of constitutional powers: proposals for strengthening Parliament by extending the parliamentary terms (as in New Zealand in 1967 and 1990), for altering the electoral system and for increased powers for the political Centre are among the measures which have most consistently been rejected in referendums. One of the most persistent findings in referendum research is that voters are prone to oppose or even reject proposals for constitutional reform which do not have cross-party support. The Irish voters' rejections of the ruling FF's attempts to introduce the first-past-the-post electoral system in 1959 and 1968 are cases in point (Manning 1978, 102).

This reluctance to support attempts to gerrymander the constitution may also be seen to explain why voters in New Zealand refused assent to extensions of the parliamentary term of the House of Representatives in 1967, which would have strengthened the position of the dominant parties (Palmer 1987, 255), as well as why Australian voters repeatedly rejected proposals which would have strengthened the Labour Party's position.

The only country in which referendums aimed at extending the power of one branch of government have succeeded is France, where the electorate backed President Charles de Gaulle's attempts to create a stronger presidency by supporting his plea for the direct election of the executive in October 1962. Yet the fact that De Gaulle lost the 1969 referendum, which was intended to curb the powers of the Senate and the local assemblies – both 'obdurate bastions of anti-Gaullism' (Wright 1978) – indicates that French voters have the same propensity to reject attempts to gerrymander the constitution. As I have said, the same is true of Ireland, where voters rejected the electoral law backed by De Valera, while on the same day electing him to serve as president of the Republic. These results supported the prediction made by L. E. H. Leckey (1899, 289), who speculated that the referendum 'would enable the nation to reject a measure it dislikes, without destroying a ministry of which it approves'.

The record of referendums on constitutional issues does not present us with a single tendency. The voters have been prone to reject controversial measures, especially if the measure in question is supported by only one side of the political spectrum (for example, the Left's rejected proposal in France in 1946 and the proposed changes of the PR electoral system in Ireland in 1959 and 1968). This pattern of rejection and adoption does not support the denunciations of the referendum of Maine and others; rather it vindicates Dicey's argument that the referendum can serve the function of an alternative second chamber.

Referendums on moral issues

The evidence regarding moral issues indicates that voters have generally supported proposed liberalisation of divorce and abortion laws, 66 per cent of which have been endorsed. This conclusion must, however, be qualified: only Italy and Ireland have held referendums on moral issues (though it should be noted that a measure for the decriminalisation of homosexuality was overwhelmingly supported by Swiss voters in 1992). An anti-abortion measure was rejected in 1985; and while some anti-abortion measures have been carried in the USA, they have later been nullified by the courts, and several anti-gay measures have carried the day in certain states (Cronin 1989, 94–95).

Italian voters have endorsed proposals for the maintenance of the divorce laws and the decriminalisation of abortion, despite massive campaigning by the Roman Catholic Church. Irish voters have, on the other hand, voted to insert an anti-abortion clause within the constitution (1983), and have voted against the repeal of the constitutional prohibition of divorce in 1986, before supporting more progressive proposals in referendums in the 1990s. These tendencies have led one observer to the conclusion that in 'Italy voters in divorce and abortion referendums proved *more* liberal than expected, while in Ireland they proved *less* liberal than expected' (Bogdanor 1994, 85).

It is, however a matter of dispute whether the voting behaviour of the Irish, as recorded in ecological data, allow us to conclude that they are resistant to changes proposed by the political elite. There was clearly a conservative tendency in the referendums on abortion in 1983 and on divorce in 1986 (at least if one considers reforms on these issues to be 'progressive').

On the other hand, one of the most striking indications of the extent of the Irish voters' conservatism is, or so it has been argued, that there is a striking coherence in consecutive conservative votes in referendums on moral issues: according to Richard Sinnott (1995), over 90 per cent of those who voted *for* the abortion ban in 1983 also voted *against* the relaxation of the ban on divorce in 1986.

Ecological data from the constituencies enable us to correlate the 'yes' vote for every constituency in each of the referendums: for instance the correlation between them in the 1983 right to travel referendums was an impressive 0.97. Yet more recent referendums seem to have produced markedly less conservative results, such as the rejection of a further restriction on access to abortions in 1992 and the support given to divorce in 1995. More recent findings based on ecological data show that the correlation between the constituencies which returned 'yes' votes in the abortion referendum in 1983 and the constituencies which returned the same results in the 1992 abortion referendum was a mere $r = 0.18$.

This result suggests a remarkable change in attitudes towards abortion. Whether a sea-change in the opinions on these issues has occurred cannot, however, be determined on the basis of an ecological study alone, but requires an analysis of survey data.

The 1983 abortion referendum had led to a constitutional amendment which stated: 'The State acknowledges the right to life of the unborn and, with due regard to the equal right to life of the mother, guarantees in its laws to respect, and, as far as practicable, by its laws to vindicate that right.' The ambiguous wording of the clause, which had been criticised by Prime Minister Garret FitzGerald (Gallagher 1996, 97), led to renewed discussion in 1992 when the Supreme Court (in the case of *Attorney General* v. *X*) ruled that a 14-year old girl who had been raped had the right to travel to the mainland for an abortion, as she had threatened to commit suicide were she refused so to do. The court interpreted the latter as a threat to the life of the mother and thus allowed X to travel for the purpose of obtaining an abortion. The court did, however, emphasise that the case was an exception to the general rule that abortion was illegal in Ireland.

The decision offended opponents and proponents alike, the former because they had sought an absolute ban on abortion in 1983 and the latter because they had sought to remove an amendment restricting the right to travel. Consequently both sides were united in the demand for a new referendum on abortion, a demand strengthened by the claims of opponents to the Maastricht Treaty, who suggested that ratification of the treaty would make it impossible to restrict the freedom to travel and consequently make it impossible to forbid abortion.

Faced with the possibility of a referendum on the Maastricht Treaty, which in effect would be a proxy for a referendum on the right to travel, *Taoiseach* Albert Reynolds promised to hold a referendum on abortion after the Maastricht referendum. The Government proposed three amendments: a less ambiguous wording of the constitutional prohibition of abortion (which excluded the threat of suicide as a risk against the life of the mother, often referred to as the 'right to life amendment'); an amendment allowing women to seek information about abortions abroad; and, finally, a clause allowing Irish women to travel abroad for abortions. The 'right to life' amendment failed to satisfy both liberals (who supported a pro-choice option) and conservatives (who wanted abortion completely outlawed). FF, the main party in government, had hoped that the proposal would satisfy the pragmatists within the main political parties. Yet the proposal was opposed by the main opposition party, FG, the Labour Party and the PDP. These parties did, however, support the right to travel and the right to information amendments. The results of the 1992 referendums were that the right to life amendment was defeated by 65.5 per cent of the voters, whereas the right to travel and the right to information amendments were carried by 62.3 and 59.9 per cent of the votes, respectively, that is, a victory for the status quo (Gallagher 1996, 92).

Such outcomes might suggest that Irish voters have become less conservative over the course of the period, not least when we consider that the majority overturned the previous ban on divorce in 1995. This interpretation appears sound as far as the 1986 and the 1995 divorce referendums are concerned, as the vote concerned almost identical proposals. Yet this interpretation is not upheld by an analysis of the abortion referendums. Survey studies have identified three categories of Irish abortion voters: conservatives, pragmatists and liberals, each category representing roughly one-third of the electorate. The conservatives are opposed to any liberalisation of the abortion laws; the pragmatists are opposed to abortion, but accept that abortions can be acceptable in cases of rape; whereas the liberals are in favour of abortion. In each of the referendums the pragmatists' votes proved crucial: they supported the 1983 proposal (on a constitutional entrenchment of the ban on abortion), whereas they joined forces with the liberals in three referendums in 1992. What appears to have been a shift in opinion towards a more liberal stance was in fact not a change in the position of the pragmatists, who, while in favour of the pro-life amendment in 1983, were not ready to endorse what many regarded as an extremist position of the Catholic Right. This finding, which is interesting from a psephological point of view, does not however answer the fundamental issue of whether voters are inherently reactionary, as hypothesised by Maine (1976).

Secular observers may find that the Irish voters' opposition to abortion and divorce is in itself evidence of reactionary conservatism. There are, however, perfectly legitimate moral and social reasons for opposing abortion and divorce; in any case, before rushing to condemn the Irish of blind, reactionary conservatism, it might be noted that they voted to abolish the death penalty in 2001.

That the Irish *have* voted conservatively is not therefore a result which in itself supports Maine's assertion that public participation has impeded reforms which the voters, had they been more knowledgeable of political issues, would have supported. It is therefore difficult to use Irish voting outcomes as an argument against referendums on the ground that those outcomes are invariably reactionary because of electorates' limited knowledge.

The voters in Ireland did not vote against the recommendations of the political elites, so they have not prevented sensible reforms proposed by the Government. Their apparent conservatism on moral issues is perhaps an example of what we might call Irish exceptionalism, i.e. a consequence of the unique influence of the Catholic Church in the Irish Republic.

Referendums on economic issues

Proposals concerning economic policies have often been rejected by voters: only 27 per cent of the referendums on economic issues have resulted in 'yes' votes, a tendency that has been interpreted as a partial verification of Maine's hypothesis. The rejection of the Danish land laws in four referendums in 1963 is perhaps the most frequently cited example of what has been interpreted as a reactionary electorate's unwillingness to support proposals which, it was claimed, were consistent with the voters' general political beliefs. It was well documented that the voters were swayed by a simplistic campaign, which (incorrectly) equated the land laws with mass nationalisation of the farmland. The Conservatives, opponents of the land laws, made much of the charge that the laws would introduce socialism, and repeated again and again that private ownership would be in danger if the laws were approved – a Conservative poster that attracted much attention showed a giant black hand reaching down and seizing a modest home. This campaign (waged by the bourgeois parties) secured the defeat of the proposals. Yet it must not be forgotten that the opposition to the proposals was part of a more general protest against the Government's breach of the constitutional convention that major economic proposals must receive the consent of all the major parties in the *Folketinget*.

The campaign against the land laws was fought on the principle of consensual government, not on the issue of the land laws themselves, i.e. a vote for the land laws was seen as an approval of the Government's breach of the consensual principles which had underpinned Danish politics since the 1920s. The fact that the bourgeois parties succeeded in their campaign against the planning and structural policies can, in large measure, be explained as a result of two factors: one-sided campaign spending and the voters' uneasiness about the Government's departure from the ideal of consensual politics. Whether these two factors were sufficient to secure the defeat of the proposals remains an open question, yet it is difficult to maintain that the result was a product solely of the voters' opposition to change; that is to say, it does not follow from the Danish result that referendums on controversial economic policies will inevitably be rejected by the voters. There is nothing inherent in referendums on economic issues to lead necessarily to rejections of the proposals (Miller 1982, 59).

The same conclusion seems to hold true for other polities, such as Sweden and Italy. Tage Erlander expressed the view that 'it becomes much harder to pursue an effective reform policy if reactionaries are offered the opportunity to appeal to people's natural conservatism' (quoted in Bogdanor 1994). This seems to be contradicted by the fact that the Swedish voters endorsed the pension scheme proposed by Erlander's own Government in 1957 – despite *massive* campaigning by the opposing Conservative Party. Erlander's view is also at odds with the fact that the Italian voters supported the Craxi Government's austerity programme in the *Scala Mobile* referendum in 1985, despite the charge of the Communists (*Partito Communisto Italiano* – PCI) that the repeal of wage indexation would jeopardise citizens' social rights and lead to the abolition of the welfare state.

The remaining referendums on economic issues, the Australian polls on social services (1946), industrial employment (1946), rent and prices (1948), prices (1973) and incomes (1973), all of which were proposed by Labour, seem to indicate that referendums on economic issues are likely to result in defeats. The social services referendum is the only Australian poll on an economic issue in the post-war era to be enacted and also the only referendum to receive tacit support from the opposition.

The general picture in the remaining referendums on economic issues has been that the Liberal–Country Party alliance has used the campaigns as a vehicle for party-political purposes and so opposed the proposals, irrespective of the merit of the proposed reforms (Aitkin 1978, 134). This strategy has often allowed an opposition to exploit the unpopularity of a government and so block the enactment of reforms which earlier had been supported by opposition parties. Yet there is no conclusive proof that such an obstructive tactic in itself has been the main reason for the ill fate of 4 out of 5 Australian referendums on economic issues. A convincing case can be made for the view that these reform proposals were rejected for the same reason as most of the other proposed constitutional amendments in Australia, namely because they increased the powers of the Federal Government (De Q Walker 1987, 89).

It is also to be doubted that the 1973 proposals were defeated as a result of the Liberal–Country Party alliance's obstructive campaign, for it is evident that the opposition played party politics with the issue. Yet the fact that the trade unions campaigned against proposals put forward by a Labour Government suggests that the proposals were hardly commonsensical and necessary, as the Labour administration had claimed. It seems plausible that voters can occasionally be deluded into voting for proposals which are in reality opposed to their long-term interests, yet there are surprisingly few instances where this has happened, California excepted. That Californian voters supported proposition 13 which 'not only [would] keep property taxes down, which it was supposed to do, but also ... [would] centralise control over many areas which no one wanted', is not, therefore, an argument against referendums on economic issues (Polsby and Wildavsky 1984, 279). There are no examples outside of California of referendums having had effects comparable to those of proposition 13.

One possible, if purely hypothetical, explanation is that voters in Europe and Oceania, unlike Californian voters, had the opportunity to consider and discuss the consequences of their decisions and so managed to arrive at more prudent decisions.

Referendums on other issues

This leaves us with the category of miscellaneous issues, like the French independence for Algeria referendums (1961 and 1962), the

Austrian, Swedish and Italian nuclear power referendums (1980, 1978 and 1987), the Irish adoption referendum in 1979, most of the popular referendums held in Italy from 1978 onwards, and Sweden's referendum on right-side driving in 1955 – the large number of issues which, for various reasons, were submitted to referendums but do not fit into the above categories. What we are interested in is whether these proposals were rejected as a result of a general conservative populism.

It would seem that the Italian popular referendums have followed a conservative pattern, as the voters have rejected all government-supported proposals since 1987. It does not, however, follow from this *apparent* pattern that the referendum outcomes in Italy reflect a general opposition to change. A strong case has, indeed, been made for the view that the popular referendum, rather than being a merely conservative weapon, was instrumental in bringing about the changes which, in 1993, led to the demise of the malfunctioning First Republic and its increasingly corrupt *partitocrazia*. Richard Katz writes:

> When the Italian voters overwhelmingly approved the referendum of the April 18–19 [1993] abrogating several sections of the senate electoral law ... they sent a message that they wanted constitutional reform. They also left the country with a fundamentally unworkable electoral system. The message was amplified by the fact that it was accompanied by several other referenda implicitly criticising the way that the parties had managed their own affairs and the affairs of the state as well as by the fact that it followed similar messages send by previous referenda. (1995, 93)

These outcomes do not support the conservative position hypothesised by Maine (1976). The Italian referendums show rather that the voters were willing to support reform, perhaps because there was a more credible alternative to the faltering First Republic (Uleri 1996, 113). Thus the (popular) referendum can, in spite of its conservative nature, be instrumental in changing the political system. It must, however, be stressed that the political climate in Italy in the early 1990s was unique, so that it would be erroneous to read a general tendency into the events which led to the demise of the First Republic. The history of referendums in Italy in the 1970s and the early 1980s showed the Italians to be cautiously conservative. It would seem that the referendums of the 1990s indicate that this pattern has changed and that the Italians have become more inclined to embrace radical change.

The persistence of a party system which reflects 'the cleavage structure of the 1920s' (Lipset and Rokkan 1967, 50) has occasionally led to situations in which the parties have failed to represent new – so-called 'post-materialist' – values. The referendum provides a possible remedy in such situations, i.e. it can (in the language of the structural functionalists) be an alternative political *aggregator* (Almond and Powell 1978, 198).

This has been the case in Switzerland especially, where the permanent four-party coalition has forced voters to find new ways of confronting novel political problems. The old parties' failure to respond to environmental problems has consequently led to a considerable growth in referendums on environmental protection, nuclear energy limitation and road traffic restriction (Kobach 1994, 143). This tendency has been less pronounced in other polities (presumably because of the absence of 'initiatives'). Yet post-materialist concerns perhaps explain the occurrence as well as the result of the referendums on nuclear energy in Austria, Sweden and Italy. It is characteristic of these referendums that all of them have resulted in 'no' verdicts: a narrow 50.5 majority of the Austrian voters defied Chancellor Bruno Kreisky's plea for a 'yes' vote in the 1978 referendum on whether to use the Zwetendorf reactor 20 miles north of Vienna; 71.1 per cent of Italian voters opposed Italian participation in nuclear power plants abroad in November 1987; and the majority of Swedish voters opted for a phasing out of the country's nuclear power stations in 1980. Those verdicts, along with similar results in Switzerland, indicate that voters have been remarkably conservative on the issue of nuclear energy. Such conservatism does not, however, mean that the voters' decisions can be explained as a consequence of conservative populism. The striking correlation between a high level of education and a negative attitude to nuclear energy in Austria (and similar tendencies elsewhere) indicate that the voters were, at the very least, capable of understanding the issues. Moreover, the experts disagreed about the 'right' answer on whether the nuclear power station posed a risk to the population. The decision was, as Ian Budge (1996, 77) has noted, 'less a technical decision and more of a political evaluation: are the levels of risk tolerable compared to the likely benefits?'

   That the voters' conclusion in some of these referendums differed from that of some of the experts does not therefore imply that the voters' decisions were wrong. The voters, like members of a jury simply weighed the evidence presented by the two sides and reached the decision that the safety issue was more important than economic benefits.

Excursus: the referendum as a *deus ex machina*

The referendum is by its very nature a conservative weapon: the voters can disapprove only of the measures put before them. This is true even of so-called plebiscites, i.e. referendums called by a political leader to secure a mandate for a controversial policy (often one opposed by the legislature). Even autocratic leaders have experienced defeats in referendums, such as the Uruguay *junta*'s surprising defeat in the plebiscite in 1980. Plebiscites rarely result in defeats, however, being, in Gordon Smith's terms (see Smith 1976), pro-hegemonic in outcome and tightly controlled in initiation.

The category of the plebiscite contains extremely varied cases, ranging from grotesquely rigged polls in totalitarian states (where support for the measures proposed is rarely below 99.9 per cent) to those initiated by democratically elected chief executives in constitutional democracies. The former instance is obviously rare in the Western world simply because its countries are democracies, though plebiscites have been frequently used in countries in post-communist states.

In Turkmenistan 99.9 per cent of the voters extended the president's mandate until the year 2000; and the president in Kazakhstan similarly won approval for a continuation of his mandate, just as Belarus' President Lukashenko, won *de facto* unlimited powers in a plebiscite in November 1996. Such plebiscites are almost identical to the classical Napoleonic plebiscite – like that in 1807 in which Napoleon asked the voters to approve his reinstatement as an hereditary emperor. Yet these plebiscites are of little interest to a study of democratic referendums. The question of interest here is how to evaluate plebiscites called in constitutional democracies.

Those who, like Henry Maine, argue that referendums are undesirable because they lead to inefficiency and deadlock may find it difficult to use this objection against plebiscitary referendums as this variant of direct citizen involvement, for better or for worse, is intended to reduce the risk of political deadlock. Proponents of efficient government supported Boris Yeltsin's use of the referendum to solve the constitutional crisis in 1993, though such use of plebiscites does raise the question of democratic legitimacy. Yeltsin had (in the aftermath of the overthrow of the Communist-dominated *Duma*) proposed a new constitution which granted him significant powers. Yet the Constitutional Court, appointed before Yeltsin had taken office, ruled that the proposal should be approved only if more than 50 per cent of the eligible voters supported it. The proposal was, according to the official figures, supported by 58 per cent of the turnout (31 per cent of the eligible voters), but the Constitutional Court's own lack of democratic legitimacy prevented it from pursuing the matter, and the constitution was approved, despite claims of vote-rigging (Slater 1996, 4).

It is arguably correct that such plebiscitary referendums give legitimacy to radical changes. It is difficult, however, to draw specific lessons from countries in the midst of democratic transition. To assess the effects of plebiscitary referendums, especially their effects on controversial political reforms, requires a study of the use of the plebiscitary referendum in a fully established constitutional democracy. The only constitutional democracy which has used the device is France.

The plebiscitary referendum in France is commonly associated with President de Gaulle, who used the provisions for plebiscitary referendums on four occasions; submitting them under article 11 of the 1958 constitution, which reads:

> The president of the Republic may on the proposal of the Government during sessions of Parliament or on the joint motion of its two houses submit to a referendum any bill dealing with organisation of public authorities, entailing approval of a community agreement, or providing for authorisation to ratify a treaty which, without being contrary to the Constitution, would affect the function of institutions.

The very inclusion of article 11 sharply distinguishes the constitution of the Fifth Republic from the constitution of the Fourth Republic which restricted the use of referendums to 'constitutional matters', declaring that 'in all matters the people shall [exercise their sovereignty] through their deputies in the National assembly'.

It is undisputed that De Gaulle interpreted article 11 in accordance with his own political interests, and that he used the plebiscitary referendum as a means both of breaking deadlocks with the Right and of acquiring popular legitimacy for controversial policies. The policy on the Algerian problem, which contributed to the downfall of the Fourth Republic, proved difficult to settle through parliamentary channels as a significant number of the deputies were opposed to Algerian independence, or as De Gaulle put it 'L'Algérie bloque tout' – Algeria obstructs everything (quoted in Wright 1989, 36).

The provisions for plebiscites provided De Gaulle with a means of bypassing Parliament, a way of breaking deadlocks. Those of 1961 and 1962 can thus be seen as examples of referendums which solved problems that had paralysed the political system, resulting not in conservatism but in dramatic change such as would have been inconceivable in their absence. The 1961 and 1962 referendums on the Algerian problem proved relatively uncontroversial, not least because De Gaulle secured a resounding endorsement of his policy. The remaining plebiscites were more controversial. The most controversial plebiscite initiated by de Gaulle was arguably his decision to call a plebiscite on the direct election of the president in the autumn of 1962. Leaders from all the non-Gaullist parties, on the Right as well as on the Left, and legal experts believed it unconstitutional to change the constitution by this route rather than by the route prescribed in article 89 of the constitution (Bell 1992, 134). The president's decision was consequently appealed to the *Conseil constitutionnel*, which supported the view of the claimants, but declared itself unable to adjudicate on the matter (Bell 1992, 134). In the referendum De Gaulle won the support of 61.7 per cent of the voters on a 77 per cent turnout, thus vindicating the view that the verdict of the people and not that of the judiciary was the 'supreme court' in France.

Objections to the plebiscite, or the plebiscitary referendum (as we might call it in democratic countries), are radically different from the objections to the referendum raised by Maine. The charge against the plebiscitary referendum is not that it stands in the way of salutary reform, but rather that it enables the executive to secure a mandate for a controversial policy by overriding the legislature (Sartori 1989, 130). Gaston Monnerville, the president of the Senate, described De Gaulle's use of the plebiscitary referendum as a 'deliberate, calculated, and outrageous violation of the constitution'. This objection ignores what historians call the 'counterfactual argument', i.e. what would have happened in the absence of a referendum. It is unlikely that the Algerian problem would have been solved had it not been submitted to a plebiscitary referendum. The opponents of the Evian agreement would have found it much easier to block Algerian independence if the proposal had not received support from the people. The plebiscitary referendum was not a *coup d'etat*, as Mitterrand argued, because De Gaulle could have been defeated. The charge that plebiscitary referendums are quasi-dictatorial is, of course, correct in totalitarian and authoritarian states where the result is rigged; it cannot, however, be sustained in relation to a constitutional democracy where there is a chance that the plebiscite will be defeated (as, indeed, De Gaulle learned to his cost in 1969).

To sum up, the plebiscitary referendum can provide the executive with a *deus ex machina* effect to overcome political deadlocks, i.e. it can assist governmental efficiency.

Referendums as a conservative weapon: a preliminary assessment

Robert Michels saw 'the incompetence of the masses' and their lack of time in which to consider the issues as 'the two principal objections' to the referendum. Yet the thrust of his argument (1959, 336) against the referendum was not just that the voters would reject measures, but that they would make decisions that are inconsistent with their long-term preferences. Referendums would, so it was argued, prevent a government from enacting necessary (but perhaps unpopular) measures, delay institutional changes and hinder the enactment of complex reforms.

The empirical evidence surveyed does not suggest that the referendum obstructs the system of representative government; nor does it support the charge that the voters are incapable of reaching informed decisions. The charge that the referendum stands in the way of 'salutary reforms' seems on the whole to be unfounded.

Voters have generally supported steps towards closer European integration, tending to favour uncontroversial constitutional changes (like the lowering of the voting age), as well as endorsing the reform of inefficient political systems (France in 1958 and Italy in 1991–93). But voters have tended to reject measures that were perceived as attempts to gerrymander the constitution (Ireland in 1958, Australia in 1974 and New Zealand in 1990).

The referendum has not, as some conservatives have hoped, halted the introduction of the welfare state; nor has it hindered the implementation of so-called structural policies and economic reforms. But the 'people's veto' has ensured that the piecemeal implementation of reforms has perhaps inadvertently accommodated the interests of majorities and minorities alike.

It is perhaps fair to say that the referendum, in Dicey's words, has been a gradualist instrument in which 'the efforts of obstructionists come to nothing [while] … the fervour of enthusiasts achieve little in hurrying on innovation' (1905, 208). This tendency is in itself a potent argument for the use of the referendum!

Note

1 There was an amendment designed to delete any remaining references to the death penalty in the constitution (this was approved by 62.08 per cent), and an amendment dealing with the ratification of the International Court (approved by 64.22 per cent).

4

Is the referendum a constitutional safeguard?

It is the *raison d'être* of the referendum to serve as a constitutional safeguard, yet we have no guarantee that it does provide voters with a Lockean check on Parliament. Indeed, it has been argued that referendums in practice strengthen the power of the ruling elites rather than the reverse. This view, which is discussed in this chapter, has been summed up by Butler and Ranney: 'Referendums are held infrequently, usually only when the government thinks that they are likely to provide a useful ad hoc solution to a particular constitutional or political problem or to set the seal of legitimacy on a change of regime' (1978, 221). This conclusion indicates that the referendum is unlikely to provide citizens with a constitutional safeguard. As Lijphart has concluded, 'when governments control the referendum, they will tend to use it only when they expect to win' (1984, 203).

This is a depressing conclusion in terms of the Diceyan view of the referendum as a constitutional safeguard. The referendum is unlikely to provide voters with a constitutional safeguard, let alone answer the question *Quis custodiet ipsos custodes*, if Parliament is to decide when it wishes to be checked. What Dicey considered an effective 'people's veto' may prove to be a constitutional paper tiger – an ineffective constitutional safeguard, which fulfils its function as a 'people's veto' only when governments miscalculate the unpopularity of a proposed measure.

Yet even critics of referendums concede that parliaments on rare occasions should be willing to hold them on issues that are unpopular among the voters but supported by the political elites (Morel 1992a, 836). One in particular exemplifies the use of the referendum to address a situation in which a parliamentary decision was considered undemocratic. The Norwegian referendum on EC membership in 1972 was, according to Lijphart, held because 'there was a strong feeling that on an issue of this nature and importance a parliamentary vote alone would be illegitimate' (1984, 204); that is to say, the pro-European Norwegian *Stortinget* (Parliament) was willing to have itself checked by its Eurosceptical electorate. This assertion is, however, based on a somewhat inaccurate interpretation of the situation. The Norwegian referendum in 1972 was called *not* as a result of a prevailing democratic sentiment, but, as (Bjørklund has shown 1982), because the political parties were split on the issue of Norway's membership of the EEC and especially because a minority of the *Stortinget* (who were opposed to Norway's entry into the EEC) skilfully managed to use this split within the major party to secure a referendum on the issue (Listhaug 1989, 91). The anti-EEC (Socialist, Communist and Liberal parties, although constituting a minority in the *Stortinget*, were able to deepen the schisms over the issue within the Labour Party to a degree which threatened to divide the party. It was, according to Bjørklund, this prospect of a rebellion within the Labour Party which more than anything else forced Prime Minister Trygve Bratteli to submit the issue to a referendum.

Yet the fundamental question in relation to the referendum's function as a constitutional safeguard concerns not only when and why they are held, but whether a government's actions are restricted by them. Dicey's support for the referendum was based on the assumption that the device would be used as a check on the excesses of unrestricted party government. Some modern observers have feared that the opposite would happen, namely that the referendum would be used as an elite-strengthening device. Based on the experience of referendums held prior to the mid-1970s, it was argued that referendums are held entirely at the discretion of elected officials, parliaments and their governments, the few minor exceptions having been compulsory referendums for constitutional amendments and some special kinds of legislation. This assertion can be tested empirically by using Gordon Smith's typology of referendums.

Smith (1976, 6) makes a distinction between two categories of referendum, *controlled* and *uncontrolled* referendums. It is in principle possible to place all referendums

> on a continuum of control, partly based on the right of initiation and partly based on the actual course of events which leads to a particular vote … A continuum running from "Controlled" through "Uncontrolled" could therefore alternatively be termed in terms of

Figure 4.1   Smith's categories

Pro-hegemonic controlled – Spain's referendum on NATO membership in 1986	Pro-hegemonic uncontrolled – Ireland's referendum on restrictions to citizenship 2004
Anti-hegemonic controlled – France's referendum on local government and Senate reform in 1969	Anti-hegemonic uncontrolled – Denmark's referendum on the Maastricht Treaty in 1992

Source: Smith (1976); examples added.

desired or intended effect, whether the referendum is supportive of the outlook and policies of the authorities or not.

It follows, when we are dealing with binary-choice referendums, that referendums can have two possible outcomes: the proposal can be adopted or rejected. Given that the result of a referendum can be either 'detrimental or supportive to a regime', Smith distinguishes between two categories, respectively, *pro-hegemonic* and *Antihegemonic* referendums. These distinctions lead to the differentiation of four categories (see figure 4.1).

On the basis of Lijphart's analysis, we could expect most to fall within the categories of 'controlled referendums', with the majority being 'pro-hegemonic': as he noted, 'most referendums are both controlled and prohegemonic' (1984, 203).

It must be stressed that these categories are ideal types; that is to say, the *real* types may be difficult to categorise. I categorise all constitutional referendums, and referendums initiated by the opposition and by citizen petition, as *uncontrolled*; I further categorise the outcome of a poll as *anti-hegemonic* if a government has campaigned against it. This leads to the distribution of referendum types listed in figure 4.1.

The results in table 4.1 falsify Lijphart's assertion to some extent. The pro-hegemonic controlled referendums account for only 20 per cent of those studied; the uncontrolled referendums, by contrast, account for 77 per cent of the total number. There is indeed some support for the assertion that governments submit issues to referendums only when they have a good reason to suppose that they will be endorsed by the voters: only five 'controlled' referendums produced 'anti-hegemonic' outcomes. But this result does not disguise the fact that the majority of referendums, 131 (84 per cent) out of a total of 156

Table 4.1 Types of referendum using Smith's categories, 1945–2003

Country	ConPro	ConAnti	UnconPro	UnconAnti
Australia	0	0	5	23
Belgium	0	0	1	0
Denmark	2	0	6	7
Finland	1	0	0	0
France	5	1	4	1
Ireland	0	0	20	8
Italy	1	0	20	28
Norway	0	2	0	0
Sweden	3	1	0	0
UK[a]	3	0	1	0
New Zealand	4	0	0	5
Austria	1	1	2	2
Total	20	5	59	72
Total %	12	3	38	46

Note: [a]The UK referendums include the border poll in 1973 and the devolution referendums in 1979 and 1997.
Changes to New Zealand's Section 189 of the Electoral Act of 1956 are included as constitutional referendums. It ought to be noted that nine of the Italian referendums were declared void due to low turnout.
Sources: Blaustein and Flanz (1997); Butler and Ranney (1994); Gallagher and Uleri (1996); Suksi (1993); C2D, University of Geneva.

were 'uncontrolled', i.e. were obligatory constitutional referendums, popular referendums, initiatives or minority veto referendums.

It might, however, be argued that Smith's definition of uncontrolled referendums is too wide, as it includes what might be called *pouvoir constituant* referendums, i.e. those held to ratify a new constitution (e.g. the Italian referendum on the constitution of the First Republic in 1948 and the French referendum in 1958, the Spanish referendum in 1976, and the Greek referendum in 1975). The notion of the *pouvoir constituant* referendum can, according to Suksi, be understood as a power of the people superior to the constitution and which does not derive from the provisions of an existing constitution (1993, 26); and, according to Klaus von Beyme, it can be defined as a 'pre-constitutional, latent and inalienable right to consent to a constitution, exercised by the people before they transfer some of their sovereignty to new political institutions' (1968, 5).

It follows from this definition that referendums on such issues are neither legally nor politically uncontrolled as they are held at the discretion of the initiators (typically the drafters of the constitution). This was so in Ireland in 1937. Eamon de Valera found it necessary to hold a *pouvoir constituant* referendum because 'there is one thing more than another that is clear and shining through the constitution ... the fact that the people are the masters' (quoted in Chubb 1988, 98). To describe such referendums as uncontrolled would be misleading, as these polls often have a quasi-plebiscitary nature (e.g. De Gaulle's use of the referendum in 1958).

It might therefore be argued that these referendums are to be categorised as controlled referendums, as it is the drafters of the constitution who initiate them. This re-categorisation does not, however, alter the conclusion that most referendums are uncontrolled, as *pouvoir constituant* referendums are relatively rare (only six of the studied polls fall in the category, namely the Italian referendum in 1948, the two referendums on proposed constitutions of the Fourth Republic in 1946 and De Gaulle's referendum on the constitution of the Fifth Republic in 1958, the Spanish referendum in 1976 on democratic government, and the Greek referendum on republican government in 1974). The result of this re-categorisation is that 80 per cent of the referendums were uncontrolled, as only 3.8 per cent of the polls were *pouvoir constituant* referendums. The general conclusion is, in other words, the same: most referendums are uncontrolled.

This is a reassuring conclusion from the perspective of Dicey's model. It is, as noted above, characteristic that Dicey proposed the introduction of an uncontrolled referendum, which, by constitutional entrenchment of certain institutions and rights, would force the rulers to submit issues to referendums. That the majority of the referendums held have been of the uncontrolled type, and that most of them have gone against the wishes of governments, suggests that the referendum can provide an effective check on the legislature. But the result neither confirms nor falsifies the assertion that the obligatory constitutional referendum provides a constitutional safeguard. Several of the referendums are in fact either popular referendums or minority vetoes. It is therefore impossible to use this result as an argument in favour of the Diceyan referendum (i.e. obligatory constitutional referendums on constitutional amendments and alterations).

Critics of Dicey's proposal have often argued that this type of referendum would depend on a government's willingness to submit itself to the control of the people. A government anxious to enact fundamental constitutional changes would thus tend to draft proposals in such a way that a referendum would be constitutionally unnecessary. A constitutional referendum like the one proposed by Dicey would, in Finer's colourful phrase, invite Parliament 'to become its own executioner': 'governments would not launch them [referendums] unless they thought they were going to win' (Finer 1980, 217). The constitutional efficiency of the referendum would, therefore, be limited. If the calling of a referendum is to be at the discretion of the government of the day, how can such a power be limited or curbed? These reservations about the Diceyan proposal seem intuitively convincing; whether they are *empirically* persuasive is another matter.

The unwillingness of parliaments to subject themselves to constitutional referendums is a matter that can be answered in part by considering how many referendums have been held under the different constitutional provisions of the respective polities. Table 4.2 lists the constitutional provisions for referendums in various countries, along with the number of referendums held under those provisions (note that this table includes only pre-regulated referendums; the UK and Norway are consequently excluded). The table shows both that constitutional referendums *are* held and that *most* referendums are constitutional referendums: 49.5 per cent of the pre-regulated referendums held since 1945 were on constitutional issues, i.e. were Diceyan referendums (that most referendums are uncontrolled is not therefore a consequence of Italian provisions for popular referendums and Danish minority vetoes).

This figure is even more impressive if we omit the deviating case of the comparatively unique Italian popular referendums: 76 per cent were constitutional if we exclude the latter category. Yet this result does not in itself undermine the charge against the constitutional referendum. Nor, indeed, does it indicate that governments or parliaments have willingly submitted constitutional proposals to the voters. It may be that these referendums were held because mechanisms for judicial review left the political elites with little choice but to submit the issues to referendums. This was in fact the main objection against the Diceyan referendum when it was debated in Britain in the early part of the twentieth century. Churchill, then a Liberal (and liberal!) home secretary, asserted that the effectiveness of the constitutional referendum as a constitutional safeguard would require the 'intervention of a judicial body of some kind' (HCD – 8 May 1911, col. 933), that is to say a judicial authority which could

Table 4.2 Constitutional provisions for types of referendum and referendums held under these provisions, 1945–97

Country	RP.	CA	PFR	MAR
Australia	Yes	Sec. 128		
Luxembourg	Yes		Art. 51	
Germany	No			
Spain	Yes	Art. 168	Art. 92	
Belgium	No			
Denmark	Yes	Art. 88,29	Art. 20	Art. 42
Finland	Yes	Art. 22A		
France	Yes	Art. 89	Art. 11	
Ireland	Yes	Art. 46		Art. 27
Italy	Yes	Art. 123,132		Art. 71[a], 75
Greece	Yes		Art. 44	
Sweden	Yes	Ch. 8. Art. (1)		
New Zealand		Sec. 189		CIRA
Portugal	Yes	Art. 118		
Austria	Yes	Art. 440		Art. 48[a]

Notes: RP = provisions for referendums mentioned in the constitution; *CA* optional referendum for constitutional amendments; *PFR* = provisions for facultative referendums on non-constitutional measures; *MAR* = minority veto and abrogative popular referendum or other constitutional provisions for semi-direct democracy.
[a] = Popular petition (respectively, *Volksbegehren* [Austria], *Iniziative di legge populare* (Italy)).
CIRA = Citizen Initiated Referendum Act 1993.
Sources: Blaustein and Planz (1997), and Suksi (1993).

'decide whether or not a given piece of legislation in fact lay within the class of constitutional legislation' (*ibid.*).

There is empirical evidence which can be interpreted as supporting Churchill's assertion. It is thus possible that the lack of judicial review in Japan enabled the ruling Liberal Democratic Government to change the constitution without holding referendums in accordance with article 96 (Stockwin 1982, 215). It is further possible that the relative political impotence of the French *Conseil constitutionnel* explains why France has yet to hold its first constitutional referendum under article 89 of the 1958 constitution.

Australia and Ireland, the polities which have held the greatest number of referendums on constitutional amendments, are notably those with the strongest traditions of judicial review. Three of the referendums held in Ireland since 1945 have in fact been initiated by the courts (Macmillan 1992). In Australia the High Court intervened in 1910 (when nationalisation of monopolies was deemed to be unconstitutional), in 1946 (when it ruled that the Pharmaceutical Benefits Act 1944 was invalid) and in 1951 (when it ruled that the Communist Party Dissolution Act 1950 was unconstitutional; see Standing Committee on Legal and Constitutional Affairs 1997).

It is, however, questionable whether this tradition of judicial review has been instrumental in forcing governments to submit issues to referendums. Only one of the referendums demanded by the Irish Supreme Court ran counter to the interests of the political elite, namely the ruling that the implementation of the Single European Act required a referendum (Sinnott 1995, 229).

The charge that the constitutional referendum would be an efficient safeguard only if combined with a strong constitutional court cannot be entirely dismissed, as the recent referendums in Ireland show. Two of those initiated by the Irish Supreme Court have concerned uncontroversial issues, such as the legalisation of contested adoptions (1979) and votes for non-citizens (1984), which the Government readily submitted to referendums. The more controversial issues, like the electoral systems referendums in 1959 and 1968, the abortion referendum in 1983 and the divorce referendums in 1984 and 1995, were in fact initiated by the Government, which in doing so submitted itself to the people's veto. That the Australian and Irish polities have had the opportunity to vote in several referendums on controversial issues is not therefore a direct consequence of judicial intervention. It is still possible that the latent threat of judicial intervention has made governments and parliaments more inclined to submit issues to referendums than they would have been in the absence of a system of judicial review. One hypothesis might be that the mere threat of judicial intervention has prompted governments to submit issues to referendums. Following this hypothesis, we would expect the number of referendums held in polities without judicial review to be significantly smaller.

It is in fact correct that the number of constitutional referendums held in Austria, Denmark and New Zealand is lower than in Ireland and Australia. Denmark has held 6 constitutional referendums; New Zealand has held 5 on section 189, while the Austrian electorate has been invited to vote in only a single constitutional referendum (the EU referendum in 1994).

Opponents of the EU have criticised the Danish Government for not holding constitutional referendums on the Maastricht Treaty (ostensibly because it would have been difficult to secure the required approval of 40 per cent of the eligible voters). Yet there is a general consensus among jurists of all political persuasions that the Danish Government has been willing to submit constitutional issues to referendums (though it should, perhaps, to be noted that the Danish Government 'decided' that the Nice Treaty did not involve transfer of sovereignty to the EU – and did not, therefore, require a referendum). In the absence of a strong – and independent – constitutional court there is no guarantee that a referendum will be held.

The same is not true for New Zealand, a country without a written constitution. The Government could theoretically have enacted the proposed changes to section 189. This has not happened, possibly because 'the discipline of pragmatic politics imposes sufficient self-regulation' (Joseph 1993, 80). The constitutional provisions for referendums have prevented the Government from acting in breach of the constitution, even when unconstrained by written constitutional checks and balances. That the provisions for referendums would be used even without the 'intervention of a judicial body of some kind' would not have surprised Dicey, who countered his critics by hypothesising that 'the electors may be trusted to resent an attempt to deprive them of legal power ensured to them by the *Referendum Act*. No party leader would risk resentment' (Dicey 1890, 499).

Whether it is this so-called logic of consequentiality (i.e. the fear of angering voters to the extent that parties might risk defeat in a general election) that has prompted politicians to submit controversial issues to referendums or whether some genuine sense of fair play (or logic of appropriateness) has spurred them to submit issues to the voters seems to depend on the specific situation (March and Olsen 1995, 7). It is possible that 'self-interested calculation can be seen as simply one of many systems of rules that may be socially legitimised under certain circumstances' (*ibid.*, 29), and it is, consequently, possible that some referendums have been called for reasons other than fear that resentful voters would be unwilling to re-elect politicians who have enacted legislation in breach of provisions for constitutional referendums. What we can conclude in any case is that constitutional referendums have been held even in countries where the executive could *de jure* have refrained from submitting an issue to the voters (although slightly more often in polities with judicial review bodies). The conclusion seems to be that constitutional referendums, contrary to what the critics have argued, do provide an effective check on the people's elected representatives.

This result does not force us to adopt the conclusion that all constitutions should contain provisions for Diceyan referendums. It is possible that ethnic and national differences in a country like, say, Belgium make even constitutional referendums undesirable. What the above discussion has shown is merely that the constitutional referendum would guarantee the people a veto on constitutional issues. The hypothesis put forward by Lijphart (1984 – that referendums are pro-hegemonic and controlled – does not stand up to empirical scrutiny. The constitutional referendum proposed by Dicey is an efficient constitutional safeguard. That is to say, the constitutional referendum provides the voters with a powerful veto on controversial issues enshrined in the constitution, yet the constitutional referendum would not help the people to set their own agenda or to express their own view on what *they* regarded as impertinently unrepresentative measures.

A controversial issue which few considered important at the time of the drafting of the constitution might later rise to political prominence. Yet the citizens can claim no right to veto this legislation unless specific constitutional provisions are made for referendums on such issues. The latter possibility has, as I show in chapter 5, prompted some theorists to go further than Dicey and demand the introduction of minority vetoes (known from Denmark) and popular referendums. These proposals have been put forward by writers who find it unlikely that a government would ever hold a referendum unless it was forced to do so. They have therefore reached the conclusion that the popular referendum (citizen-initiated vetoes on ordinary legislation) is necessary to prevent parliaments from enacting legislation opposed by the majority of citizens. It might, however, be questioned whether that conclusion is empirically demonstrable. Some governments have in fact been willing to submit non-constitutional issues to unpre-regulated referendums when a decision would be illegitimate in the absence of a referendum (Sweden's referendum on the EU being a case in point). Yet the people cannot count on that eventuality unless it can be shown that unpre-regulated referendums are mainly called when there is popular demand for a referendum. Whether this is likely can perhaps be determined by studying countries which have no provisions for referendums, countries such as Norway and the UK.

Comparative perspectives on referendum initiation

Dicey famously noted that the majority of British voters around 1900 were unionists and free traders, but that the Unionist Free Traders were in the minority in the House of Commons. This is, as the reader will be aware by now, a quite common objection against purely representative democracy. The Norwegian referendum in 1972 provides the classic case of the same problem, i.e. of a discrepancy between the voters' views and the views of the politicians. The Norwegian psephologist Ola Listhaug wrote:

> While no more than 30% of the members of parliament were against membership at any point before the referendum, all public opinion polls conducted in the two years before the referendum showed a majority of voters against membership ... The EEC issue can thus be interpreted as a case where the representative democracy did not work. (1989, 91)

It is possible that politicians feel compelled to submit such issues to the voters irrespective of whether they are constitutionally obliged to hold referendums. There are apparently several examples of referendums that were called to secure the legitimacy of parliamentary decisions on controversial issues. The Norwegian Labour Government, which was accused of manipulation when it took Norway into NATO without a referendum, sought to secure the legitimacy of a decision concerning membership of the EEC, and decided to hold an advisory referendum on the issue. Canada's Conservative Prime Minister Brian Mulroney decided to hold a referendum on the Charlottetown Accord to provide, via a vote by 'all Canadians', the kind of legitimacy which the constitutional process sorely lacked (LeDuc 1993) Sweden's Prime Minister Ingvar Carlsson (a Social Democrat) agreed to submit the issue of Sweden's membership of the EU to the voters after the leader of the opposition, Carl Bildt (a Conservative), had convinced him that 'this important national decision had to be preceded in Sweden, as well as in several other European countries, by direct popular involvement' (Ruin 1996, 177).

It is possible that such willingness to submit controversial issues to referendums diminishes the need for the introduction of a referendum along Diceyan lines (or the above-mentioned popular referendums), for what need is there of legislation if the political decision-makers are willing to submit issues to referendums when demanded by the people? Yet we cannot infer from these cases that such non-regulated referendums are likely to be called when representative democracy, so to speak, fails. Nor can we infer that the above referendums were held as a result of a popular demand. Bjørklund has asserted that most of these (unpre-regulated) referendums were held as a result of parties' tactical considerations, thus questioning the validity of Dicey's contention that the referendum would be inimical to party interests (Bjørklund 1982, 248). According to Bjørklund, the referendum is a mechanism used by a minority within a party who believe that a majority of the citizenry will support them. The minority in the Norweigian Labour Party knew that they could not change party politics, but they believed – rightly, it turned out – that a vote among the citizens would go their way. When the request for a referendum is accepted, two conditions are important to its proponents: parties that are split and a strong commitment on the part of the voters.

Bjørklund's analysis is a powerful one when applied to the Scandinavian countries, especially Norway, and it is augmented by the consideration that other Scandinavian referendums follow the same pattern. The Danish referendum on membership of the EEC in 1972 was likewise triggered by internal disagreement (especially among the Social Democrats), just as the Swedish referendum on nuclear energy in 1980 was a result of Prime Minister Oluf Palme's attempt to maintain unity within the Social Democratic Party. These examples suggest that Bjørklund's model may have general utility and that such *ad hoc* referendums are unlikely to provide efficient safeguards against the parties' interests.

Referendums in the UK

It has occasionally been proposed that a referendum might be held on a particular issue, but the proposals do not appear to have been taken seriously. And there has been no support at all for the idea that the initiative and the referendum should be adopted as a permanent institution of government, as it is in Switzerland, so that the representatives could be by-passed. Views of this kind have found favour among peoples of British extraction in both Australia and the United States, but in Britain itself they have never acquired any kind of influence'.

Thus wrote Birch (1964, 227–8) in a seminal analysis of the British constitution.

If this observation was pertinent in 1964, when his book was published, it ceased to be so in the 1970s, when referendums were held on the future status of Northern Ireland, continued British membership of the EEC (the forerunner of the EU), and on devolution (self-government) for Scotland and Wales. While no referendums were held during the years of Conservative rule (1979–97), a plethora of plebiscites have been held since Tony Blair's New Labour was elected to power in 1997.

The referendum is now a part of the UK's constitution – if one that is sparingly used. This in itself is a breakthrough, for until as recently as the 1990s the referendum's status as a constitutionally legitimate device was questioned. Foreign Office Minister Tristan (now Lord) Garel-Jones said in the House of Commons, in a debate about the Maastricht Treaty, that the referendum was 'an abdication of the responsibility of the House and of the Government of the day' (HCD – vol. 204, 21 February 1992, col. 627). Garel-Jones's position was not confined to the political right, nor was it new.

In 1945 leader Clement Atlee responded to Winston Churchill's proposed referendum on the continuation of the wartime coalition by stating that he could not

> consent to the introduction into our national life of a device so alien to all our traditions as the referendum, which has only too often been the instrument of Nazism and Fascism. Hitler's practices in the field of referenda and plebiscites can hardly have endeared these expedients to the British heart. (Quoted in Bogdanor 1994, 36)

Interestingly, it was Atlee's own party, Labour, which in the early 1970s decided to embrace the referendum. This was not, it should be added, indicative of a new-found enthusiasm for direct participatory democracy: the referendum was seen as a mediating device used to avoid a bitter internal split over membership of the EEC.

In 1972, when the Conservative Government under Heath took Britain into the EEC, the majority of the Labour Party's MPs followed the party line and voted against UK membership. Yet, a significant group within the party, which included Shadow Chancellor of the Exchequer Roy Jenkins, led a rebellion and voted with the Conservative Government. This posed a problem for the Labour Party. Aspiring to get back into power – and capitalising on the increasingly unpopular Conservative Government's decline in the polls, Labour needed to show that it was capable of returning to power without being damaged by internal splits over policies.

The referendum proved to be the device that rescued the Labour Party. By agreeing to disagree, it could claim that a vote for Labour would not – at least not automatically – be a vote for withdrawal from the EEC. The people would be given a choice – they would, politically speaking, be allowed to have their cake and eat it: they could vote for a party at a general election and – if they so chose – vote against that party's policy at a later date. As the leading Labour politician, Jim Callaghan (prime minister 1976–79) observed that the referendum (to which he had previously been opposed) would be 'a rubber life raft into which the whole party will one day have to climb' (quoted in Butler and Kitzinger 1976, 12). Or, as it was put by his colleague – and rival – Tony Benn: 'a referendum would get [the European issue] out of our system and leave the party united: the party was divided at this stage and we should accept the fact that this would resolve it' (quoted in Wright 2000, 145).

The Labour Party was not, however, always committed to the referendum. Indeed, in a debate in the House of Commons in 1967, Wilson, then prime minister, rejected the very idea of the referendum, on the grounds that 'decisions of great moment of this kind have to be taken by the elected government of the day, responsible to this House. The constitutional position is that whatever this House decides on this matter, or any other matter, is the right decision' (HCD – vol. 731, 14 July 1966, col. 1718). Wilson, ironically, was the first prime minister to submit a major policy issue to a UK-wide referendum. The Roman statesman and rhetorician Marcus Tullius Cicero had a point when he noted that 'consistency has never been a virtue in a politician'.

The issue of continued membership was eventually submitted to the voters in June 1975, by which time the Labour leadership had changed course. Having been opposed to UK membership while in opposition, the party leadership now supported it – with the exception of some left-leaning members of the Cabinet, most notably Tony Benn, the energy minister. On 5 June 1975, an overwhelming majority of 17 million voted for continued membership; only 8 million voted 'yes'.

A case could be – and indeed has been – made that the 1975 referendum follows a pattern identified by Bjørklund's thesis that referendums result from political parties' attempts to paper over internal splits over 'valence issues'. Analysing Scandinavian referendums in the 1970s, Bjørklund concluded that 'a government [or party] … which is divided on an important issue … may embrace the referendum as a mediating device' (1982, 248).

There is much to be said for this interpretation when analysing the decision to submit the 'European' issue to a referendum. But, does this interpretation stand up to close scrutiny when we analyse the other British referendums? The view I put forward here is that a broader model is required to make sense of the dynamics of referendums in the UK – and, indeed, in other countries.

A typology of referendums in comparative perspective

The question remains, however, of whether Bjørklund's model, while theoretically stringent, is not overly parsimonious – does it, perhaps, take the principle of Ockham's Razor a little too far? Other referendums held later do not, on the face of it, seem to support Bjørklund's model. For instance, Blair's Labour Government decided in April 2004 – after some political dithering – to allow the UK's citizens to vote on the European constitution. Yet, the party was not split over the issue. Does that falsify Bjørklund's model – or does the model need expansion?

Borrowing from – and slightly extending – a typology developed by Laurence Morel (2001), it is possible to differentiate five types of referendum:

• decision-solving referendums;
• legislative referendums;
• plebiscitary referendums;
• legitimating referendums;
• opposition referendums;
• tactical referendums.

Decision-solving referendums are proposed when a government is split over an issue. Like the UK's Labour Government, the Norwegian Labour Government was split over the EEC issue in 1972. To avoid a broadening of the rift Prime Minister Trygve Bratteli decided to submit the issue to a referendum (Bjørklund 1982, 248).

Legislative referendums are called when minority governments (and presidents) are unable to get policies through the parliamentary system, and so resort is had directly to the voters. French President Charles de Gaulle, unable to win approval for his proposed direct election of the executive in 1962, went directly to the voters to win a popular mandate. Another often-cited example is that of the Danish Prime Minister Poul Schlüter submitting the Single European Act to the voters when, in 1986, he failed to win approval for the Maastricht Treaty in the *Folketinget* (Morel 2001).

Plebiscitary referendums are called when a government (or a president) wants to strengthen its mandate. In 1992 French President François Mitterand decided to submit the Maastricht Treaty to a popular vote – ostensibly – to strengthen his own position; in the event Mitterand only narrowly won approval. Another example – though a democratically questionable one, at that – is the Russian referendum in 1993, when President Boris Yeltsin sought a mandate for his new constitution – and indeed for himself (Slater 1996, 4).

Politically obligatory referendums are public votes on controversial issues that are deemed to warrant the direct approval of the citizenry. An example is the Swedish referendum on membership of the EU. The Swedish constitution did (and does not) require that referendums are held on transfers of sovereignty, yet Prime Minister Invar Carlson, a Social Democrat, agreed to submit the accession treaty to the voters after his predecessor Carl Bildt (a Conservative) had convinced him that 'this important national decision had to be preceded in Sweden, as well as in several other European countries, by direct popular involvement' (Ruin 1996, 177).

Opposition referendums are proposed by opposition parties to prevent the enactment of legislation to which they are opposed. A classic example is the Danish referendum on planning laws in 1963 (Qvortrup 2000). Using a provision that allows the minority to demand a referendum if they can gather signatures from one-third of the MPs, Centre–Right parties ensured that the planning laws were submitted to the electorate (which rejected the proposals). Another – albeit unsuccessful – proposal for a referendum was the UK's Conservative Party's proposal of a referendum on the repeal of 'section 28' (which bans the promotion of homosexuality in schools).

Tactical referendums are used by a party to strengthen its hand electorally or to cause embarrassment to other parties. An example of this kind of referendum could be (see case studies) New Labour's proposal of a referendum on Scottish and Welsh devolution.

The 1975 referendum, as we have seen, was used overtly as a mediating device. The same – or so it might be argued – was true in the case of the referendum on Scottish and Welsh devolution (self-government). In the latter case, large sections of the Labour Party's backbenchers opposed the Government's policy to establish devolved parliaments in the two nations. To fend off another split the Government grudgingly accepted the submission of the policies to referendums in the two nations (both of which were lost – though in the case of Scotland only because the number of 'yes' votes did not constitute the required 40 per cent of the eligible voters).

On closer scrutiny, however, this categorisation fails to appreciate the nuances of the debate leading up to the decision to hold a referendum, a decision that was by default – not by design. Bjørklund has noted that 'those whose standpoint would be voted down if it went through the channels of representative democracy can embrace the demand for a referendum on the issue. In the absence of a referendum the battle is lost' (1982, 247). This was exactly the situation for the anti-devolutionists. The Scotland and Wales Devolution Bill (which was introduced into the Commons in 1976) did not include provisions for a referendum at all, ostensibly because the Government underestimated the opposition to the bill from Labour backbenchers who were, in Bogdanor's words, 'unenthusiastic, if not positively hostile, to devolution' (1996, 227).

Anxious not to bring down the Government by defeating the devolution proposals, the opponents of the Scotland and Wales Devolution Bill demanded a referendum before the legislation received royal assent. This prompted the Government to withdraw the original Bill in favour of two separate Bills (introduced in November 1977), both of which contained a provision for a consultative referendum. By this time, however, it had become clear that a parliamentary defeat for the devolution Bills would result in the dismissal of the Callaghan Government. This meant that the Labour opponents of devolution had to devise new ways of inflicting damage on the proposals, without actually preventing their passage through Parliament. To that end George Cunningham, a Scot elected in an English constituency (precinct), tabled an amendment which stipulated that the proposal – once approved by Parliament – had to be supported by at least 40 per cent of the eligible voters in either nation.

For this analysis, that the Callaghan Government eventually fell victim to a no-confidence motion – after the referendums had failed – is not the most important lesson to be drawn. Interest here is rather in why the referendums were called in the first place. Unlike the referendum in 1975 the devolution referendum was not used as a mediating device; rather the decision to submit the issue to the voters was a result of the dynamics associated with – what Morel (2001) calls – an 'opposition referendum'. A minority of the Labour Party used its 'blackmail potential' (Sartori 1976). The decision was not, as it had been in the early 1970s, an agreement to disagree; rather the Government was forced to make concessions for fear of failing to win parliamentary approval for the Bills.

Yet, like the decision to hold a referendum on the EEC, the decision to hold a referendum on devolution was taken to ensure that the Labour Party avoided a damaging split (in the event only one MP, the Scottish pro-devolutionist Jim Sillars left the Labour Party, eventually joining the Scottish Nationalist Party). While not a paradigmatic case of party mediation, the 1979 referendums on devolution were, at the very least, a result of internal disagreements. Is this, after all, true of British referendums in general?

While Bjørklund's analysis of the Scandinavian votes in the 1970s conformed to his theory (referendums are mediating devices embraced to avoid splits within governments, coalitions and parties), the more recent referendums in that part of the world have not supported the Bjørklund's theory. The Norwegian Government – and the parties that supported it – were not split over the issue of EU membership in the early 1990s, nor was the Swedish Government. The 1994 vote 'was ... not preceded by any conscious decision at all, a mandatory referendum on the EU issue being by this time in effect a silent dimension of the political system' (Wyller 1996, 142). It would seem, in other words, that the decision to call referendums in Scandinavia (with Denmark as the possible exception) had become a convention of the constitution: the referendums were *politically obligatory*.

A similar analysis, it might be argued, could be made of the decision to hold a referendum on the European constitution. Having been on the back foot over the issue, Tony Blair in April 2004 bowed to political pressure and declared that Britain would not ratify the European constitution unless it had received the approval of the majority of the voters in a referendum. Before coming to power Tony Blair had expressed support for a 'greater use of referendums'. The referendum, Blair had stated, 'gives citizens a veto over proposals to change their system of government' (1996, 34). His apparent commitment to politically obligatory referendums was not a passing fancy: in 1994 he had professed that in the event of 'a major constitutional change there clearly is a case for ensuring that the decision can be ... taken by the British people' (*Sunday Telegraph*, 11 December 1994). Can we therefore conclude that the UK's referendums have become politically obligatory rather than decision-solving referendums? In answering this question there is need to consider the initiation of individual referendums.

Labour's referendum proposals in 1996: the Case of Scotland (and Wales)

'Mandelson's decision had all the hallmarks of one of his classical [sic] media operations.' Thus concluded *Scotland on Sunday* (30 March 1996). What the paper referred to was the way in which Labour's spin doctor supremo had leaked Blair's decision to hold a referendum on devolution in Scotland (the referendum for Wales was an afterthought).

This was a new development. Only a week before the decision, I had asked Peter Mandelson about his view on the possibility of holding a referendum on the issue. He was not amused. 'That is constitutionally unnecessary. What a silly idea.' Now Mandelson – and the Labour leadership – had come round to the idea – 'A week in politics is a long time', as Harold Wilson had observed.

By leaking the decision to hold *two* referendums in Scotland (one on devolution and a separate one on whether the new Scottish Parliament should have tax-raising powers) Labour had – it seemed – wrong-footed the Conservatives. John Major, the prime minister, was to give a speech the following Tuesday, in which he would deliver his views on constitutional change. Being on the defensive, the Conservatives hoped – with some justification – that they would be able to capitalise on the public uneasiness over Labour's proposals for constitutional reform. The devolution question seemed to be one of the few, if not the only, potential vote-winner for the Scottish Conservatives. Scottish Secretary Michael Forsyth's constant references to the 'tartan tax' seemed to damage Labour's endeavours to be seen as a business friendly party. In full pursuit of his strategy, Forsyth had even challenged Labour to hold a referendum on the issue before a devolution Bill was eventually passed in the Houses of Parliament (*Scotland on Sunday*, 30 March 1996). Mandelson's stage-managed leak of the decision put the Tory Government on the receiving end. Speaking on BBC TV on Sunday 30 June, Michael Forsyth found it hard to explain why he repudiated the very same decision that he had challenged the Labour Party to make less than a week before. The impression, as summed up by the *Economist*, was that the Labour Party positioned itself as the defender of the people's rights and the

Tories, by implication, appeared 'atavistic and undemocratic'. The publication reached the same conclusion when the Labour Party repeated its success by declaring that a future Labour Government would hold a referendum before the UK would join a single currency. Opinion polls conducted in March 1996 showed that 60 per cent of UK's electors were opposed to EMU, while only 20 per cent were in favour. This had prompted John Major to announce his conviction that a referendum on joining a single European currency could be 'a necessary step', a view which was adopted as official policy soon after. This commitment to a referendum seemed to secure peace inside the Tory Party: the referendum was, as *The Times* put it, 'a cost free option which might buy off some sceptics' (8 March 1996). The Government, which had rejected Tory backbencher Nicholas Budgen's proposed Bill 'to provide for the holding of referendum on whether the United Kingdom Government should continue to work towards a single European currency' (*ibid.*, 8 June 1996), now supported an identical measure for tactical reasons. The referendum had once more been utilised by a party as a tactical device, only this time Labour was on the receiving end. By proposing a referendum, the Government had succeeded in portraying Labour as opposing the people's right to decide an important constitutional matter.

It seems that the Labour Party was divided over its options in response to the Conservative's tactical move. Shadow Chancellor Gordon Brown was initially hostile to the idea of a referendum, whereas other members of the Shadow Cabinet, most notably Shadow Foreign Secretary Robin Cook, were in favour of one (*New Statesman*, 22 November 1996). It came as a surprise that a member of the Shadow Cabinet, Margaret Beckett, speaking on the television programme *A Week in Politics*, declared that the party would 'come out with a statement calling for a referendum before Britain joined a single European currency' (Channel 4, 16 November 1996). On *Breakfast With Frost* the following day, Gordon Brown communicated that it would 'be necessary to consult opinion during the next Parliament through a referendum' (BBC1, 17 November 1996).

This decision produced the desired effect. Only hours later the prominent Tory Euro-sceptic William Cash attacked the prime minister, arguing that the Conservatives had 'got to say no to the single currency'. Another prominent Euro-sceptic, Sir Teddy Taylor, even saw the Labour policy shift as an opportunity for the Government to 'get out of the EU altogether'. These statements were predictably rejected by Europhile Tory MPs such as Edwina Currie and Quentin Davis (BBC1, *News*, 18 November 1996). A statement from the chairman of the Conservative Party, Dr Brian Mawhinney, saying that the Labour announcement was 'a smoke-screen to divert people's attention from the fact that they [Labour] plan a massive transfer of power from London to Brussels' (*Independent*, 18 November 1996), seemed only to make matters worse, and did not seem to alter the impression that Labour had once more succeeded in using the referendum to display the divisions inside the Tory Party while itself avoiding an internal debate on the issue (the latter perhaps indicates that Bjørklund's model goes some way in explaining the party's decision). The *Economist* (23 November 1996) commented:

> With the referendum on a single currency Mr. Blair is shooting the Tories' fox. Before this week's pledge the Tories could look forward to fighting the election on the basis that they would consult the people. After it ... they will have to find a new anti-European device – and the search is already causing Tory pros and antis to break their truce on Europe.

This interpretation was shared by the *Observer*: 'The Labour Party has fire-proofed itself in the run up to the election, put pressure on Conservative Eurosceptics to raise the stakes, forced the Government to rule out membership during the next Parliament and equipped itself to enter if it chooses' (17 November 1996).

It is difficult to find in the latter two cases evidence to give conclusive support to Bjørklund's theory; these cases are rather examples of the use of the referendum as a tactical device. It is, to be sure, possible that the Labour Party was internally split on both issues, yet it is difficult to maintain the *New Statesman*'s conclusion that Jack Straw, allegedly an opponent of devolution, 'wanted referenda before setting up regional assemblies in England and insisted that Scotland would have to adopt the same procedure for uniformity's sake' (13 September 1996), just as it is difficult to liken Robin Cook's alleged scepticism regarding the EMU to the 1970s' rebellion over EEC membership. There may have been internal differences on both issues, but not to a degree that threatened the unity of the Labour Party. Yet the opportunity to wrong-foot the Conservatives rather than the importance of party unity seems to have given Labour its taste for referendums. Moreover, the party realised that both issues were regarded with scepticism by many of the voters. Devolution and the EMU were issues that were 'too hot to handle'. By submitting them to referendums, a Labour Government would not risk alienating voters who supported their other policies while being opposed to devolution and EMU. Moreover, the fact that the voters, according to the opinion polls, supported the use of referendums must have had an influence on Labour's new enthusiasm for referendums; an opposition party which relied on focus groups and private opinion polls had an incentive to endorse referendums, especially as it was a cost-free option, one which in addition embarrassed John Major's Government.

'The referendum had more to do with political expediency than constitutional principle or democracy'. Thus concluded Dennis Kavanagh (1996, 60) in his analysis of the referendums in Britain in the 1970s. The same conclusion, it seems, can be drawn with regard to the British referendums initiated and held in the late 1990s. Whereas the referendums in the 1970s seem to conform to Morel's typology (the 1975 referendum as a decision-solving Referendum and the 1979 referendum as an opposition referendum), the referendum proposals for, respectively, Scottish and Welsh devolution and the European currency, were held as a result of electioneering considerations. They were, to coin a new term, 'tactical referendums'.

This addition to Morel's typology does not, of course, imply that all British referendums were of this category. The referendum on the Good Friday Agreement in Northern Ireland was not, it seems, a result of party-tactical considerations, but rather a consequence of the bi-partisan commitment of both Government and opposition to submit any peace deal for Northern Ireland to the voters. Yet, the fact that party-political and party-tactical considerations – on the basis of this analysis – seem to have played a large part in the decision to adopt referendums in Labour's 1997 and 2001 manifestos does suggest that the referendum is more than the people's veto that theoreticians intended it to be.

At the time of writing, Blair's Labour Government has bowed to demands for a referendum on the European constitution. Some might argue that this referendum is a (rare) example of what Morel (2001) calls a 'politically obligatory referendum'. That is certainly a possibility. Yet, it seems at least equally plausible that the decision to submit the European constitution to the voters was an attempt to shoot the Conservatives' electoral fox – that a vote for the Labour Party in an election would be a vote for the European constitution. The referendum card was played for tactical reasons. Some may see this use of the referendum as opportunistic – and perhaps it is. Yet it is also proof that the referendum allows the voters to distinguish between measures and politicians. That the voters may, occasionally, vote against the wishes of their elected leaders is one of the costs governments will have to learn to live with if they keep using the referendum as a tactical device.

Whatever one thinks of this use of the referendum, it seems beyond reasonable doubt that the referendum has become part of the British constitution, and that Birch's assertion from the early 1960s is no longer accurate.

UK referendums: the story thus far

All but one of the eight significant referendums in the UK have been held under Labour administrations, the single exception being the 1973 border poll in Northern Ireland (see table 4.3). Within a year of taking office, the Labour Party elected in 1997 had submitted four constitutional issues to referendums: Scottish devolution; Welsh devolution; reform of London's system of government (the election of a mayor and an assembly: and the Good Friday Peace Agreement in Northern Ireland. Moreover, the Government remained committed to referendums on the single currency, the electoral system and the establishment of elected chambers in the regions. Given this spate of plebiscites, one might expect an increasing use of (semi-)direct democracy in the UK. This development is unlikely; the UK is not likely to become a new Switzerland, although it seems likely that it will join Ireland, Denmark and France as a frequent user of referendums. It is certainly conceivable that the referendum will play a more prominent part in UK politics than previously. The referendum will not become a part of everyday life, but will be used only when it is deemed necessary to legitimise a political decision or when a political party sees a tactical advantage in using the referendum. However, it may be speculated that the latter use of the referendum is likely to play a lesser role in the future than it did in the late 1990s, not least because its recent uses have shown that the referendum is or can be a double-edged sword. The referendum is not a risk-free option: indeed, it can backfire and cause considerable political embarrassment. The Welsh referendum in September 1997 is a reminder that even the most popular government risks defeat at the polls. An observer of that referendum noted:

Table 4.3 Referendums in the UK, 1973–98

Referendum	Turnout (%)	Yes vote (%)
1973 Border poll (Northern Ireland)[a]	58.6	98.9
1975 EEC (United Kingdom)	64.5	67.2
1979 Welsh devolution (Wales)	58.8	20.3
1979 Scottish devolution (Scotland)	63.8	51.6
1997 Scottish devolution (Scotland)	60.4	74.3[b]
		63.5[c]
1997 Welsh devolution (Wales)	50.1	50.3
1998 Reform of London government	34.1	72.0
1998 Good Friday Peace Agreement (Northern Ireland)	81.0	71.1

Notes: [a] The referendum was boycotted by the nationalists. [b] Vote on devolution.
[c] Vote on tax-varying powers for the new Parliament.
Sources: Based on Balsom, (1996); Denver *et al.* (2000).

Seldom in political history can there have been so nerve-racking and uncertain an election outcome; at 3 a.m. the BBC's *Wales Decides* programme had predicted the outcome of the referendum as a narrow rejection of the Labour government's proposal for a Welsh Assembly; by less than an hour later, confirmation of the final result from Carmarthenshire in south west Wales sealed a slim overall vote in favour. (McAllister 1998, 149)

The Welsh referendum, like the one held in London a few months later, showed that the Government, despite having an overwhelming majority in favour of change, was vulnerable to the opposition's claim that the proposed changes failed to arouse public enthusiasm. Neither referendum gave the seal of approval to the changes. The (at best) lukewarm endorsement of the proposals for London and for Welsh devolution was in marked contrast to the results of the referendums in Scotland and Northern Ireland. On 11 September 1998, 74.3 per cent of the Scottish voters endorsed the Government's proposal for devolution on a 60.4 per cent turnout (63.5 per cent voted to give the new assembly tax-varying powers). The result proved that devolution was the settled will of the Scottish people, as predicted by the late Labour leader John Smith.

The referendum was more a national celebration of ancient statehood re-emerging (perhaps somewhat like the Norwegian referendum in 1905). An authoritative survey of the referendum concluded, 'an electorate which was well informed about an issue made a clear decision which led to a major constitutional change' (Denver *et al.* 2000, 186). Supporters of devolution had feared that there would be a low turnout, as there had been in 1979. In the event, the turnout (44 per cent) was considerably higher than that for the previous year's local elections. The ringing endorsement of a relatively high turnout was a success for the Government and for the parties which favoured devolution. The same conclusion can be reached about the 1998 referendum on the Good Friday Peace Agreement in Northern Ireland.

The political parties of Northern Ireland (except the Democratic Unionist Party – DUP) and the governments of Ireland and the UK had reached an agreement on a new constitutional settlement for Northern Ireland in the spring of 1998. The previous Conservative administration had promised that any deal would have to be approved by the people of Northern Ireland in a referendum. The massive endorsement of the agreement (71.1 per cent in favour) settled the question of whether the proposals put forward by the parties were legitimate. Citing the referendum result proved to be an effective way of countering arguments by opponents and was arguably one of the factors which encouraged the parties to seek a resolution to the post-referendum hiccups.

The referendums in Scotland and Northern Ireland thus seem to have fulfilled the hopes of the advocates of referendums, contributing to the legitimising of the Government's proposals for constitutional changes by enabling the voters to show their support for the policies. The two referendums arguably bestowed greater legitimacy on the decisions than would have been the case had politicians by themselves handled the issues. The referendums held under the Labour Government elected in 1997 did not undermine representative government. The referendums were supplementary to representative government. However, the unenthusiastic support for the proposal for Welsh devolution perhaps shows that the referendum should be used only to settle matured constitutional or exceptionally salient issues.

Last thoughts

I began this excursion by asking whether a government would be willing to hold referendums if and when a particular decision was seen as illegitimate by the people or whether it would hold referendums only in order to pursue its own political interests; I asked also whether politicians would be likely to submit issues to referendums should such public consultations be demanded by the people. The simple answer is that a popular demand for referendums is rarely, if ever, a sufficient reason for submitting an issue to a referendum, although popular demand for referendums is certainly one of the factors behind the decision to submit an issue to a poll. The net result is that a unpre-regulated referendum (as it is known from the UK) will rarely be used as a constitutional safeguard. This conclusion is troubling if one maintains that the referendum should perform the function of a 'people's veto', for the referendum does not seem to be much of a check on the political parties if it is the parties themselves that referendums for party-tactical reasons. We must therefore consider if there are ways in which Parliament can be prevented from 'arrogating to itself that legislative omnipotence which of right belongs to the people' (Dicey quoted in Wright 1994, 18).

5

The minority veto and the popular referendum: two case studies

'People shall be judge', stated John Locke, for 'who [else] shall be judge whether his Trustee or Deputy acts well, and according to the trust reposed in him, but he who deputes him?' (1988, 427). We have found that by and large the constitutional referendum provides citizens with a safeguard against Parliament's alleged temptation to legislate beyond its mandate. But the question is whether this safeguarding function is enough to satisfy the normative criteria of liberal constitutionalism? Locke found that the people should have a say on matters 'of great consequence' (*ibid.*). Dicey believed that those matters would be the constitutional issues, perhaps a reasonable inference in an age when the public sector was small and at a time when the consequences of the State's actions were comparatively limited. Yet the development of biotechnology, nuclear energy and weapons of mass destruction is a vivid illustration that decisions nowadays can be of 'great consequence' without necessarily being constitutional. This has led champions of referendums to conclude that access to the 'people's veto' must be extended from the constitutional veto to, say, minority vetoes and even popular referendums.

These demands, which are analysed in this chapter, give rise to issues which may render such extensions incompatible with our other normative ideals, especially the 'principle of participation'. It is possible that the criteria of liberal constitutionalism require the introduction of, say, the popular referendum. Yet it is equally possible that the introduction of this device would be inimical to the criteria of democracy drawn up in chapter 1. In other words, what we must find is a device which meets both conditions, i.e. allows the citizens to veto all matters 'of great consequence' without undermining the criteria of democracy – an enlightened citizenry, high turnout, minority protection, etc.

There are two possible candidates for a solution to this problem: the minority veto (which allows a minority of the MPs to demand a referendum) and the popular referendum (which allows a specified number of citizens to demand a referendum on a law already enacted). The problem with these mechanisms is that they are exceptionally rare; the minority veto is used only in Denmark, whereas the popular referendum is used only in Italy, Switzerland and some American states. This relative rarity forces us to abandon the comparative approach in favour of a case-study approach.

The Danish minority veto: an historical overview

The minority veto has often been discussed by Danish scholars and practitioners in hypothesising about politicians' evaluations of the device. Yet it is noteworthy that the conclusions regarding the effects of the minority veto have been based almost exclusively on anecdotal evidence (Qvortrup 2000). Such evidence may complement empirical findings, but it does not provide us with material which allows us to draw general conclusions about the effects of the minority veto. It is therefore necessary to carry out an empirical study of Danish politicians' evaluations of the minority veto which in turn requires us to understand the context of the Danish referendum debate.

Yet an empirical case study of the effects of a particular institution cannot be detached from an understanding of historical, political and cultural circumstances. The historical origins of particular institutions are often said to influence the behaviour of the political actors, whose knowledge of the origins of particular institutions induce them to act in accordance with a given *logic of appropriateness* that for an outsider may appear wholly illogical or perhaps even irrational. We must therefore begin with a historical overview of the Danish referendum in order to understand the context within which it is used.

It has been claimed that the provisions for referendums in Denmark were enacted to protect the minority (Svenson 1996). There can be little doubt that the referendum has been favoured most vigorously by the minority parties in the *Folketinget*, especially if they were in opposition. The Social Democrats, the first Danish party to advocate the use of the referendum (as early as the 1870s), gradually lost interest in referendums after becoming in the 1930s the largest party in the *Folketinget*. The Conservatives, once fierce opponents of the device, gradually became sympathetic to the referendum in the 1930s, when they became a minority party.

The first serious attempt to introduce the referendum in Denmark was made by the Radicals, a social liberal party which had broken away from the Liberals (*Venstre*) in 1905. In 1909, the leader of the party, Ove Rode, called for the introduction of legislative initiatives and constitutional referendums. Rode suggested that a minimum of 300,000 voters should be constitutionally entitled to call a referendum (*Rigsdags Tidende* 1909–10, vol. I, col. 39), a suggestion which, in Rode's view was 'supported by parallel tendencies in all other developed democracies'(*ibid.*, col. 851). This proposal was supported by the Social Democrats, but rejected by both *Venstre* and the Conservatives.

Yet the Conservatives and (more reluctantly) *Venstre* soon changed their minds, at least as far as the constitutional referendum was concerned. In 1915, the Radical (minority) Government under Thomas Zahle managed to convert the bourgeois parties to the referendum cause by arguing that the introduction of the referendum would be a safety valve, which could prevent a future Social Democratic Government from nationalising the farmland. The Conservatives and *Venstre*, furthermore, feared that the Social Democrats would attempt to abolish the Upper House, the *Landstinget* (which was controlled by *Venstre* and the Conservatives), if they won a majority in a general election. The two parties therefore agreed that any future changes in the constitution would require the consent of at least 45 per cent of the registered voters.

The philosophy behind this proposal was, as a Government White Paper on the reform made clear, that constitutional changes 'ought not to be enacted unless a substantial majority of the population favours a constitutional change, nor if the proposed change failed to attract the interest of the voters, i.e. engage the voters to a degree that they decide to take part in the referendum' (quoted in Eiggard 1993, 346, n. 8). This strategy almost backfired when the Radicals, the Conservatives and *Venstre* sought approval for the constitutional changes which would enable North Schleswig to re-enter the Danish Kingdom in 1920. The Social Democrats urged voters to abstain, a strategy which almost proved successful: the proposal was supported by only 46.5 per cent of the registered voters.

Enthusiasm for the referendum seemingly cooled off during the 1920s. The Social Democrats had reiterated their support for a people's initiative in 1920, though this time they suggested that

100,000 voters and not 30,000 voters should be entitled to call a referendum. Their proposal was soon withdrawn, perhaps because the Social Democrats became the largest party in the *Folketinget* and formed the party's first government in 1924.

The referendum debate was largely dormant until, in 1936, Thorvald Stauning, the Social Democratic prime minister, proposed the introduction of a 'plebiscitary mechanism' which would allow the Government to call a referendum on proposals opposed by the majority in the *Rigsdagen* (*Forfatningskommissionen Årbog 1937–1938*, 77). This proposal, which would have strengthened the Government's powers considerably, forced the opposition to reconsider its position on referendums. It prompted the Conservative Party and *Venstre* to propose the introduction of citizen-initiated popular referendums as an alternative to the existing upper chamber.

This radicalism ostensibly shocked the Government. The opposition parties had until then been weakened by their almost uncritical defence of the existing institutions. Yet their change of heart seems with the benefit of hindsight to be understandable. *Venstre* and the Conservatives' majority in the *Landstinget* had dwindled. The Upper House, which had previously been a brake on change, now seemed to be a threat to the interests of the bourgeois parties, as the Social Democrats had become the largest party in the *Landstinget*. It was ostensibly this prospect, rather than principled ideals, which convinced the leader of the Conservatives, John Christmas-Møller, that the introduction of citizen-initiated referendums would provide a more efficient check than a bicameral legislature on the excesses of the majority parties in Parliament. As he put it:

> It must be considered as a possibility that the opinion of a majority in Parliament is not always congruent with the opinion of a majority of the electors. The Conservatives, therefore, demand that a provision for a referendum be included in the Constitution, but in a way in which such a plebiscite … only can be initiated by a minority of the members of Parliament, or by a certain number of the electors. A plebiscite which only can be initiated by the Government, or by the members of Parliament who support the Government, is in our view without constitutional value. (*Rigsdags Årbogen 1938–1939*, 38)

The Conservatives supported both the referendum as a minority veto (initiated by a minority of MPs) and the popular referendum (initiated by the voters). This enthusiasm was, however, viewed with unease by some of the backbenchers of the Conservative Party, especially the outspoken traditionalist Victor Pürschel, who favoured a reform of the two-chamber system rather than the introduction of the referendum. The same view was in the end taken also by *Venstre*. This split made it difficult for Christmas-Møller to force the Government to make concessions.

After prolonged negotiations Christmas-Møller had to settle for the following compromise: 'When a bill has been passed by the *Rigsdagen*, two-fifths of the members in a session of the joint *Rigsdag*, called by at least fifteen members, can demand a referendum ... Referendums shall, further, be called if a third of the members in the *Rigsdag* are supported by fifteen per cent of the electors' (*Grundlovsforslaget 1938–39*, article 61). This proposal failed to win the support of the required 45 per cent of the registered voters in the referendum on 23 May 1939, mainly because *Venstre* and some Conservative backbenchers urged the voters to abstain. The result was a double defeat for the Conservative Party, which split when Victor Pürschel founded the party *Nationalt Samvirke* (National Co-operation) in opposition to the leadership's campaign for a 'yes' vote. The failed attempt to change the constitution in 1939 did not dampen enthusiasm for referendums. All the major parties realised that an alternative to the *Landstinget* was needed. The *Venstre*–Conservative Government (led by the former's Knud Kristensen) consequently invited the other parties in the *Folketinget* to take part in negotiations over a new constitution, in general, and alternatives to the *Landstinget*, in particular, negotiations which commenced in 1946. One of the main features of what became the 1953 constitution was the introduction of the provision for minority vetoes in what is commonly referred to as the 'artice 42 referendum'.

Denmark's minority veto is not in fact a homegrown idea, but was inspired by a failed attempt to introduce a similar mechanism into the British constitution. The Tory peer Lord Balfour of Burleigh suggested in March 1911 that a minority of 200 members of the House of Commons be given the right to call a referendum on a measure that both houses of Parliament had adopted (Bogdanor 1981, 93). This proposal did not win support and was soon forgotten in Britain. It was, however, introduced in Denmark (though it is unlikely that there was a connection between the two proposals).

For the bourgeois parties and the Radicals the prospect of a mechanism which would challenge the power of the Social Democrats was attractive, especially as the parties had reached agreement about the abolition of the *Landstinget*. What was intended as a warning thus inspired Bertel Dalgaard, the Radical member of the Constitutional Commission, to call for the introduction of the minority veto, which in his words would provide 'a safety-valve which can be used against the government if the socialists should wish to enact revolutionary reforms' (*Forfatningskommissionen Udvalg Et*, 12 February 1952).

The intention was not to transform Denmark into a referendum democracy, but rather to introduce a mechanism that would force the Government to negotiate with the opposition. The Conservatives' chief negotiator, Aksel Møller, thus stressed that minority referendums were 'likely never to be used as the government would be deterred from enacting or even proposing legislation which could provoke the minority to demand a referendum' (*ibid.*, 8 August 1952).

It was on the basis of the conception of the referendum as a mechanism of minority protection that the parties reached agreement on article 42, section 1 of which reads:

> Where a bill has been passed by the *Folketinget*, one-third of the members of the Folketinget may within three week days from the final passing of the Bill request of the Chairman of the *Folketinget* that the Bill be submitted to a referendum. Such a request shall be made in writing and signed by the members making the request.

There are, however, limits to the use of this procedure. Section 6 of the article excludes finance Bills, supplementary appropriation Bills, government loans, civil servants' (amendment) Bills, salaries and pension Bills, naturalisation Bills, expropriation Bills, taxation (direct or indirect) Bills, as well as treaties introduced for the purpose of discharging existing treaty obligations. It is perhaps a testimony to the parties' reluctance to use the provisions for minority referendums that article 42 has been used only once, namely to decide the fate of the land laws (*Jordlovene*) in 1963.

The minority clause had almost slipped into oblivion when it was suddenly revived by a Conservative MP, the former judge Knud Thestrup, who suggested that artice 42 should be used to hinder the enactment of four laws that were bitterly opposed by the opposition parties, i.e. *Venstre*, the Independents (*Dc Uafhængige*) and the Conservatives in 1963.

It is open to question that opposition to the bills would have led to a referendum were it not for the increasing animosity between the Government and the opposition in the months prior to the third reading of the Bill. The Social Democrats and the Radicals (who formed a coalition government) had used their majority – of a single member – to enact a far-reaching economic package, the so-called 'total solution' (*Helhedsløsningen*), which outlined the economic policies for the immediate future, as well as containing a number of quite radical economic measures.

The Conservatives, *Venstre* and the small libertarian Independents Party found the enactment of the *Helhedsløsningen* a demonstration that the Government had abandoned the constitutional convention according to which such packages were subject to negotiations between government and opposition. Their anger was exacerbated as the Government had appointed one of the two members for Greenland, Mikael Gams, as minister for Greenland in return for his support.

The prospect of the Government enacting measures without negotiating with the opposition prompted the bourgeois parties to consider ways in which they could regain their influence. Resistance to the land laws was instrumental in this. The opposition parties were not opposed to the land laws as such.

The disapproval of the Government's Bill was a principled one, rather than one based on disapproval of the proposals. The thrust of the opposition parties' charge was that Prime Minister Jens Otto Krag had abandoned consensus-seeking initiatives, which had been the norm in Danish politics even under majority governments (Einhorn and Logue 1988, 311).

It was on the basis of this development that Erik Eriksen, the leader of the Opposition, called a referendum in which the Government's position was overwhelmingly defeated. It thus seems that the provision for referendums served to bring about what Dicey had referred to as a 'people's veto'. But, equally importantly, the result subsequently forced the parties to reach a negotiated solution in accordance with the notion of democracy outlined in chapter 1 of this book. This solution was recognised by Prime Minister Krag, who, once the result was known, conceded that 'the task is to find ways in which we can reach broad agreements. Was that not the strongest appeal to the political parties, the opposition as well as the government, that new proposals must be made, and that the negotiations must start again?' (quoted in *Aktuelt*, 22 July 1963).

It has been argued that this result has had a lasting effect on the Danish political system. The prospect of unpopular Bills being submitted to referendums has, according to some observers, tended to facilitate consensus democracy – an interpretation summed up thus by constitutional lawyer Max Sørensen: 'it is evident that the fact that a referendum can be requested by a minority in the Folketinget will encourage broad agreement in legislation which might affect the interests of large sections of the society' (1973, 183). The analysis of the Danish minority veto thus led to the tentative conclusion that article 42 has served the purpose of encouraging politicians to seek negotiated solutions in order to avoid the risk of being defeated at the polls. As Bogdanor has noted, 'a government, however large a majority it may enjoy, is prevented from carrying legislation which arouses the active disapproval of the electorate. In such a situation the referendum serves to encourage the politics of agreement' (1981, 71).

While this interpretation may have applied in the aftermath of the land laws referendums, it is by no means certain that the minority referendum would have the same effect today. An empirical analysis is required to determine the matter. The provision has not been used since 1963, and it seems – on recent evidence – to have drifted into political oblivion. The Danish minority referendum is not, therefore, well suited to the task of ensuring compliance with the Lockean dictum that 'the people shall be judge'. The provision has not directly provided the voters with a safeguard against the 'elected dictatorship'. Article 42 has, it seems, been conducive to co-operation between the major parties. Yet, the problem as regards article 42's compatibility with the Lockean dictum emerges only in the rare instances when the anti-system parties represent views shared by the majority of the voters, but by only a tiny minority in Parliament.

The problem, according to the spokespersons for these parties, is that the majority in the *Folketinget* often exceeds two-thirds of the members, and so the minority is not large enough to initiate a referendum, as was illustrated by the Radicals' failed demand for a referendum in 1955. The party sought support for a referendum on the majority's decision to accept the deployment of German troops on Danish territory, a decision backed by the three largest parties in the *Folketinget*, *Venstre*, the Social Democrats and the Conservatives, which together amounted to more than 90 per cent of the members. Yet there was significant public opposition to the plan, which would have allowed German soldiers to re-enter Denmark only ten years after the Second World War. There was, however, little that the Radicals could do, as they were significantly short of the required sixty MPs. A similar situation emerged in 1969 when 40,000 citizens signed a petition for a referendum on the abortion law. The majority of the *Folketinget* took little notice of the protest, and did not consider submitting the law to a referendum since a mere eighteen members of the *Folketinget* had signed a petition for a referendum to be held in accordance with article 42.

There is, then, compelling evidence that article 42 fails to provide the voters with a check on the majority. It might therefore be argued that a different mechanism is needed, namely a mechanism which allows the citizens to demand a referendum on any given law. This shortcoming has prompted smaller parties, like the Socialist People's Party, the Progress Party, the Radicals and the Danish People's Party, to demand the introduction of citizen-initiated referendums. Asked if she supported the introduction of Italian-style popular referendums, Pia Kjærsgaard, leader of the far-right Danish People's Party, answered:

> Yes I fully support [the Italian provision], a given number of citizens should be entitled to demand a referendum on any given issue. One is sometimes told that the citizens are too ignorant to decide on issues, and that some issues are so fundamental and of such consequence that they must be left to the politicians. I do not agree. I believe that some issues are too important to be left to the politicians. By giving the people the initiative to correct the majority we can make sure that the politicians opinions are in line with the opinions of the people. (Correspondence with the author, 18 February 1998)

This view is echoed in a Bill introduced by the Progress Party in 1995. The accompanying memorandum expressed the belief that a popular referendum would provide the voters with a popular veto. 'There are situations when the majority of the representatives' views are not shared by a majority of the voters and it is in these situations that the referendum can be used to make sure that the politicians stay on the path chosen by their electors.' In a written communication to the author, Kim Behnke, Progress Party spokesman, expressed the view: 'As a voter one might support one party on tax-issues but be opposed to the same party's policies on moral issues ... We believe that this can be remedied by allowing 20,000 to demand a referendum' (3 July 1996).

The fact that the anti-abortionists were able to gather 40,000 signatures on an issue that was opposed by a handful of MPs suggests that the popular referendum, which was championed by Christmas-

Møller in 1938, may well provide a more efficient safeguard than the minority veto and almost certainly a safeguard closer to the Lockean dictum.

The abrogative referendum

As always, the question to be considered is would it work? The popular referendum, or the popular veto, has received considerable attention since the French Revolution. An embryonic version of the popular referendum was introduced in article 59 of the Montagnards' constitution drafted by Marie-Jean de Condorcet, which was in force between August 1792 and July 1794. It has, however, been employed only in relatively few countries: Switzerland, Italy, Uruguay, some American states and some German states (see the Appendix to this chapter).

Article 89 of the constitution of the Swiss Confederation stipulates that 'federal laws and generally binding federal decrees must be submitted to the people for approval or rejection if 50,000 Swiss citizens entitled to vote so demand' (De Q. Walker 1987, 211). This provision has been used 122 times since 1875, resulting in the repeal of a total of 61 laws (Treschel and Kriesi 1996, 192). It has been asserted that the mere possibility of popular referendums encourages consensus government. Indeed, this was given as the reason for the Danish Progress Party's proposal in 1995. In a memorandum, Kim Behnke, the party spokesman, wrote:

> The referendum experience in Switzerland shows that the federal politicians spend more time drafting and revising proposed legislation in order to avoid the citizens demanding referendums – as they are likely to if they are displeased with ill-considered legislation. It might thus he argued that the most important effect of the referendum is that the citizens decide not to demand referendums. (Danish Parliament, *Beslutningsforslag*, no. B2, 2 – part of the infamous *Rigsdags Årbogen*)

There is some support for this view among Swiss scholars of the Swiss referendum experience. Leonard Neidhart has argued that Switzerland's 'referendum democracy' had been transformed into a 'negotiated democracy' because the mere possibility that the voters would demand a referendum spurred the parties to reach a compromise solution. Moreover, recent research has shown that where provisions for citizen-initiated polls exist the elected parliamentarians tend to be more responsive to the views of their citizens (Feld and Kirchgässer 2000). This finding may be supported by the consideration that Swiss voters have requested referendums on 12.8 per cent of the total of 1,787 acts that *could* have been subjected to referendums – 3 per cent of Swiss acts have been successfully challenged in referendums (Linder 1998, 99). Moreover, the Swiss referendum provides the safeguard which is lacking in Danish politics, especially as MPs from small parties like the Swiss environmentalists can 'use the threat of referendums to influence parliamentary deliberations' (Kobach 1993, 256). A recent study concluded, perhaps rather hastily, that

> compared to purely representative systems, direct democracy [in Switzerland] leads to a different type of communication among citizens and also between citizens and representatives. The opportunity of deciding for themselves on political issues provides citizens with incentives to collect more information. Because citizens are better informed, politicians have less leeway to pursue their personal interests ... Citizens feel more responsive for their community: tax evasion is lower than in representative systems. (Feld and Kirchgässer 2000, 287)

This seems to be an exaggeration, yet the thrust of the argument is supported by my findings in this book. The question is, however, can the Swiss system be emulated?

Dicey had his doubts; 'the referendum', he wrote, 'might probably change its character and working when transplanted from the Alpine republic to the insular monarchy' (1890, 501). This appears to be a sound objection, as the unique political culture of direct democracy in Switzerland makes it difficult to make comparative projections regarding the effect of the popular referendum on the basis of Swiss experience. Switzerland remains a special case, a *Sonderfall*, a polity with a unique tradition of democracy in the 'first world of the referendum'.

The popular referendum in Italy

The popular referendum in Italy, known as the *referendum abrogativo*, constitutes a special case of the popular referendum, as the citizens can both reject bills passed before their promulgation and abrogate measures which already are in force. The Italian referendum is not, therefore, a purely conservative device. While New Zealanders, for example, can petition a referendum on any issue if they can collect signatures from 10 per cent of the voters, Italians can petition a referendum on an already enacted law if it is requested by 500,000 voters or 5 regional councils.

The difference between the Italian and the Swiss popular referendum provisions is that the former allows the citizens to repeal any law on the statute book, whereas the Swiss provision allows the voters only to veto a bill within ninety days of its publication. The request for a popular referendum in Italy must subsequently be approved by the Constitutional Court, which ensures that no referendum is called on matters concerning international treaties, budgetary laws or pardons, all of which are exempted by the provision. This limitation on the use of the referendum has been further constrained by the Constitutional Court, which has interpreted article 75, the *referendum abrogativo*, quite narrowly. The Constitutional Court has thus rejected 29 of 75 proposals for popular referendums (Uleri 1996, 175).

The Italians have, these restrictions notwithstanding, held forty-eight popular referendums between 1974 and 1995. The *referendum abrogativo* was included in the Italian constitution of 1948. Yet the provision was deeply mistrusted by the political parties, which feared that uncontrolled use of the popular referendum to challenge the legislation could yield anti-hegemonic results. The parties consequently failed to implement the provision for popular referendums until 1970.

The decision to implement article 75 was not the result of a growing commitment to direct democracy, but was based rather on a calculated risk, namely that the *Democrazia Cristiana* (DC – Christian Democrats) would be able to exploit the provision in a semi-plebiscitary fashion. In addition, it was hoped that the referendum could resolve the internal disagreements over the issue of divorce between the secular parties and DC in the ruling coalition. DC opposed divorce, while the divorce proposal was supported by the secular parties in the coalition, as well as by the largest opposition party, the Communist Party of Italy (PCI).

In an attempt to save the coalition, DC proposed that a divorce law be enacted on the condition that it was later submitted to a popular referendum (should that be requested by the prescribed 500,000 electors). In this way DC could please both its coalition partners by enacting a divorce law, while at the same time staying loyal to the party's Roman Catholic principles by securing the right to campaign against the law in a future referendum.

The main reason for implementing article 75 was to preserve coalition solidarity; as such it can be likened to Harold Wilson's decision to hold a referendum to avoid a split within the Labour Party and, indeed, to Swedish Prime Minister Tage Erlander's decision to call a referendum on the supplementary pension plans to avoid the break-up of the Centre–Left government in 1957.

DC believed, wrongly as it turned out, that it was possible to utilise the popular referendum to serve the party's interests. While DC succeeded in its aim of keeping the coalition together, it lost the referendum, which resulted in overwhelming support for the proponents of the divorce law, who secured 59.3 per cent of the vote of an impressive 88.1 per cent turnout (Hine 1993, 155).

This outcome prompted the Radical Party (*Partito Radicale*) to use the referendum in order 'to encourage greater public involvement in politics', and as a means of 'forcing reforms of what it regarded as outmoded and repressive laws' (Spotts and Weiser 1986, 121). This strategy was encouraged by a unique provision in article 75 which allows the voters to repeal *sections* of laws rather than laws in their entirety. This allowed the Radical Party to call for the repeal of a section of the law passed by Mussolini that made abortion 'a crime against the health and integrity of the race'. In doing so the Radicals sought to clear all restrictions on abortion; as such, they tried to make *progressive* use of what was intended as a conservative device.

Abortion was one of Italy's most fiercely debated issues of the 1970s. The World Health Organisation (WHO) estimated that 800,000 illegal abortions were performed in Italy every year – the highest number of illegal abortions in Europe (Spotts and Wieser 1986, 121). Legislation aimed at lifting restrictions on abortion was, however, blocked by DC which had vocal support from the Vatican. Yet the attempt to scrap a section of the Mussolini law from the statute book opened up the prospect of a complete liberalisation of the abortion laws, an undesirable prospect for moderate supporters of the legalisation of abortions, such as the Socialists, the Republicans and the PCI, as well as for DCs (though for other reasons). A referendum on the abortion issue could have been damaging for the growing collaboration between the PCI and DC (an understanding between the two parties was at that time seen as prerequisite for a solution to economic and political crises in Italy). None of the so-called 'relevant' parties in the Italian legislature was enthusiastic about the prospects of another referendum, not least because psephological studies had indicated that the parties in the governing coalition were split on the issue. These studies had shown that middle-class DC electors had voted in favour of the divorce law, while Socialist electors in rural areas had voted against the law. That is to say, the electors had massively rejected the recommendations of their parties and had voted in accordance with their convictions. These consequences undoubtedly played a role in the parties' hostility towards the referendums proposed by the Radicals, not least because the latter overtly championed the referendum as an alternative to a party system which had failed to represent the electors on important issues.

It is, however, open to question whether such party-tactical considerations were the sole reason for the parties' reservations over the proposed popular referendum on abortion. An understanding of the abortion referendum debate must include more than an analysis of the parties' strategic considerations, not least because the pro-abortion parties regarded the proposed repeal of the abortion section as too radical. This highlights a theoretical perspective: it has been suggested that referendums are inconsistent with democracy because voters are presented with simplistic alternatives. This was particularly true for the abortion referendums, which offered an artificially simplistic choice between complete liberalisation and complete criminalisation of abortions, both of which were unacceptable to opponents and proponents of the abortion law. In order to avoid a referendum on a choice between two equally radical options, the parties in Parliament sought to use a provision of article 75 which allows Parliament to pass a new law 'in harmony with the aims of the promoters of a referendum' within ninety days. These negotiations resulted in the enactment of the so-called 'Law 194' (1978), which legalised abortion at the State's expense for women aged 18 years and over, subject to certain specified medical conditions.

The threat of a referendum had again facilitated a compromise solution, as well as forcing the parties to negotiate. Rather than threaten representative democracy, the popular referendum spurred a compromise solution which the elected representatives had been unable to reach. The abortion law was, however, anathema both to the radical Catholics and to feminist groups and the Radicals.

Both the anti-abortionists and the Radicals consequently sought to repeal the new statute by targeting sections of it, the former in order to ban abortion altogether, the latter to legalise abortion. Neither of these proposals won the support of the majority of the voters in the referendum in 1981: 32 cent supported the Catholics' attempt to criminalise abortion, while only 11 per cent supported the Radicals' quest for complete liberalisation (Marradi 1976).

This pattern was repeated in Parliament's efforts avoid referendums between radical alternatives on such issues as asylums for the mentally ill (1978), military justice (1981) and the so-called 'cost-of-living bonuses' in 1982 (LaPalombara 1987). Although the first nine referendums in Italy failed to repeal any statutes, the preceding debate seems to have encouraged the political parties to enact laws which they perhaps would not otherwise have done.

However, it must be noted that there is a 50 per cent rule in article 75. The repeal of a law must be supported by at least 50 per cent of the voters in a referendum in which the turnout exceeds 50 per cent. This requirement was not met in the so-called anti-Berlusconi referendums in June 1995 (in the referendums to ban a private company from owning more than one TV channel and commercial advertising in films). The referendums in 2000 also failed, this time because of low turnout. Indeed, the fact that all abrogative referendums since 2000 have failed because of low turnout perhaps questions whether the abrogative referendum remains the potent force it once was in Italian politics.

What is certain, however, is that the referendum did make a difference: it has been 'a stimulus for Parliament to act' (Pasquino 1992, 21) and perhaps served to ensure that Parliament refrained from enacting unpopular laws. The popular referendum yielded some of the same results as did the Danish minority veto, though without making the citizens dependent on a minority in Parliament. In its heyday the Italian popular referendum established a 'minimal consensus between different groups' (Luthardt 1994, 70), tending to facilitate compromise rather than undermine it. These findings suggest that the popular referendum is a more efficient safeguard than its critics have anticipated.

Unlike the Danish minority veto, the Italian provision has ensured that a government, however large its majority, is prevented from enacting legislation that is contrary to the will of the people. This was most emphatically shown in the referendum on a reform of the electoral system in 1991, in which a majority of 95.6 per cent of the voters of a 62.5 per cent turnout voted to abolish multiple preference voting at Chamber elections, despite massive party opposition to the proposal, which was supported by only one party, namely the reformed Communists, the PDS.

It seems fair to conclude that the referendum in Italy – in the 1980s and in the 1990s – allowed the voters to express views different from those of their favoured parties. The use of the referendum has thus vindicated its proponents, as the results of the 1981 referendums showed that those 'opposed by parties representing 95 per cent of the electorate had won support of a third or more of the voters' (Spotts and Wieser 1986, 120). This effect of the referendum has been most tangible within DC (and the party's allies in the Roman Catholic Church).

To take but one example, the referendum in 1974 allowed DC voters to oppose policies specifically promoted by the hierarchy of the Catholic Church, the elite group which had a dominating influence on DC. The influence of the Church was generally unpopular among the voters. An average of 71.3 per cent of the respondents in a survey carried out in 1972 supported the statement that 'the Church should stay out of politics'. A total of 60.6 per cent of DC's voters supported this view, whereas only 3.5 per cent of them agreed with proposition that 'the Church should be more actively involved in politics' (Marradi 1976, 129). The introduction of the popular referendum allowed secular voters to continue to support DC's economic policies without having to support the party's stance on moral issues.

The fact that Italian voters have been able to 'distinguish between measures and men' is yet another vindication of Dicey's credo that the referendum would be the best possible check on party government. As Gordon Smith noted in connection with the divorce referendum, its importance lay in the fact that for the first time a large number of loyal or traditional DC supporters felt free to stray from the party while remaining DC voters (Smith 1975, 297).

The popular referendum and the normative criteria

There has often been something illogical about the selection of issues to be submitted to a referendum. Charles de Gaulle called a referendum on whether to establish a regional tier of government in 1969, but failed to hold a referendum on whether the UK should be allowed to join the EEC. His successor Georges Pompidou, by contrast, saw no need for a referendum on establishing a regional tier of government, yet he held a referendum on the entry of the UK, Denmark and Norway to the EEC. The same lack of consistency exists in the Danish minority veto; the bourgeois parties initiated a referendum on the land laws in 1963, while no referendum was held when almost identical proposals were enacted by a bourgeois government five years later.

There is only one constitutional means by which such inconsistence selections illogicalities can be legimised, and that is to politically make the initiation of a referendum dependent on the extent of popular demand. The only mechanism which meets this criterion is the popular referendum, which, to use a Lockean term, allows the people to decide if a bill is 'of great consequence'. With the popular referendum, the people are not dependent on constitutional provisions, a specified number of legislators or splits within the major parties. That the people can demand a referendum on laws they consider important makes the popular referendum an ideal 'people's veto'. This view has been summed up by Spotts and Wieser's contention that the popular referendum was 'encouraging political interest, allowing direct expression of the public's views, and bringing decisions closer to the people'. They found that most of the claims made on behalf of the popular referendum had 'been amply fulfilled', not least because its employment had shown it to be 'an instrument beyond the control of the parties [which] forced them to take stands on issues' (1986, 121).

As for potential shortcomings, Spotts and Weiser acknowledged the ease with which 'a referendum [might be set] in motion [so] that a small number of people [could] start the process over issues … of interest only to a tiny minority'; they accepted furthermore that there was a risk that an 'improper use of the referendum could sour the public's interest and defeat the very purpose of engaging the public in topical social issues' (ibid., 122). On the basis of evidence relating to referendums held prior to 1985, however, the authors concluded that 'so far referenda have done far more good than harm' (ibid.).

Whether that conclusion can been sustained in the light of the considerable number of referendums held since 1987 is, however, debatable. Only 9 referendums were submitted to the voters between 1970 and 1987, whereas between November 1987 and June 1995 a total of 28 popular referendums were held. The most notable consequence of these referendums was that the turnout dropped from an average of 80.5 per cent in the former period to one of only 61.9 per cent in the latter period, according to one opinion poll (La Republica, 14 June 1997), apparently because voters felt 'saturated' by referendum campaigns (ibid.).

This declining turnout raises serious doubts about the attractiveness of the referendum to voters, and might in principle lead to a situation where the majority which votes for, say, the repeal of an act does not correlate with the majority of voting-age citizens. This problem has been summed up by Kris Kobach (1993, 350):

The legitimacy of the referendum stems from the assumption that its results expresses the will of the majority. But the lower the participation level, the greater the possibility of distortion (in which the percentage voting yes varies considerably from the percentage that would have resulted if all citizens had voted). In these instances of high voter apathy a mobilised special interest may be well poised to take advantage of the situation. Trooping to the polls in great numbers while most of the electorate stays at home, an active minority can defeat a position held by the majority of citizens. The result is what I describe as a false majority (in which the final verdict on the proposal, had all citizens voted, would have been different).

There is evidently a possibility that Italian referendums will result in such false majorities, yet the risk is diminished by the stipulation that a law can be repealed only if more than 50 per cent of the electors actually vote (all referendums since 1997 have been declared void because the turnout requirement has not been met). It is further important to note that the voters, while abstaining on non-controversial issues, have voted on issues of major constitutional importance. The turnout in the referendum on the abolition of state funding for political parties in 1993, in fact, surged to 77.0 per cent, a figure only 0.1 per cent lower than the turnout in the referendum to abolish PR in Senate elections in the same year. An increasing number of referendums may generally result in declining turnouts, yet the voters have, as we saw in chapter 1, a 'civic reserve', i.e. skills and commitments available for issues important to them (Almond 1992, 99); moreover, the salience of the issues submitted to the voters is certainly a factor that affects the turnout. Nigel Smith commented (in personal communication with the author, 25 April 2004): 'a high turnout requires a credible problem and a credible solution'.

It is often hypothesised that frequent referendums lead to a declining interest in politics and voter apathy, and that these in turn strengthen the rule of elites as well as increasing the influence of the middle classes. The Italian data, though based on sources less scholarly than the Californian and Swiss data, do not deviate significantly from these findings. The Italian voters score high on measures of knowledge. More than 50 per cent had an 'adequate' knowledge of the issues when measured by the Hertig–Grunner criteria (*La Republica*, 14 June 1997). The popular referendum may not be a political panacea, yet the evidence does not support those who criticise the referendum as undemocratic and potentially dangerous.

Appendix: Referendums in Germany

The Germans have by their own admission suffered from a *Plebis phobic der Nachkriegsära* (referendum phobia of the post-war era); no nationwide referendums have been held in Germany. Yet it is noteworthy that popular referendums have been held at the local level, and that the provision for these referendums has had an effect, even when no actual referendum has been called.

That the provision for the referendum in itself increases the responsiveness of Parliament is perhaps illustrated by the planned referendum on the abolition of grammar schools, which was never held in the German state of North Rhein Westphalia because the state government abandoned the proposal when it became clear that the law would be challenged in a referendum (Ludthardt 1994, 70). While popular referendums are rare in North Rhein Westphalia, they are frequently used in Bavaria (and occasionally in Hessen). Article 74 of the Bavarian constitution allows 10 per cent of the voters (roughly one million people) to demand referendums (so-called *Volksbegehren)* on bills proposed by the state legislature.

Bavarian voters have had the opportunity to vote in 14 popular referendums since 1967, only two of which have led to an outright rejection of legislation proposed in a given area. Yet it has generally been the case that the Christian Social Union (CSU) Government (which has enjoyed a virtual monopoly of power in Bavaria) has had to modify proposed legislation after negotiations with the opposition parties (predominantly the SPD). An example of this pattern of compromise government is provided by the referendum on religious schools in 1968. The CSU Government had proposed a law which would strengthen the rights of religious schools. The Free Democrat Party (FDP) had in vain sought to gather the necessary signatures for a referendum, but had failed (although they did obtain signatures from 9.2 per cent of the citizens). The apparent unpopularity with some aspects of the proposed law prompted the SPD to launch a campaign for a referendum on some of the controversial aspects of the law. The second attempt succeeded. The prospect of a referendum prompted the CSU to seek a compromise with the SPD, yet the FDP and the more radical Catholic fractions within the CSU boycotted the negotiations. The compromise (which recognised the special status of Roman Catholicism without discriminating against other denominations) won the referendum (76 per cent voted in favour). The referendum had not just provided a check on an otherwise popular party (the CSU) but had facilitated a compromise solution. This indicates that the consequences of the German referendums are strikingly similar to those of the Swiss and Italian popular referendums.

Conclusion: bringing it all back home

The American Declaration of Independence expresses Thomas Jefferson's belief in a system of government under which the elected rulers derived 'their just powers from the consent of the governed'. Political thinkers, philosophers and laymen and women have been divided as to what this means in practice. Some – like Schumpeter (1976) – believed that democracy is – at best – a delegation of power to elected representatives, while others, like Benjamin Barber (1984), believed that democracy is best exercised directly by the people.

While the latter view may sound theoretically attractive, the former view has generally been regarded as the only realistic possibility in large modern states. Democratic government requires deliberation and a balancing of the views of differing communities' legitimate interests. Yet this soundly based commitment to representative – or indirect – democracy cannot disguise the in-built shortcomings and flaws of the system. 'Log-rolling' (vote-trading) and 'rent seeking' (the provision of a private good for a special-interest group at the expense of the commonwealth) are well-documented features of all systems of representative government.

This book has made a case for the view that some of these problems could be remedied by different mechanisms of direct democracy, especially by the referendum. Log-rolling would not be possible in a referendum, as it would be impossible for millions of voters to strike deals with one another as party leaders do. The same is evidently true of rent-seeking: it is possible for a special-interest group to influence targeted politicians, but not even the most sophisticated system of direct-mailing would make it possible to lobby millions of voters in the same way.

The referendum, therefore, should not be seen as an alternative to representative government. In fact, it was in order to prevent the degeneration of representative democracy and party government that proponents of referendums, from Machiavelli, through Rousseau to Dicey, have advocated that the electorate be allowed to vote on laws already enacted by its representatives (Qvortrup 2003).

The referendum is a complement to representative democracy; a mechanism for improving the prevailing system. It is a means of checking what Christopher Lasch (1996) termed 'the revolt of the elites'. The idea – as well as the practice – is that the mere risk of a referendum will encourage the elected representatives to govern with due regard to the wills and the sentiments of their ultimate masters: the people. The threat of a referendum will encourage politicians to legislate responsively for fear that their enactments be nullified by a 'people's veto'.

However, such theoretical arguments are insufficient to convince sceptics. While sound in theory, these arguments for (a modest) use of referendums hinge on the citizens' ability to reach sound and carefully considered conclusions.

Many observers, from Plato to Chris Patten, have doubted that the citizenry is capable of reaching such decisions. Michael Oakeshott, the conservative British philosopher, candidly summed up this objection to the referendum (which he called the plebiscite): 'The plebiscite is not a method by which "mass man" imposes his choices upon his rulers; it is a method for generating a government with unlimited authority to make choices on his behalf. In the plebiscite "mass man" achieved final release from the burden of individuality; he was emphatically told what to chose' (1991, 380).

The problem with this line of reasoning is that it is empirically unfounded: voters, more often than not (as I have shown), do not do as they are told. In 49 per cent of all referendums held in Western democratic countries since the end of the Second World War the result has been a defeat for the positions favoured by governments.

This does not, of course, prove that voters are knowledgeable. Ignorance – possibly exacerbated by deceptive advertising (see Appendix A) – *can* influence the voters – though the evidence in support of this suspicion remains slender (see below). In fact, comparative studies of voter knowledge suggest that voters have a (surprisingly) detailed knowledge of the issues. To take but one example, 80 per cent of the Swiss voters could mention at least one fundamental feature of the proposals submitted to them. Further, the voters – while not having an encyclopaedic knowledge of the issues, – have generally been able to use 'cues' and 'short-cuts' to decide on issues, generally voting in accordance with their preferences. Arthur Lupia, as noted in chapter 1, found that citizens tend to vote in accordance with their preferences in 96 per cent of the cases.

Another objection used against referendums is that voters are inherently conservative; that they invariably resist change. As already noted, this is not the case: roughly half of all referendums result in a 'no' vote, which hardly constitutes proof of inherent blind conservatism.

Pericles noted famously that Athens' system of government 'favours the many instead of the few; this is why it is called a democracy' (Thucydides 1954, 102). He was only partially right: 'democracy' is more than this. Government by the people does not allow the majority to oppress the minority. Where does this leave the referendum? Being a majoritarian device, some have feared that the referendum would have the effect of legitimising tyranny by the many (Bell 1978). It is true that Hitler and Mussolini abused the referendum to this effect. Yet, these plebiscites were grossly rigged and were not representative of modern referendums. Who could sensibly claim that the referendum on Scottish devolution could be compared with Hitler's referendum on Austria's inclusion in the Third Reich?

While there have been a handful of referendums that were directed against minority groups (e.g. AIDS sufferers) at the local level in American states, there have been no successful national referendums that have led to the oppression of minorities. It seems that the charge that referendums can be used to discriminate against minorities belongs to a bygone age. Perhaps, Alexis de Tocqueville was right when he noted that 'a new science is needed for a world in itself quite new' (1988, 13).

The referendum is not a panacea. Sometimes turnout has been dismally low; at other times politicians have submitted issues to the voters for party-tactical considerations (Morel 2001). More often than not, however, the referendum has allowed the people – the ultimate sovereign – to have the final say on controversial issues. While the referendum is not a solution to all conceivable political problems, its occasional use (especially in systems where the citizenry has the right to call a referendum, as in Italy and Switzerland) can increase the legitimacy of political decisions. Moreover, the mere possibility of an issue being submitted to a referendum in many cases has, arguably, provided a check on politicians over-eager to legislate and regulate without due consideration to the consequences.

Sceptics may well be unconvinced; and pragmatists will continue to ask 'Will it work?' To this one can only reply, quoting Jeremy Bentham, that the 'utility of this remedial process would depend entirely upon the way it was administered; yet the rejection of a means so salutary can only originate in culpable indifference anxious to save it self the trouble of discovering expedients' (1931, 107).

Appendix A

Campaign spending in ballot campaigns

> Other rights, even the most basic, are illusory if the right to vote is undermined. (*US Supreme Court in Wesbury v. Sanders* [1964])

The aim of this appendix is to determine the effect of campaign spending in ballot campaigns, taking as its point of departure a case study of Californian referendums, followed up by case studies of Denmark, the UK and Austria. Discussion is structured around the following problems:

- Does money affect the outcome of referendums?
- Who spends the most in ballot campaigns and are there theoretical considerations which can explain spending discrepancies?
- Are referendum results more vulnerable to campaign spending than are those in candidate elections?
- What are the preconditions for efficient campaign spending?
- Is the Californian pattern universally applicable?

Conventional wisdom has it that the biggest winners in Californian referendums and initiatives 'in recent years have been admen and lawyers, not voters' (*Economist*, 13 October 1990, 21). A survey thus showed that 82 per cent of the respondents agreed that 'In those proposition races where one side of an issue has enough money to pay for expensive campaign advertising, the outcome does not usually represent the will of the people but the interests of big campaign contributors' (Field Institute 1983). It is, therefore, unsurprising that 'the most frequently heard criticism of the referendum is the role that big money plays in direct democracy campaigns' (Bell and Price 1988, 103).

This claim is, if it can be empirically sustained, a potential death blow to the many arguments in favour of referendums and initiatives that have been advanced by political theorists and philosophers. It is difficult to uphold laudatory claims about direct democracy if it is the case that the richer side invariably prevails. It is not difficult to see that referendum outcomes which effectively are *bought* by the richest bidder are at odds with the Dahlian norm that the 'preferences of each citizen ought to be taken equally into account in determining the final outcome' (Dahl 1989, 6).

The question is, however, whether the assertion that the richer side invariably wins is supported by empirical findings. In a seminal article Ronald I. Allen found it difficult to sustain 'the fear that monied interests will be able to use the initiative at a national level to their advantage by hoodwinking the people' (1979, 1033). Other writers have reached the opposite conclusion, that 'campaign expenditures are the single most powerful predictors of the vote' (Zisk 1987, 90).

Such contradictory assertions call for a detailed study of the actual effects of campaign spending in referendums, which, unlike the studies from which those claims come, is firmly rooted in a general theoretical model with supporting empirical evidence.

The case of California

California is, after Switzerland, the polity in which the largest number of issues has been submitted to direct decisions by the voters (Möckli 1994, 147); it is, furthermore, the polity in which campaigners have spent the largest sums of money on campaigns. California thus seems to be ideally suited to an inquiry into the effects of money in referendum campaigns; or, put differently, if money does not affect outcomes in California, then money is unlikely to have a decisive effect elsewhere.

That interest groups could distort referendum results through massive spending was not considered to be a serious risk when the referendum was introduced in California in 1911. Indeed, the referendum was introduced with the aim of reducing the influence of well-funded interest groups. The Southern Pacific Railroad, to give one example, enjoyed a monopoly of political influence in the legislature. 'It was also said that newspapers and public officials were controlled, and that party conventions did the bidding of railroad attorneys' (Bredsdorf 1975, 923).

It was believed that referendums would reduce the influence of lobbyists, interest groups and the party machine. For while lobbyists easily could influence, if not bribe, a few hundred parliamentarians, it would be difficult, so it was argued, to do the same with millions of voters. The referendum was introduced to effect 'a shift in power and a shift of influence in favour of causes whose adherents were numerous and passionate but not well financed and well connected' (Lowenstein 1982, 608). Or, as Elihu Root, a campaigner, said, 'the ideal is to prevent ... the great railroad companies, the great insurance companies, the great telephone companies, the great aggregations of wealth from using their corporate funds directly or indirectly [for the] advancement of their interests as against those of the public' (quoted in Hart and Shore 1979, 622). The growing use of money did, however, result in increased fears about the possibility of *buying* the desired result in a referendum. Such fears resulted in the passage of the Political Reform Act of 1974, which limited the spending in state-wide campaigns (Lowenstein 1982, 622). A similar measure, enacted by the legislature of Massachusetts was, however, invalidated by the US Supreme Court in the case of the *First National Bank of Boston et al. v. Bellotti* (1978, p. 14).

In deciding whether Massachusetts had the right to prohibit large corporations from contributing money to referendum campaigns 'not materially affecting the property, business or assets of the corporation', the US Supreme Court overruled an earlier decision made by the Massachusetts Supreme Court which had upheld the law. Associate Justice Lewis F. Powell based his decision on the *alleged* fact that there 'had been no showing that the relative voice of corporations has been overwhelming or even significant in influencing referenda' (*ibid.*) The US Supreme Court also rejected the proposition that one-sided spending posed 'a threat to the confidence of the citizenry in government' (*ibid.*). On the basis of these assumptions the court ruled that constraints on the use of money would lead to unfair restrictions that would favour the other side of the issue. The Court, furthermore, argued that limits on campaign spending would prevent the public from considering all aspects of an issue if one party was barred from contributing information relevant to the debate (*ibid.*).

This ruling was repeated in 1981 in *Citizens Against Rent Control v. City of Berkeley* (1981), in which the US Supreme Court overruled a decision by the Californian Supreme Court permitting local authorities to introduce limits on campaign spending. Writing on behalf of the majority, Chief Justice Warren Burger held that 'there is no significant state or public interest in curtailing the debate and discussion of a ballot measure' (*ibid.*).

Burger found that the referendum was consistent with the intentions of its original initiators who sought to employ it against attempts to influence elected politicians. As he argued: 'Referenda are held on issues not on candidates for public office. The risk of corruption perceived in cases involving candidate ejections simply is not present in a popular vote on a public issue' (*ibid.*).

The conclusion that the effect of campaign spending is minimal in ballot campaigns seems to be vindicated by recent referendums, such as the referendum in 1988 on proposition 103, an initiative aimed at reducing the cost of car insurance by 20 per cent. Insurance companies and law firms spent a total of $76 million in a bid to secure the defeat of the proposition, while the proposers spent a mere $4 million (Lupia 1994,). The opponents of proposition 103 thus spent more than President George Bush did in his nationwide presidential campaign in the same year (California Commission on Campaign Funding 1992, 283). This massive disparity did not prevent the voters from endorsing the proposition. This result might be seen as a falsification of the view, advanced by David Magleby, namely 'that voting intentions coincide with disparities in campaign spending' (1984, 150).

In a much-cited study of the campaign (Lupia 1994), it was argued, rather convincingly, that massive campaign spending enhanced voter competence by increasing the information available to them. Massive spending, Lupia argued, precipitated the mass media's interest in the campaign, which, in turn, revealed the economic interests behind it, allowing the voters to evaluate the proposals more thoroughly.

Bowler and Donovan (1998c, 147) have seen this – and similar findings (Magleby 1994) – as an indication that 'spending ... may occasionally have the paradoxical effect of raising opposition to a given proposal'. They based their conclusion on the often-cited assertion that voters tend to vote 'no' when in doubt (*ibid.*, 43). In addition they cite evidence from the 1990s suggesting that voters make decisions on the basis of considerations about 'Who's behind it'? If the voters realise that, say, Philip Morris (the tobacco manufacturer) is behind a measure to prevent the passage of a restriction on smoking, they will take this into account when voting. Bowler and Donovan write: 'when a group such as the Philip Morris Company ... finances a yes campaign and media attention emphasizes the source of the funds, many voters are given a cue about "who's behind it" without having to review the ballot pamphlet' (*ibid.*, 150). On the basis of this argument they suggest that 'campaign spending has the potential for enhancing voter competence in direct democracy'; indeed, 'even one-sided spending can contribute to the voters ability to reason on the basis of party and ideology' (ibid., 163).

But how much money does it take to increase awareness? A lot if we are to believe the authors, who acknowledge that 'for every $1 million, roughly an additional 1 per cent of the voters become aware of the proposition' (ibid., 152). This, even for the free-spending Californian political environment, is quite a considerable outlay for such a return, though it must not be forgotten that a proposition in California has to compete with a dozen or more others. As I will show (see pp. 153–5) in the case study of Austria, smaller amounts appear to suffice in the 'second world' of the referendum.

More importantly, however, Bowler and Donovan (1998c) assume both that campaigners have to disclose their funds and – equally dubiously – that a critical press will scrutinise the campaign. Whether this is a true reflection of the press in an age of media moguls, spin and 'infotainment' is open to question. Still other political scientists, though of a less theoretical persuasion, have reached a conclusion strikingly similar to Bowler and Donovan's. David Butler has, in fact, asserted that excessive campaign spending can backfire as the voters become over-exposed to a particular point of view (1980, 14).

There is, however, conflicting evidence. Studying 276 local referendums in California in the period 1983–1988 David Hadwiger found that 'for every 1 per cent increase in the proportion of pro-ballot measure spending, there was a [0].15 increase in the proportion of pro-ballot measure vote' (1992, 543). Yet even a perfect correlation between campaign expenditures and campaign results does not prove that money is the decisive factor in ballot campaigns: it is possible that the richer side simply happens to be the more popular side. A good case has, in fact, been made for the view that proposition 13 (an anti-tax measure) was approved by the voters because they supported the measure, rather than because the measure was endorsed by rich interest groups (Walker 1987, 77). To draw the conclusion that referendum results are influenced by expenditures requires more than a statistical analysis: it requires an understanding of the dynamics of a ballot campaign.

The case of proposition 18

Proposition 18, a constitutional referendum initiated by the California legislature in 1970, may provide a classic example of a ballot campaign in the Golden State. The proponents of the measure sought to add two exceptions to the constitutional provisions which had hitherto required that petrol taxes and licence fees be used only for the improvement of streets and highways. The proposed provision would allow the legislature to allocate the funds raised from petrol taxes and licence fees to finance measures to reduce pollution. The proposal was, however, vehemently opposed by a coalition of oil companies, teamsters, auto clubs and road-builders, as well as by the Chamber of Commerce. In short, the proposition was opposed by organisations, all of which feared that the measure would run counter to their interests. This powerful coalition raised a total of $333,446, while the measure's proposers raised a total of only $26,635,214 (all figures from Lowenstein 1982).

It seems unlikely that this disparity in spending was without effect. A poll conducted a month prior to the vote showed that a majority of 69 per cent supported the measure, with only 22 per cent opposed to the constitutional amendment. Four weeks later the proposal was defeated in a 54–46 per cent vote (*Los Angeles Times*, 23 October 1970 and 4 November 1970). One of the factors contributing to the defeat may have been the 'no' campaign's emphasis that the constitutional amendment could lead to higher taxes. In the last three weeks of the campaign the opponents spent $123,000 on billboards with the simple message: 'More taxes? NO. NO' (*Sacramento Bee*, 3 January 1971).

By using their financial superiority the opponents of the proposal thus effectively turned the discussion away from the environmental issues and towards a debate about the desirability of higher taxes. The 'no' campaign avoided attacking the programmes which would have benefited from the passage of the amendment, apparently because of the widespread support for environmental causes which existed at the time (*ibid.*, 15 October 1970). The claim that the enactment of the proposition would have increased the level of taxation was criticised by economists, yet their objections to the campaign failed to make the headlines (*ibid.*, Letter to the editor, 28 October 1970) – perhaps an indication that Bowler and Donovan's assumption (1998c) about the critical press has its limitations.

The net result was that the opponents succeeded in defeating the proposition, perhaps because, as an editorial writer of the *LA Times* put it, 'a sufficient number of voters were deluded into opposing proposition 18' (6 November 1970).

Excursus: money and candidate elections

It is important to note at this stage that campaign spending, including its effects, is equally well established in *candidate* elections. Mueller, citing US examples, has shown that the possibilities of buying a result are equally real in a representative democracy (1989, 210). That it is, to a certain extent, possible to *buy* a referendum result does not, therefore, undermine the case for referendums any more than it undermines the case for representative government. Moreover a system of direct democracy is not vulnerable to post-election influence in the way that a representative democracy is: lobbyists and interest groups will find it difficult to target the voters in the same way as they can target a handful of MPs. The latter phenomenon, which is known as 'rent-seeking', is a clear case of the influence that interest groups can have on legislatures. There are several studies which show that interest groups have influenced a legislature's deliberations in a way which is impossible in a referendum. Coughlin (1985) found that the unions' contributions to congressmen had a notable effect on the latter's voting pattern, and Tosini and Tower (1988) reached the same conclusion in a study of the textile industry's influence on congressmen's voting patterns on the Textile Bill of 1985. That is to say, we cannot claim that referendums are undesirable because the voters fall prey to the influence of organised interest groups. The same is true for a system of representative government.

Moreover, a study of fifty-two constituencies in Californian State House elections in 1992 gives us an indication of the effect of campaign spending in candidate elections. All of the selected constituencies were 'unsafe' (i.e. neither of the two parties had consistently won the constituency seat over a twenty-five year period). The seat was won by a margin of more than 15 per cent in 33 constituencies, in 32 of them by the candidate who spent more money. The remaining 19 seats were won by a margin of less than 15 per cent, in 14 of them by the higher spending candidate. In sum, 46 of the 52 seats were won by the bigger spender!

These figures are no more alarming than the figures for referendums, although both give rise to serious problems for democratic legitimacy. Yet the findings effectively undermine the argument that candidate elections are preferable to referendums because the outcome is less likely to be influenced by campaign spending.

Campaign spending as a collective action problem

This short history of proposition 18 adds additional support to the hypothesis that the well-funded groups have an advantage in ballot campaigns. The opponents of proposition 18 secured support from large companies and firms, while the proponents had to rely on donations from individual citizens – citizens who were 'numerous and passionate but not well financed and well connected'. Standard Oil of California contributed $45,000, Mobil Oil contributed $30,000 and the Gulf Oil Corporation $20,000221. This pattern is far from unique: a study by the California Commission on Campaign Financing (CCCF) reveals that 66 per cent of the funds spent in ballot campaigns between 1952 and 1992 was donated by large companies, while contributions by individuals accounted for only 12 per cent of the total amount spent. This tendency is underlined by the fact that large contributors were even more dominant in the eighteen most expensive initiatives in the history of the Californian referendum (CCCF 1992, 380; Magleby 1994).

This discrepancy might be explained theoretically: one of the problems which faced the proponents of proposition 18 was that they sought to win support for the public financing of a public good, i.e. a cleaner environment, so that everyone would, almost by definition, benefit, however marginally, by its passage. The problem for the supporters of proposition 18 was that they faced a group of companies which would suffer significant economic and financial losses if public funds were to be allocated away from road-building to the benefit of environmental causes. The proponents of the proposition were thus akin to what economists call a 'latent group'. The number of people who would benefit from the passage of the proposition was almost infinite, yet few individuals contributed to the campaign as each person would have reckoned that his or her contribution was unlikely to be decisive. Thus the group which would benefit from the proposed constitutional amendment was united by the belief that one member's contribution or failure to contribute to the collective good would not significantly affect any other member. Or, as American economist Mancur Olson expressed it: 'an individual in a *latent* group … cannot make a noticeable contribution to any group effort, and since no one in the group would react if he makes no contribution, he has no incentive to contribute' (1965, 50). The individual citizen had an incentive to be a free-rider, expecting that other citizens would pay the costs of the campaign.

Table A.1 Campaign contributions (as %) in Californian ballot campaigns, 1952–92

Labour	1
Issue groups	5
Political groups	7
Office holders	9
Individuals	12
Businesses	66

The opponents of proposition 18 faced a less difficult task. To use Olson's phrasing, the group of opponents were akin to what is called an 'intermediate group', that is, a 'group in which no single member gets a share of the benefit sufficient to give him an incentive to provide the good himself, but which does not have so many members that no one member will notice whether any other member is or is not helping to provide the good' (*ibid.*). The group which would benefit from the defeat of the proposal, and hence benefit from contributing to the campaign, was so small that it was impossible for any single actor to free-ride. It would be noticed if one of the oil companies failed to contribute to the 'no' campaign, whereas an ordinary citizen's failure to contribute to the 'yes' campaign would go unnoticed. This created a strong incentive for the opponents to contribute to the campaign, while it allowed the proponents to free-ride.

Using this simplified model we can hypothesise that the risk that proponents of a provision for a collective good will be outspent by business interests is greatest if the proposals affect actors in markets characterised by so-called monopolistic or oligopolistic competition, i.e. in situations where the actors cannot free-ride, for in those cases the cost of the campaign will (often) be funded either by a small group of competitors in an oligopolistic marked or by the monopolist – in the former case because free-riding is impossible, in the latter because the monopolist has the incentive to provide the costs of the campaign. Examples of situations in which monopolists have provided the full costs of a campaign are comparatively rare: the only prominent examples are various gun-control measures in which the National Rifle Association has carried the full cost of a 'no' campaign. The most common situation is that a group of competitors, in a market characterised by oligopolistic competition, share the costs of a campaign. An illustrative instance is provided by proposition 5, the anti-smoking measure submitted to the Californian voters in 1978.

The initiative called for the establishment of separate sections for smokers and non-smokers. This measure was opposed by five tobacco companies, which betweem them contributed $6,245,752 out of the total of $6,373,163 spent to defeat the proposal. The proponents, by comparison, raised a total of only $659,382. There were no large contributions made to the proponents' campaign (FPC 1978, G.5).

It seems likely, though it is by no means proven, that this discrepancy in spending can be attributed to the free-rider problem. The large number of non-smokers had no incentive to contribute, as each of their campaign contributions would have been infinitely small. The tobacco companies, by comparison, had a strong incentive to contribute to the 'no' campaign, as none of the companies could free-ride, and because, of course, the enactment of the proposal was likely to result in a reduction of their profits.

This explanation, along with the statistical evidence showing that 66 per cent of the campaign contributions were made by larger companies and firms, support the hypothesis that the referendum device, at least in California, discriminates against ordinary people for whose benefit the device was originally introduced. This conclusion does not, however, explain why the difference in funding affects the results.

Agenda-setting: the role of advertising and the media

Finance has often appeared to be the decisive factor, especially in defeating proposals – the same tendency is not pronounced in one-sided campaign spending for a proposal. Yet there are examples of underdog results when public sentiment has prevailed over the interests of large corporations. Not even the $21 million spent by the tobacco companies could guarantee the defeat of proposition 99, a proposal for higher duties on tobacco products submitted to the voters in 1988 (CCCF 1992, 393). Yet such examples are, as I have said, comparatively rare. Greater spending proved successful in 68 per cent of the referendums in 1968–1980, and in 74 per cent of the referendums in 1978–1999. The question is what accounts for this effect of campaign expenditure, i.e. is there a general theoretical explanation of this tendency?

The largest share of campaign expenditures goes on television advertising and, to a lesser degree on radio-spots and billboard campaigns. This may appear surprising in view of the failure of empirical studies to show that the influence of the mass media and commercials can alter voters' perceptions to a significant degree. This does not, however, indicate that such advertising is ineffectual, for while advertising in the mass media 'may not be successful in telling the readers what to think it is stunningly successful in telling its readers what to think about' (Cohen quoted in Siune 1992a, 152): that is to say, the media (and hence advertisements) have an 'agenda-setting function' (*ibid.*, 153). Whether the big-spending side in a campaign (often the 'no' side) manages to sway the minds of the voters seems to depend on its ability to control the agenda.

Nevertheless, ability to control the agenda is no guarantee that the bigger spender will prevail, for while it might produce a deluge of arguments in favour of its case the voters may still conclude that the arguments forwarded by the other side have greater merit. This was, allegedly, the case in the campaign against proposition 20 in 1972. Proposition 20, initiated by members of the Lower House of the Californian Congress, aimed at the establishment of a land-use planning agency which was to oversee the environmental protection of the Californian coastline. The opponents spent $1,185,246 in a bid to defeat the proposal, while the supporters of the proposition spent only $251,308. The opponents spent their money on radio advertisements and a massive billboard campaign with the simple message 'If you like to spend hours on the Ocean Beach, vote no!' and 'The beach belongs to you, vote no!' These apparently popular messages backfired when the press started to question the accuracy of the claim that the passage of proposition 20 would lead to the closure of beaches, perhaps an early example of the 'who's behind it?' hypothesis advanced by Bowler and Donovan (1998c)! The press reports unequivocally showed that the claim was unfounded (see, e.g., *Sacramento Bee*, 3 November 1972). Continuing reports on the – allegedly – false claim eventually prompted the attorney general to issue a legal opinion in which he criticised the campaign. The ability to control the agenda seemed to have backfired here: instead of capitalising the issue's popular appeal, the opponents of the proposition suffered the consequences of a poorly conducted campaign. The measure was approved by 55 per cent of the voters (Lowenstein 1982, 533).

Another, more recent, example of the failure of the better-funded interest groups to control the agenda is provided by the 1996 campaigns on tort reform. The proponents sought to present the reform as a pro-consumer initiative. The media, however, found that the organisation conspicuously named Voter Revolt was little more than a front for the interest groups backing the initiative.

Vast financial superiority does not guarante either a successful outcome or control of the agenda. Money does, however, bestow a distinct advantage. The importance of controlling the agenda has often been used to divert attention away from a popular measure by highlighting the likely consequences of its enactment. In his study of Californian referendums over 1968–80 Lowenstein found that the winning side in most of the successful campaigns had, as a rough rule, succeeded in shifting attention away from the actual issues to a principled discussion about increasing taxation or to a debate about First Amendment rights (*ibid.*, 563). He also showed that these negative campaigns had been successful despite polls showing that the less-well-resourced side was some way ahead prior to the start of the campaign (*ibid.*, 609). That the strategy of winning the middle ground proved efficient is, perhaps, an indication of the validity of the model of voting developed by Tullock in his sadly overlooked *A Mathematics of Politics* (1967).

The median voter in a direct democracy

Tullock's book is concerned mainly with candidate elections, yet it seems that the model is equally – perhaps even better – suited to referendum and initiative campaigns. Building on the model developed by Downs (1957), Tullock assumes that voters' preferences are relatively fixed. Bringing about shifts in the voters' preferences through advertisements would, consequently, require an unlimited amount of money. Indeed, the campaign expenditure required to bring about a shift in voters' political dispositions would, in all likelihood, exceed the benefits of the desired result of the referendum. The campaigner must, according to Tullock, show that the proposal or stance in question coincides with the disposition of the majority of the voters. (1967, 16). The strategy in a referendum campaign is thus akin to that of the two parties in Downs's hypothetical model of party strategies in a two-party system (1957, 28). Both sides seek to adapt their policies so that they appeal to the median voter; that is, they formulate their policies in order to win support rather than to convert the voters to a proposed policy.

This tendency was exemplified during the 1972 campaign against proposition 18, a measure which would have toughened California's anti-obscenity statute, removing from the definition of 'obscenity' the requirement that 'the material be utterly without redeeming social importance'. Proposition 18 was initiated by Christian fundamentalists, yet it was apparently supported by the general public, as well as by the governor, Ronald Reagan (*LA Times*, 7 October 1972). The proposition was opposed by a powerful coalition of theatre owners, publishers, teachers and magazine distributors. The opponents outspent the proponents by $773,224 to $162,899 – Playboy Enterprise Incorporated alone contributed $125,000 to the 'no' campaign (Hyink, Brown and Thacker 1975, 130).

This was insufficient: the popular support for the measure made it necessary for the opponents to shift the debate from a discussion of obscenity towards one which highlighted the undesirable consequences of the proposal. The opponents thus stressed that the measure would lead to a ban on movies such as *True Grit* and *Love Story*, and generally result in censorship in violation of the First Amendment of the US constitution. The 'no' campaign also produced radio and newspaper advertisements saying 'No to obscenity. No on censorship. No on proposition 18'. This was undoubtedly a misleading description, since a vote for the proposition would have toughened the obscenity laws (*LA Times*, 'Editorial', 26 October 1972). The opponents even claimed, though apparently without much justification, that the measure would outlaw sections of the Bible! (*Sacramento Bee*, 5 October 1972). The emphasis on freedom of speech enabled the opponents to divert attention from the popular anti-obscenity issue and towards a principled debate about First Amendment rights. Through massive spending on advisements and television commercials featuring movie-stars and celebrities – the opponents purchased television-spots all through October 1972 in which the actor John Wayne expressed his objection to the proposition (*LA Times*, 2 November 1972) – the 'no' side captured the agenda. Through this strategy, the opponents, it seems, succeeded in changing the focus of the campaign.

The 'no' side may not have changed the voters' view about obscenity, but it successfully conveyed the coincidence of its stance with the majority's reverence for First Amendment rights. The proposition was defeated by 68 per cent of the voters (Secretary of state, statement of the vote, 7 November 1972). The opponents of the measure seem to have prevailed because, as predicted by Tullock, they showed that their position coincided with that of the majority of the voters: they succeeded, not because they convinced the voters of the merits of their views, but because they had sufficient money to control the agenda through advertisements and billboards, and were able to identify the voters' views by conducting costly opinion polls (Price 1992, 547). They did not 'buy' the votes, but by using the results of expensive private opinion polls they could target their messages to coincide with the views of the voters. This finding not only supports Tullock's hypothesis but highlights the role of spin-doctors. That televised advertisements, at least in recent years, have been designed to suit the views of the respondents in opinion polls seems to increase the probability that they yield the desired result (from the point of view of the richer side). Put differently, spin-doctors can safely communicate a simplified message to voters provided that the message is consistent with the view of the majority. It is only by communicating that its stance coincides with the view of the majority of the voters that a campaigning side can be relatively certain of success. Money *can*, in other words, be a decisive factor if, and only if, the side with more money can dominate the agenda in a way which shows that its position and that of the voters are essentially the same.

These selected cases indicate that the side which spends more freely can influence the result of a referendum if it succeeds in controlling the agenda. Campaign spending cannot 'buy' the result, and it is still possible that an attempt to control the media will fail because the media's focus is on an agenda other than that of the side seeking control (this was the case in the debates about proposition 20 in 1972 and proposition 103 in 1988). Nevertheless, there are few examples of campaigns in which the side with money to spend has failed to control the agenda.

There are, to be sure, examples of underdog campaigns which have successfully taken control of the agenda. The successful campaign for proposition 15 in 1976 (a measure which restricted the use of land in California for new nuclear power plants) shows that a group of committed activists can succeed in focusing the media's attention on issues, and that can compensate for lack of spending power. Despite being outspent to the order of $4,033,590 to $1,257,132 the 'yes' side succeeded in getting the safety issue on the agenda, which resulted in televised hearings. Proposition 15 was, however, as Lowenstein (1992, 527) has rightly acknowledged, a special case as it received intensive coverage in the media. Few referendums receive media attention: there is, as political scientist Gail Hands concluded, 'relatively little news or electronic coverage by most stations except for colourful or controversial issues' (quoted in Cronin 1989, 1176). The consequence of this is that the majority of the voters receive their primary information from television advertisements rather than the news media (Zisk 1987, 248). This evidently gives the well-funded groups an advantage, allowing them to set the agenda and so influence the result. 'Television ads', as Cronin noted, 'reach more people, including the less well-informed potential voters who typically make up their minds late in the campaign about whether and how to vote' (1989, 117). That being so, it is not surprising that David Schmidt concluded that 'money, or the lack of it, is certainly a factor in the outcome [although] the advertising strategy usually [is] more decisive than money alone' (1989, 36).

That money plays such a decisive role in Californian plebiscites apparently hinges on the almost limitless access to the mass media which money can buy. This makes it easier to dominate the agenda in the USA than it is in the UK where political advertising is banned on local radio-stations. It is, therefore, debatable that campaign spending on referendums would have the same effect in such other polities as those of the UK and Denmark. Yet, even in countries where such advertising is allowed (e.g. Austria) there may be cultural and political differences which have an influence on the effect of campaign spending or the lack of campaign funds.

Effective campaign spending: Austria 1994

The referendum on EU membership in 1994 was the first held in Austria since the ill-fated plebiscite on the Zwetendorf nuclear reactor in 1979 (a referendum which the Government lost – see chapter 3). It seems that the governing coalition of Social Democrats and the Centre–Right People's Party was intent on avoiding the experience of the previous referendum. The Government spared neither effort nor money to ensure that the people cast their votes in support of EU membership.

Needless to say, a brief snapshot of the Austrian campaign in 1994 cannot do justice to a long endeavour rich in nuance and political subtlety. Yet, while acknowledging the ever-present caveats, it is, at the very least, noteworthy that the Austrian campaign seems to have followed the pattern identified in California (though with the notable difference that the proponents won after a campaign dominated by one-sided spending). Austria, unlike the UK, Denmark and Ireland, does not prohibit political advertisements and commercials in the broadcast media. The 'yes' side took advantage of this, and, according to Nielsen Media Research, spent 47 million Austrian shillings (approximately £2.5 million) on a state-of-the-art advertising campaign developed by Demner and Merlicek (the 'no' side spent roughly one-tenth of that amount).

The televised commercials, as would be expected from the analysis above, targeted the median voter by focusing on economic issues – a sensible choice as Europe was in the throes of a deepening recession (brought about by the collapse of the European ERM in the autumn of 1993). By dominating the media, through a professional campaign, the 'yes' side was able to set the agenda in a way that marginalised the opposing parties, i.e. the Greens, the Communist Party and the Freedom Party, the main opposition party.

Bowler and Donovan (1998c, 161), as has been seen, have hypothesised that 'spending leads to more awareness and participation'. The Austrians certainly became well aware of the campaign and the issues: according to research by IFES (on file with the author) 73 per cent of all voters could recall the most recent 'yes' poster (in comparison, Beneton, as a brand, was recognised by only 55 per cent of the respondents to a Gallup poll). Further, the percentage recalling the proponents' televised ads was 86 per cent (compared to only 46 per cent recalling the most recent Coca-Cola ad).

This level of recognition seemingly translated into a considerable growth in EU awareness: the proportion of the respondents who were not interested in the EU was reduced by 50 per cent within a year. One would have expected, following Bowler and Donovan (1998c, 149), that this awareness would have led to an increased 'no' vote – of the 'Who's behind it?' variety, not least because the two newspapers with the widest circulation, *Täglich Alles* and *Ganze Woche*, were vociferous opponents of EU-membership (Pelinka and Greiderer 1996, 28).

There is little evidence of this in the IFES figures: 63 per cent of the voters found the Government's information trustworthy and only 23 per cent agreed with the statement 'The Government's campaign had considerable influence on the final result'. The *Bundeskanzler*, Prime Minister Franz Vranitzky, on the other hand, was in no doubt. In the immediate aftermath of the campaign he boldly declared that 'the work of the advertising agency has obviously not been wasted … otherwise we would not have achieved this success' (IFES 1994, 3).

Following this analysis, it is tempting to reject Bowler and Donovan's view that 'well-financed interests are typically unable to "buy" public policy' (1998c, 163).

Some might see the Austrian campaign as proof that a result can be bought by the biggest spender. This is an understandable conclusion, though not one that can be deduced from the data. Indeed, the fact that the 'yes' side received government money while the 'no' side had to raise its own funds makes this Austrian campaign somewhat unusual. Thus in Ireland the Supreme Court has ruled that government money may not be spent on a campaign (*McKenna* v. *an Teoiseach* [1995]). In the UK the Political Parties, Elections and Referendum Act 2000 both limits campaign spending as well as offering bloc grants to either side in a campaign.

Appendix B

Regulation of referendums

Referendums – and especially initiatives – are rare in most Western democracies. They have become the centrepiece of the political system only in Switzerland and, since the 1970s, in Italy. The legislative initiative is practically unknown outside of America. Only in New Zealand can the citizens initiate legislation – but they have done so on only three occasions since 1995.[1] The Swiss can merely propose constitutional amendments, but these are often defeated – the voters have endorsed a mere 12 of a total of 104 proposed constitutional initiatives. (It should, however, be noted that the constitutional initiative has been used to pass laws which in other polities would have been enacted by ordinary statutes; see Ludthardt 1994, 43.)

These differences between countries have led observers to the conclusion that there are 'two worlds' of the referendum: one where their potential for making or unmaking policies is ever present in the minds of the legislators or lobbyists, and a *second* world where referendums are used only infrequently, usually to seal the legitimacy of a controversial policy change or a change of regime (Butler and Ranney 1978, 222).

The comparative rarity of the referendum in the second world has, moreover, led observers to the conclusion that referendums in those polities are unimportant and devoid of controversy; in short, the referendum in those polities appears to be a democratic curiosity, with few, if any, practical implications. In one sense, however, nothing could be further from the truth. Referendums are, to be sure, rare. That in itself, however, does not indicate that they are unimportant. In fact, it sometimes seems that the fewer the number of referendums held the wider are their implications; that is, their infrequency is inversely correlated with their consequences. Norway's referendum (in 1972) on membership of the EEC (the forerunner of the EU) led to a break-up of the party-system, as did the referendums on the electoral system in Italy in 1993. The French referendum on a reform of the Senate and local government in 1969 led to the resignation of President Charles de Gaulle, and James Callaghan's Labour Government was forced to resign following the unsuccessful referendums on devolution for Scotland and Wales in 1979.

No American plebiscite has had deleterious consequences for the party system and no governor has resigned following a defeat of an initiative. In short, no American plebiscite has (with the exception of that over proposition 13 in 1978) had consequences which even remotely resemble the effects of referendums in Europe. In general, American referendums and initiatives have few constitutional implications. The reverse is true in Europe, where almost every referendum has considerable constitutional and political implications, and, given their effect, it is somewhat odd that the referendum is practically unregulated in those polities.

Regulation can take many forms, some of which are inevitable in a democratic system: for example, the act of voting, the location of the polling stations and the size of the ballots are issues which are necessarily regulated. These issues are often uncontroversial and, as such, they are not discussed in this appendix. The forms of regulation discussed here are the often controversial restrictions imposed on the initiative and referendum process (henceforth the I–R process). These restrictions, which often are introduced to ensure a fair outcome, are:

- limits on campaign contributions;
- limits on campaign spending;
- pre-election judicial review;
- post-election judicial review;
- single-issue restrictions;
- super-majorities;
- disclosure laws;
- higher signature requirements. (Gerber 1999, 37)

Most of the twenty-three American I–R states have imposed several of these restrictions on the citizens. The reverse is true in Europe and Australia, where only one or two of the restrictions are in force.

Pre-legislative review has been a dominant feature in Italy, but nowhere else. Super-majorities are known from Denmark, the UK (in the latter case only in the 1979 devolution referendums) and Italy, and most recently from Canada (the Clarity Act stipulates that the voters in any future secession referendum must provide a clear expression of the will of a clear majority); a similar requirement is being debated in Israel at the time of writing. The super-majority provisions have led to the defeat of several laws in Italy and, in the UK, to the defeat of the devolution proposal for Scotland in 1979.

None of the polities have imposed restrictions on campaign spending (with the notable exceptions of the Canadian province of Quebec (*Loi sur les electiones et les réferendums dans les municipalties*, LRQ, CE-2.2) and the UK. In the latter country the Political Parties, Elections and Referendums Act 2000 limits campaign expenditure to a maximum of £5 million for the two designated campaign groups and for the largest political parties). In both Ireland and Canada the courts dismissed challenges to limit expenditures in ballot campaigns, arguing in both cases that such restrictions are incompatible with the constitutional provisions for freedom of speech. In Australia the High Court (Supreme Court) has, on similar grounds, invalidated provisions to restrict broadcasting of political commercials on radio and television during campaigns (*Australia Capital Television Pty Ltd* v. *Commonwealth of Australia*, [1992]).

Not all countries are as unregulated as are Ireland, New Zealand, Australia and Scandinavia, however. The British Broadcasting Act of 1990 – introduced by Thatcher's Government – bans all political advertising on ITV (the commercial channel) and local radio stations. Yet most polities have notably few regulations operating on the process of (semi-)direct democracy.

The classical exception to the rule is the Quebec Referendum Act of 1978, the official objective of which was to guarantee the democratic nature of referendums by promoting equality between the two sides, especially in respect of the information provided to them. In order to prevent the distortion of campaigns by wealthy individuals, the Act requires that so-called referendum committees use a special fund to cover the expenses they incur during the campaign. Each committee may spend up to $1.00 per eligible voter; the state contributes to a committee's fund an amount set by the National Assembly, and the committee may then raise other funds up to the $1.00 limit. Individual citizens may donate a maximum of $3,000 to each committee, while companies, charities and legal entities are not allowed to contribute funds.

The Act was, however, ruled unconstitutional in 1997 by the Canadian Supreme Court, which argued that it was inconsistent with the Canadian Charter of Rights and Freedoms which protects freedom of expression and association. Although the court acknowledged the need for spending limits, the Act was considered objectionable because it gave a campaign's political parties a virtual monopoly on information. As the Canadian Supreme Court noted:

> In its egalitarian aspect the Act [was] intended to prevent the referendum debate being dominated by the most affluent members of society. At the same time, the Act [promoted] an informed vote by ensuring that some points of view are not buried by others. This highly laudable objective, intended to ensure fairness of the referendum on a question of public interest, [was] of pressing and substantial importance in a democratic society. (*Libman* v. *Quebec (Attorney General)*[1997])

The National Assembly in 1999 enacted a new law incorporating the court's recommendations. The comparative lack of regulation of referendums does not, however, imply that politicians are categorically opposed to regulation.

The following extract from a front-page article in the UK's *Guardian* indicates that regulation of referendums is a contentious issue even in a country which has held only one nationwide referendum:

> Labour yesterday proposed tight spending in its own future referendum campaigns which would effectively thwart attempts by maverick Euro-sceptics like billionaire Yorkshire businessman Paul Sykes to bankroll a campaign against the EU's single currency. The move came on a day when a group of business leaders, headed by Lord Marsh, a Labour cabinet minister in the 1960s, launched a million-plus Business for Sterling campaign designed to offset what they claim is a multi-million pound pro-Euro campaign funded from the EU information budget. Labour's proposals would not stop Lord Marsh, his allies at the wealthy Institute of Directors or the 100,000 strong Federation of Small Businesses from campaigning. But it would limit their individual donations to £500,000 – 10 per cent of the proposed national maximum allowed to parties ... Mr. Sykes said last night: 'The suggestion that individuals would be limited in what they could spend to promote a cause they believed in would be anti-democratic. It's meant to stifle debate.' (*Guardian*, 12 June 1998)

The opposite is true in the USA, where state governments have been prone to regulate the initiative lest the people should employ this device to introduce legislation opposed by the legislators.

The fundamental question is why Western European politicians have been disinclined to introduce restrictions. Are there political reasons for their unwillingness to impose constraints or is it the result of a distinctive political culture, as claimed by some students of public administrations? These latter scholars point to the striking contrasts between approaches to public policy in the USA and in Western Europe. Whereas West European civil servants usually enjoy a close and co-operative relationship with non-governmental representatives (e.g. of business, the trade unions, etc.), in the USA the regulatory process is – for historical reasons – highly legalistic and contentious. These differences explain why issues which in Europe would be resolved through corporatist bargaining are resolved through legislation in the USA.

The failure to introduce restrictions on the referendum process seems to reflect the fact that it is governments in Europe and Australia which typically sponsor the legislation that is submitted to the voters. Government, business and trade union leaders have little incentive to introduce restrictions that make the enactment of *their* law more difficult. The voters can-at most-veto proposals drafted and enacted by the legislators.

Interestingly, proposals for restrictions of campaign spending have occurred only in the aftermath of a defeat of a government-sponsored measure or when it is feared that interest groups had raised sufficient funds to wage a successful campaign against a government-initiated proposal. There is a lot to be said for this public policy interpretation, yet it is clearly less applicable in an analysis of the regulation of referendums than in an analysis of, say, environmental policies or occupational safety.

The main difference between the two worlds of referendums is that plebiscites in the 'second world' primarily perform the role of being a check on governments (or the majority in the parliament in multi-party systems). Most referendums in the 'second world' are constitutionally obligatory referendums on fundamental constitutional changes, changes that – for constitutional reasons – are implemented only if the people endorse them (Butler and Ranney 1978, 222).

These provisions are typically inserted in the constitutions as checks against governments and parliamentary majorities. The elected law-makers in the USA have an incentive to restrict citizen involvement, i.e. an incentive to create obstacles to prevent citizens from enacting legislation that is against the interests of the legislators. European and Australian legislators, by contrast, have an incentive to reduce obstacles in order to increase the probability of the successful passage of their own proposals (proposals which follow a process of elite bargaining). These well-endowed and influential groups have no interest in introducing limits on campaign spending, nor would they benefit from public disclosure laws.

Indeed, such regulations might add to the citizens' mistrust of the political class, and hence increase the risk of a 'no' vote in a referendum on a law initiated by the political class. For, as Austin Ranney noted,

> it is much harder to buy an election if everyone knows that the effort is being made; grossly excessive contributions and expenditures may well provoke a backlash among the voters and cause them to vote the other way. Hence ... full publicity is one of the best guarantees available against the excessive influence of money on election outcomes. (1981, 92)

This logic – as I showed in Appendix A – is not restricted to the second world of referendums. Olson's study of the 1991 Washington term-limit initiative (1-533) campaign illustrates how lavish one-sided spending calls attention to an initiative and to the group backing the proposal. Early on in the campaign the 'yes' side was well ahead in the polls. Contributions came from the previously unknown organisation Citizens for Congressional Reform (CCR). By mid-October the media reported that the CCR was located outside of Washington and that it was funded by businessmen connected to the GOP. The widespread support evaporated following the revelation and the measure was defeated by an 8 per cent margin. Knowing which side of an issue parties, groups and elites are promoting might allow more voters to decide where they stand on an issue – we might think of it as the 'Who's for it (who's against it)?' cue.

Disclosure laws could reveal who is behind an issue, which explains why governments – typically backed by organised interests – are reluctant to introduce disclosure laws that would expose them to unwelcome scrutiny of the true beneficiaries of the proposed changes. A government proposing a legislative change is – for obvious reasons – rarely interested in such attention. It is, therefore, unsurprising that disclosure laws are almost unknown outside the USA (again the notable exceptions being Canada and the UK).

This conclusion goes some way in explaining why the people's representatives (who typically seek to prevent the passage of initiatives) in the USA are in favour of regulation (that would expose the financial backers of initiatives) and why legislators in Europe and Australia (who seek to ensure the passage of their own proposals) are opposed to disclosure laws. Public knowledge of the vast amounts spent by proponents in, say, the controversial referendums on European integration (the 'yes' side typically outspends the 'no' side by a factor of ten to one) is likely to generate suspicion, which increases the probability of a rejection of the proposal.

That governments outside of the USA are less enthusiastic about regulation – if not positively hostile to it – is not a consequence of idealism or theoretical conviction, but is rather a result of the fact they have other incentives than American state legislators, i.e. European governments/legislators are not faced with initiatives demanded by the people. The Government in New Zealand did not consider restrictions on the process in the first referendum on the electoral system in 1992 (a referendum in which the Government campaigned for the continuation of the first-past-the-post electoral system), but it was suddenly in favour of restrictions in the second referendum when the people, in 1993, had to choose between electoral systems all of which were opposed by the Government.

Yet, as sceptics are sure to point out, this explanation does not cover all cases; indeed, it does not explain two notable anomalies: the Quebec Act, which, in fact, was passed by *Parti Québécois* (PQ) Government (PQ had fought desperately for the passage of the 1980 proposal for so-called sovereignty association) and the Political Parties, Elections and Referendums Act, introduced by a political party with an overwhelming majority in the House of Commons.

Why was Tony Blair pressing for the introduction of restrictions on campaign spending in the UK? Possibly because the PQ and New Labour – credibly enough – believed that the 'no' side in the referendums would be bankrolled by, respectively, Anglo-Canadian interest groups from Ontario and the other English-speaking provinces and wealthy Euro-sceptics.

The pattern outlined here does not amount to a universal law of political science; it is rather a tendency. However, the tendency is not – or so it seems – a result of the frequency or the number of referendums. The number of polls held in Switzerland and Italy approach the number held on the USA's west coast, yet the direct democracy processes in these countries are comparatively unregulated; no restrictions on campaign spending and campaign expenditures have been introduced in either of the two countries, disclosure laws are unknown and regulation of media access is non-existent. This is possibly because these countries are dominated by referendums rather than initiatives (less than 25 per cent of the polls in Switzerland are constitutional initiatives, whereas initiatives are more common than referendums in the USA).

The difference in the level of regulation is thus a function of the institutional provisions for one of the two main forms of direct democracy. The process is regulated in polities where initiatives are common, whereas the reverse is true in polities where the citizen's involvement is restricted to participation in referendums. The restrictions depend on the governments' interests: the initiative creates an incentive for regulation, while the referendum creates an incentive against regulation of the I–R process. It is of course, true that the political and administrative culture of the USA differ from those of the other countries. We should never underestimate those differences, yet it seems that the politicians' incentives are a more obvious reason for the differences in the schemes of regulation.

These impressions do not amount to a general theory of direct democracy regulation. The schemes of regulation vary considerably, yet a pattern can be discerned. The USA is easily the most regulated country, not because US politicians are more prone to regulate than are the Europeans and the Australians, but because regulation makes it more difficult for the people to co-legislate and pass laws opposed to the will of the legislators (and the interest groups). The politicians in Western Europe, on the other hand, have an incentive not to regulate the process, as to do so would increase the probability of defeat for their own proposals. In short referendums are seldom accompanied by regulation.

What all this amounts to is a simple, yet undisputed, maxim of politics: politicians tend, all other things being equal, to strengthen their own influence and power – if necessary, at the expense of others.

Note

1   Citizen Initiated Referenda Act 1993; the signature requirement is 10 per cent of the eligible voters.

Majority requirements for referendums

Increasingly, a low turnout in referendums is seen as a threat to their legitimacy (e.g. in Wales, in 1997, when only 25.1 per cent of the voters voted for devolution, or in Ireland, in 2001, when the Nice Treaty was defeated on a turnout of less than 35 per cent). Some countries have attempted to this situation has been sought dealt with through the introduction of qualified majority provision. This appendix presents an overview of existing provisions in North American, Oceanian and European democracies. Majority requirements are differentiated into five kinds:

- qualified;
- eligible;
- geographical;
- turnout;
- ethnic.

In June 1802 the Swiss people as a whole voted on the text of the Second Helvetic Constitution. That constitution was ratified, though 92,500 voters rejected it, while only 72,500 voted in favour. Why? It was announced prior to the referendum that abstentions would be considered 'yes' votes; because 167,000 abstained the 'yes' side prevailed (Aubert 1978, 39). Unusual, perhaps, or was it unfair? Before answering, it is perhaps worth mentioning the example of majority requirements in Weimar Germany. In 1926 93.3 per cent voted for the confiscation of royal property, and three years later 94.5 per cent voted for the repudiation of the war guild (reparations). Both referendums were declared void. Why? Because the Weimar constitution required that the majority constituted a majority not only of the voters but of the *eligible* voters. Was that fair and acceptable?

Democracy, we are often reminded, means the rule of the people.

Lack of clarity is a feature of many 'neat' definitions, and this one is no exception. What is meant by 'the people'? Do we understand it to refer to all the people or just a majority? And do we mean a majority of those voting or of those *eligible* to vote? Needless to say, considerable energy has been spent on the more theoretical aspects of these questions. The aim here is not to rehearse these arguments but to present an overview of provisions in place, using the methods of comparative politics.

The attraction of the referendum device is that – for better or for worse – it can be seen as the ultimate system-legitimising device. Yet democracy involves more than just majority rule. Indeed, it is often argued that referendums produce a caricature of democracy; as Magleby noted, 'the actual experience with direct legislation demonstrates that the process is structured in ways that limit effective participation for some voters, and the agenda of issues may only serve to intensify conflict and lead to politics of confrontation' (1984, 180–1).

Both of these considerations are to be borne in mind when we consider referendums on territorial and ethnic issues, for these shortcomings have led to a widespread tendency to regulate the referendum, by introducing qualified majorities, majority quorums, etc.

The legitimacy of a referendum rests on the decisiveness of its outcome. No one in this day and age of democracy is likely to argue against 'the voice of the people' as expressed in a convincing and decisive majority. However, a close result obviously decreases the legitimacy of a referendum. There are a handful of examples of referendums which were decided by a whisker (e.g. the Danish Maastricht referendum (51–49 per cent) in 1992, the French Maastricht referendum (51–49) in 1992, the Quebec secession referendum (50.1–49.9) in 1995, and the Irish divorce referendum (51–49) in 1995. Close results are rare: referendums are normally decided by wide margins. Only a handful of the 200 referendums held in the Western democracies have been decided by close margins: as many as 'two-thirds of referendums have produced results in the 60–40 percent range' (Butler and Butler 1994, 4).

The potential problems arising from a close outcome are frequently discussed in polities which employ the referendum. There have been special majority requirements in Denmark, Britain, New Zealand and – somewhat exotically – at one time in Gambia. For methodological reasons – following a 'most similar cases approach' (Przeworski and Teune 1970) – this appendix considers will only relatively comparable democracies. Moreover there is a considerable number of legal cases challenging special majority requirements at the state level in the USA. The same is true of Canada, where the Supreme Court, in 1998 ruled that a special majority requirement be enacted lest a narrow majority of the voters in Quebec should vote for secession without prior negotiations with the rest of Canada. The Canadian Government has, through the Clarity Bill (C-20), sought to implement those recommendations. The rationale behind the Government's Bill has been to ensure that the outcome of a future referendum in Quebec reflects the settled will of the citizens of the province.

As the Canadian minister of inter-governmental affairs, Stephane Dion (herself from Quebec), has argued:

> You don't break you a country with support of 50% plus one. That's just never happened. On the contrary, outside the colonial context, referenda held as a part of a successful process of secession have always generated majorities of over 70%. Separatist leaders around the world say: 'let my people vote under fair conditions and you'll see that they want to separate'. They are not saying: 'half of my people want to separate. (Quoted in Qvortrup 2000, 190)

The Bill stipulates that the outcome of the referendum must be 'a clear expression of a will by a clear majority of a province that that province cease to be part of Canada'. However, the Government has refrained from stipulating a specific percentage below which the result of a referendum becomes legally void.

The Canadian Bill is – in many ways – comparable to Israel's Bill proposed by the *Likud* politician Silvan Shalom, later foreign and finance minister. In 2000, in an attempt to wreck a proposal for a referendum on Israel's occupation of the Golan Heights, proposed by Prime Minister Ehud Barak (Labour), the Bill stipulated that a qualified majority of 50 per cent of the eligible voters had to vote in favour of the proposal for it to be valid. The Bill was, however, overtaken by events: the re-ignited tensions in Israel in the summer of 2000 made the question of withdrawal obsolete.

Provisions for special majorities are not rarities in most democracies – though many countries do without them. The following requirements may be differentiated:

- *Qualified majority proper*: a specified percentage – e.g. 60 per cent of the voters – must approve the proposal (known from constitutional changes in some American states). This requirement once was used in Gambia in 1965; it is currently in use in Lithuanian amendments of article 1 of the constitution.

- *Eligible majority requirements*: a majority, representing a specified percentage of the eligible voters, must support a proposal (e.g. constitutional amendments in Denmark must be supported by the majority, which in that country represents at least 40 per cent of the registered voters).
- *Geographical (double majority) requirements*: the majority of the citizens as well as the majority of the states (or cantons) must support a referendum in a federal state (known from constitutional referendums in Australia and Switzerland).
- *Turnout requirements*: a proposal is enacted only if the turnout in the referendum surpasses a specified threshold (cf. the Italian constitution's stipulation that the turnout must be higher than 50 per cent for the result to be valid).
- *Ethnic majority requirement*: the majority of a specified ethnic group must support a proposed change (e.g. South Africa's referendum on the abolition of apartheid in 1992 in which only white South Africans could vote).

Qualified majority requirements

Pure qualified majorities are rare. Constitutional changes in New Zealand had to be approved by 64 per cent of the voters in 1908–14; a similar provision was applied in Gambia in 1965, though not in the 1996 referendum on the new constitution of the small African country. Nationwide qualified majority provisions are currently in force in Lithuania where 75 per cent of the total electorate must vote in favour in order for a proposed amendment of article 1 of the constitution to be valid. Qualified majority requirements exist in some state constitutions in the USA: the constitution of West Virginia thus stipulates that political sub-divisions may not incur bonded indebtness or increase tax rates beyond those established by the state constitution without the approval of 60 percent of the voters (Magleby 1984, 50).

One possible reason for the apparent dearth of similar provisions is that the high threshold is unacceptable to the large majority; another is that the requirement is unnecessary as most referendums – contrary to the general perception – are decided by wide majorities. The Canadian Clarity Bill stipulates that a future referendum on Quebec's independence would have to be 'decisive' – endorsed by more than 50 per cent plus one – yet the Bill does not, as noted above, prescribe a specific percentage, perhaps because a qualified majority requirement has been deemed politically unacceptable in Canada. Litigation over similar requirements in the USA have, however, been unsuccessful. The courts thus rejected a challenge to the provision in the constitution of West Virginia (Dane Waters, Initiative and Referendum Institute, personal communication to the author, 2000).

Eligible majority requirement

That 50 per cent of the eligible voters must support an agreement for this to come into force might seem an unusual requirement, though instances of its application are known. Such requirements are, however, extremely rare. They have never been used in those countries that have held referendums most frequently: France, Australia, Switzerland, Italy and Ireland. On the other hand, special majority requirements are common in new democracies in Eastern Europe, and five new democracies have introduced these provisions (See table C.1).

The best-known example of the registered voters' requirement is, perhaps, the, so-called, 40 per cent rule (or Cunningham Amendment), introduced by the Labour backbencher George Cunningham, before the Scottish and Welsh devolution (home rule) referendums in the late 1970s. The Cummingham Amendment stipulated that the majority in the devolution referendum should represent not only the majority of those voting, but at least 40 per cent of the eligible voters. Another example of the registered voters' requirement is the Danish constitution's article 88 which stipulates that

> a constitutional Bill shall within six months after its final passing be submitted to the Electors for approval or rejection by direct voting ... If majority of the persons taking part in the voting, and at least 40 per cent of the Electorate has voted in favour of the Bill as passed by the Parliament, and if the Bill receives the Royal Assent it shall form an integral part of the Constitution Act.

These requirements may seem sound in theory, yet they have often proved unworkable in practice. The Scottish electorate voted in favour of devolution (51.6 per cent 'yes' votes) on a 63.6 turn out), but the result was declared void as the majority represented only 32.9 per cent of the electorate. The outcome did not increase the legitimacy of

Table C.1   Majority requirements in new democracies (established since 1974)

Country	Majority requirement
Albania	Simple majority.
Bosnia-Herzegovina	Simple majority
Bulgaria	Simple majority
Croatia	Majority of registered voters in separation referendums (article 135)
Czech Rep	Simple majority
Hungary	25% quorum
Latvia	Turnout requirement: 50% quorum
Lithuania	Turnout requirement and absolute majority of 50% (75% of voters must support constitutional amendment of article 1 of the constitution)
Macedonia	Turnout requirement: majority of voters support the proposal and more than 50% of the total electorate votes
Moldova	Registered voter requirement: majority of registered voters
Poland	Turnout requirement: majority of voters (50% quorum on sovereignty)
Portugal	Registered voter requirement: majority of registered voters
Romania	Simple majority
Russia	Majority of voters
Serbia/Montenegro	Simple majority
Slovakia	Turnout requirement: majority of voters support proposal and more than 50% of the total electorate votes
Slovenia	Majority of voters
Spain	Majority of voters
Greece	Simple majority
Ukraine	Majority of voters

Source: Lesage (1995), IRI-Europe, and C2D, University of Geneva.

the process, being rather viewed as a desperate attempt by the English to hold on to Scotland at any price.

The Danish provision has proved no more workable and has even yielded farcical outcomes, most notably when a 91.8 per cent majority in favour of a constitutional amendment in Denmark was declared void because the majority represented only 44.5 per cent of the electorate (45 per cent of the eligible voters had to support the proposal according to the Danish constitution of 1920).

The introduction of a majority of the eligible/registered voters requirement is likely to be unnecessary in a referendum concerning ethno-nationalist referendums. The fact of the matter is, however, that the problem of a low turnout is almost non-existent in ethno-nationalist referendums. The turnout in the East Timor 1999 vote was a full 94 per cent and that in the Northern Ireland 1998 referendum was 81 per cent (see DeDuc 2003). These turnout rates are not unusual in ethno-nationalist referendums because these issues arouse an interest far in excess of that generated by more mundane issues like wage indexation (Italy 1985), nuclear energy (Austria 1979) or divorce (Ireland 1995), and it is therefore almost certain that the majority almost would represent a majority of the registered voters.

The problem of a low turnout – and of a close result – could be resolved by making the result *advisory* only, an arrangement that would allow the MPs to interpret the result. It is unlikely that a majority in the legislature would go forward with a narrow victory, just as it is unlikely that a majority would overrule the people if they have voted massively in favour of an agreement. It is becoming increasingly dubious that it would be politically possible for a legislature to go against the majority of the voters (even on a low turnout). As Lawrence LeDuc has put it: 'Legally binding or not, governments in modern democracies would be ill advised to ignore a formal vote of their citizens on an important public issue' (2002, 73). That seems a correct judgement. No result has been ignored since the Swedes' votes against their government on the issue of right-side driving, in 1955, and the lowering of the voting age in Denmark in 1953.

Critics argued, prior to the vote in Scotland in 1979, that the 40 per cent rule would, in effect, allow abstainers to be treated as 'no' voters. This is not, however, an accurate legal assessment, as Parliament – under British (and, perhaps, Israeli) constitutional law – ultimately decides whether the result should be binding or not. Yet the situation is very different if the referendum is mandatory, i.e. binding and not advisory, as was the case in Denmark in 1939. Such an outcome (a rejection despite a 91.8 per cent 'yes' vote) could have been avoided with an advisory referendum, and perhaps that experience of the 40 per cent rule illustrates one of the advantages of a flexible constitution.

Table C.2   Majority provisions in established Western democracies

Country	Majority requirement
Australia	Geographical requirement: majority of voters and majority of states
Austria	Simple majority
Belgium	No provisions for referendums
Canada	Under debate
Denmark	Registered voter requirement: 30 per cent of voters, 40 per cent of voters on constitutional changes
France	Simple majority
Finland	Simple majority
Germany	No provisions for referendums
Iceland	Simple majority
Ireland	Simple majority
Italy	Turnout requirement: 50% of the registered voters
Luxembourg	Simple majority
Malta	Simple majority
Netherlands	Simple majority
Switzerland	Geographical requirement: simple majority and majority of cantons
United Kingdom	Simple majority (40 per cent of registered voters in 1979)
USA	No provisions for nationwide referendums

A special version of the majority of the registered voters' requirement exists in several American states (e.g. Wyoming and Minnesota).
Article 52(f) of Wyoming's constitution stipulates that if the votes in
favour of a measure are in excess of 50 per cent 'of those voting in the
general election' the measure shall be passed, a provision that has led
to some rather paradoxical results. A constitutional amendment in
Minnesota – on the introduction of the initiative, incidentally – failed
although 53.3 per cent had supported the measure; 12 per cent of those
voting in the general election had failed to vote. The requirement (in
Wyoming) has recently been challenged in the courts, a challenge
rejected by the federal court:

> We believe that the State of Wyoming has a legitimate and reasonable
> interest in seeing that an initiated measure, for example, is not
> enacted into law unless it is approved by a majority of those voting

in the general election in which the initiated measure is being considered. If Wyoming wants to make it 'harder,' rather than 'easier,' to make laws by the initiated process, such is its prerogative, and, in our view, does not violate the First Amendment. A state understandably wants to … make it difficult for a relatively small interest group to enact its view through an initiated measure. (Information provided by Dane Waters, Initiative and Referendum Institute)

Geographical (double majority) requirements

This requirement is a notable feature in federal states. Constitutional changes in Australia and Switzerland must be supported both by a majority of the voters and by a majority of the states, or cantons. Article 128, section 4, of the Australian constitution states: 'If in a majority of the States a majority of the electors voting approve the proposed law, and if a majority of all the electors voting also approve the proposed law, it shall be presented to the governor-general for the Queen's assent.' Article 123 of the Swiss constitution states that 'the revised Federal Constitution or the revised part of it, as the case may be, shall enter into force if it has been approved by the majority of the Swiss citizens casting a vote and the majority of the Cantons'.

These provisions were concessions to the smaller states as a means of safeguarding local – or cantonal – prerogatives. Whether these requirements are suitable for a unitary state like Israel is an open question. The fact of the matter is, however, that the requirement has had relatively little effect on the fate of the proposals submitted to the Swiss and Australian voters. Only 8 of 43 proposals have been approved in Australia, but only 5 have not been approved because they failed to reach a double majority. The figures for Switzerland are even less impressive: only 6 of 143 proposed constitutional amendments have been rejected because they failed to achieve the double majority (in 1866, 1955, 1970, 1973, 1975 and 1983). The double majority requirement is not, therefore, a particularly effective barrier to change.

Turnout requirements

The legitimacy of a referendum stems from the belief that the result expresses the will of the majority of the people. The lower the turnout, however, the greater the possibility of distortion (in which the percentage voting 'yes' varies considerably from the percentage that would have resulted had all the citizens voted). In these instances of high voter apathy a special interest group of committed citizens may well take advantage of the situation by trooping to the polls in great numbers while the majority of the electors stay at home.

An attempt to avoid this problem can be made by stipulating that a qualified majority must support the proposal. Article 75, section 4 of the Italian constitution states that 'the proposal submitted to referendum shall be approved if a majority of those eligible have participated in the voting, and if it has received a majority of valid votes'. That is, the proposal is approved only if the turnout is above 50 per cent. This stipulation has proved a severe obstacle in recent years; all seven Italian referendums held in 1997 failed as a result of the 50 per cent requirement (see Barbera and Morrone 2003, 202). The provision is an effective safeguard against so-called 'false' majorities (a minority's exploitation of voter apathy).

Ethnic majority requirement

Ethno-nationalist referendums are seldom conducted on a nation-wide basis. Only those living in the area typically vote on plebiscites affecting the territorial integrity of a state (e.g. East Timor in 1999). A variation of this type of referendum is to restrict the franchise to members of a particular ethnic group, e.g. the settlers in the occupied territories or the Jewish citizens of Israel. An opponent of the peace deal has argued:

> The state of Israel was established against the wills of the Arabs, and its fate, for better or for worse, should therefore be decided only according to the will of the Jews. This is the approach we should be taking to the referendum Prime Minister Ehud Barak has promised on the withdrawal from the Golan in return for an agreement. (*Jerusalem Post*, 2 December 1999)

The strongest objection to this proposal is that it is very likely to be intolerable to the international community. The 1983 referendum on a new constitution for the Republic of South Africa – in which the franchise was limited to whites – was condemned by the international community, precisely because the electorate was limited to white and coloured South Africans. It should be noted, however, that the international community hailed the 1992 referendum on the abolition of apartheid (from participation in which Blacks were excluded), for two reasons: it followed a process of elite bargaining; and it prevented the ultra-rightist parties from denouncing the negotiations with the ANC as politically illegitimate and against the stated will of the people.

Yet an emulation of the South African experience is not an option because the country was not a democracy but a racist oligarchy at the time. Unsurprisingly, therefore, there are no examples of similar requirements in democratic countries.

Conclusion

It is difficult to make a strong case for either of the above models. Special majority requirements rarely have the intended effect. As far as the majority requirement is concerned, the only lesson to be learned is that efforts must be made to ensure that the electorate is as wide and as inclusive as possible.

A case can be made for the view that a close result threatens the legitimacy of the outcome; yet, specific requirements are unlikely to increase the legitimacy of the result. It might be stipulated that the turnout should be above 50 per cent lest a controversial policy be enacted against the knowledge and will of the voters. But that situation – which has occurred in Switzerland – is unlikely to be a problem in Israel where the turnout-rate usually is above 75 per cent.

Special majority requirements (e.g. qualified majority requirements and registered voters' requirements) are comparatively rare. They have frequently been challenged in the courts, though thus far unsuccessfully. The proponents of qualified majority requirements can, perhaps, take heart from the fact that the Canadian Supreme Court has endorsed the use of special requirements. The political use of referendums indicates that such provisions (e.g. the Shalom Bill and the Canadian Clarity Bill) tend to be unnecessary. Most referendums are decided by a clear margin, so that to introduce qualified majority requirements makes the process unnecessarily rigid. What should be sought are rather mechanisms to make the use of the device more flexible. Stipulating that the referendum be advisory rather than binding could achieve that end.

Bibliography

Adonis, Andrew and Geoff Mulgan. 'Back to Greece: The Scope for Direct Democracy', *Demos Quarterly*, no. 3, 1994.

Aitkin, Don. 'Australia', in Butler and Ranney (eds), *Referendums: A Comparative Study of Practice and Theory* (Washington, DC: American Enterprise Institute, 1978).

Alderson, S. *Yea and Nay: Referenda in the United Kingdom* (London: Cassell, 1975).

Allen, Ronald. 'The National Initiative Proposal', *Nebraska Law Review*, vol. 58, no. 4, 1979.

Almond, Gabriel. 'Civic Culture', in Bogdanor (ed.), *The Blackwell Encyclopedia of Political Science* (1992).

Almond, Gabriel and G. Bingham Powell. *Comparative Politics: System, Process, and Policy*, 2nd edn (Boston, MA: Little, Brown & Company, 1978).

Almond, Gabriel and Sydney Verba. *The Civic Culture: Political Attitudes in Five Nations* (Princeton, NJ: Princeton University Press, 1963).

Andersen, J. G. and J. Hoff. 'Lighed i den politiske deltagelse', in Gunnar Sjöblom, Hans Jorgen Nielsen and Morten Madsen (eds), *Demokratiets Mangfoldighed* (Copenhagen: Forlaget Politiske Studier, 1995).

Andersen, Poul. 'Dansk Folkeafstemning om Love', *Nordisk Administrative Tidsskrift*, vol. 47, no. 1, 1966.

Anderson, Raymond. 'Adoption and Operation of Initiative and Referendum in North Dakota', unpublished PhD thesis, University of Minnesota, 1962.

Arblaster, Anthony. *Democracy* (Buckingham: Open University Press, 1994).

Arington, Michael. 'English Only Laws and Direct Legislation', *Journal of Law and Politics*, vol. 7, 1991.

Arterton, F. C. *Teledemocracy: Can Technology Protect Democracy?* (Newbury Park CA: Sage, 1987).

Arterton, F. C. 'Political Participation and Teledemocracy', *Political Science and Polities*, vol. 21, no. 3, 1988.

Ashead, Maura. 'Sea Change on the Isle of Saints and Scholars: The 1995 Irish Referendum on the Introduction of Divorce', *Electoral Studies*, vol. 15, no. 1, 1996.

Aubert, Jean-François. 'Switzerland', in Butler and Ranney (eds), *Referendums: A Comparative Study of Practice and Theory*, (1978).

Auer, Andreas. 'Le Referendum populaire en suisse et en étates-unis: droit positive, histoire, et fonctionnement', *Revue française de droit constitutionnel*, vol. 7, 1991.

Austen, John, David Butler and Austin Ranney. 'Referendums 1978–1986', *Electoral Studies*, vol. 6, no. 2, 1987.

Australian Law Journal, 'Current Topics', vol. 62, 1988.

Bachrach, Peter and Morton Baratz. 'Decisions and Non-Decisions: An Analytical Framework', *American Political Science Review*, vol. 57, September 1963.

Balsom, Denis. 'United Kingdom: Constitutional Pragmatism and the Adoption of the Referendum', in Gallagher and Uleri (eds), *The Referendum Experience in Europe* (1996).

Balsom, Denis and Ian McAllister. 'The Scottish and Welsh Devolution Referenda', *Parliamentary Affairs*, vol. 32, no. 4, 1979.

Barbera, Augusto and Andrea Morrone. *La Repubblica dei referendum* (Bologna: Il Mulino, 2003).

Barber, Benjamin. *Strong Democracy: Participatory Politics for a New Age* (Berkeley: University of California Press, 1984).

Barber, Benjamin. 'Participation and Swiss Democracy', *Government and Opposition*, vol. 23, no. 1, 1988.

Bardi, Luciano. 'Italy says "No": The Referendums of May 1981', *West European Politics*, vol. 4, no. 3, 1981.

Barker, Rodney and Xania Howard-Johnson. 'Politics and Political Ideas of Moisei Ostrogorski', *Political Studies*, vol. 23, no. 4, 1975.

Bartle, Martin. 'Initiatives and Experiments', *Demos Quarterly*, no. 3, 1994.

Bastos, G. Marques de. 'La sélectivité de la participation', in Hans-Peter Kriesi (ed.), *Citoyenneté et démocratie directe: compétence, participation et décision des citoyens suisses* (Zurich: Seismo, 1993).

Becker, T. L. and R. Scarce. 'Teledemocracy Emergent', paper presented at the American Political Science Association, Washington, DC, 1980.

Beigbeder, Yves. *International Monitoring of Plebiscites, Referenda and National Elections* (Dortrecht: Martinus Nijhoff, 1994).

Bell, Charles and Charles Price. *Californian Government Today: Politics or Reform?*, 3rd edn (Chicago, IL: Chicago University Press, 1988).

Bell, Derrick. 'The Referendum: Democracy's Barrier to Racial Equality', *Washington Law Review*, vol. 54, no. 1, 1978.

Bell, John. *French Constitutional Law* (Oxford: Clarendon Press, 1992).

Benedict, Rob and Lauren Holland. 'Initiatives and Referenda', paper presented at the American Political Science Association, Washington DC, 1980.

Bentham, Jeremy *The Theory of Legislation*, ed. C. K. Ogden (London: Kegan Paul, 1931).

Beyme, Klaus von. *Die verfassungsgegebende Gewalt des Volkes: Demokratische Doktrin und politische Wirklichkeit* (Tübingen: J. C. B. Mohr, 1968).

Birch, A. H. *Representative and Responsible Government. An Essay on the British Constitution* (London: George Allen & Unwin Ltd, 1964).

Bjørklund, Tor. 'The Demand for Referendum. When Does it Arise and When Does it Succeed?' *Scandinavian Political Studies*, vol. 5, no. 3, 1982.

Blackburn, Robert. *The Electoral System in Britain* (London: Macmillan, 1995).

Blair, Tony. 'Democracy's Second Age', *Economist*, 14 September 1996.

Blaustein, Albert and Gisbert Flanz (eds). *Constitutions of the Countries of the World* (New York: Ocean Publishers, 1997).

Bogdanor, Vernon. 'Referendums and Seperatism II', in Austin Ranney (ed.), *The Referendum Device* (1979).

Bogdanor, Vernon. *The People and the Party System. The Referendum and Electoral Reform in British Politics* (Cambridge: Cambridge University Press, 1981).

Bogdanor, Vernon (ed.). *The Blackwell Encyclopedia of Political Science* (Oxford: Blackwell, 1992).

Bogdanor, Vernon. 'Western Europe', in Butler and Ranney (eds), *Referendums around thee World* (1994).

Bogdanor, Vernon. *Politics and the Constitution. Essays in British Government* (Darthmouth: Aldershot, 1996).

Bogdanor, Vernon. *Power and the People: A Guide to Constitutional Reform* (London: Victor Gollancz, 1997).

Bowler, Shaun and Todd Donovan. 'Direct Democracy and Minority Rights', *American Journal of Political Science*, vol. 43, 1998a.

Bowler, Shaun and Todd Donovan. 'Two Cheers for Direct Democracy or Who's Afraid of the Initiative Process?', *Representation: Journal of Representative Democracy*, vol. 35, no. 4, 1998b.

Bowler, Shaun and Todd Donovan. *Demanding Choices: Opinion, Voting, and Direct Democracy* (Ann Arbor: Michigan University Press, 1998c).

Brazier, Rodney. *Constitutional Reform: Re-shaping the British Political System* (Oxford: Clarendon Press, 1991).

Bredsdorf, Nick. 'The California Initiative Process', *Southern California Law Review*, vol. 29, no. 4, 1975.

Bryce, James. *Modern Democracies* (London: Macmillan, 1921).

Buchanan, James and Gordon Tullock. *The Calculus of Consent* (Ann Arbor: Michigan University Press, 1962).

Budge, Ian. *The Challenge of Direct Democracy* (Cambridge: Polity Press, 1996).

Buksti, Jakob. 'De politiske problemer omkring den fysiske planlægning og opbygningen af et planlovssystem i Danmark', *Nordisk Administrativt Tidsskrift*, vol. 58, no. 4, 1977.

Burgess, Michael. 'Constitutional Reform in Canada', *Parliamentary Affairs*, vol. 46, no. 3, 1993.

Burke, Edmund. 'A Vindication of Natural Society', in *The Works of the Right Honourable Edmund Burke*, vol. 1 (London: John C. Nimmo, 1887).

Burke, Edmund. 'Speech to the Electors in Bristol', in *Works* (London: Bohn's Standard Library, 1902).

Butler, David. 'United Kingdom', in Butler and Ranney (eds), *Referendums: A Comparative Study of Practice and Theory* (1978)

Butler, David. *Referendums: Guidelines for the Future* (London: Hansart Society, 1980).

Butler, David and Gareth Butler. *British Political Facts* (London: Macmillan, 1994).

Butler, David and Uwe Kitzinger. *The 1975 Referendum* (London: Macmillan, 1976).

Butler, David, Howard Penniman and Austin Ranney (eds). *Democracy at the Polls: A Comparative Study of National Elections* (Washington, DC: American Enterprise Institute, 1981).

Butler, David and Austin Ranney (eds), *Referendums: A Comparative Study of Practice and Theory* (Washington, DC: American Enterprise Institute, 1978).

Butler, David and Austin Ranney. 'Summing up', in Butler and Ranney (eds), *Referendums: A Comparative Study of Practice and Theory* (1978).

Butler, David and Austin Ranney. 'Practice' in Butler and Ranney (eds), *Referendums Around the World* (1994a).

Butler, David and Austin Ranney. 'Theory', in David Butler and Austin Ranney (eds), *Referendums: The Growing Use of Direct Democracy* (London: Macmillan, 1994b).

Butler, David and Austin Ranney. *Referendums Around the World* (London: Macmillan, 1994c).

Byrne, Tony. *Local Government in Britain*, 6th edn (London: Penguin, 1994).

California Commission on Campaign Financing (CCCF). *Democracy by Initiative – Shaping California's Fourth Branch of Government* (Los Angeles, CA: Centre for Responsive Government, 1992).

Capelletti, Mauro. *Judicial Review in the Contemporary World* (Indianapolis, IN: Bobbs-Merrill, 1971).

Caramani, Danielle. 'La Perception e l'impact des votations féderales', in Hanspeter Kriesi (ed), *Citoyenneté et démocratie directe: compétence, participation et décision des citoyens suisses* (Zurich: Seismo, 1993).

Casey, John. *Constitutional Law in Ireland* (London: Sweet & Maxwell, 1992).

Chimenti, Anna. *Storia dei Referendum: dal divorcio alla riforma ellttorale* (Rome: Laterze, 1993).

Chubb, Basil. 'Government and the Dail: Constitutional Myth and Political Practice', in Brian Farrell (ed.), *De Valera's Constitution and Ours* (Dublin: Gill & Macmillan, 1998).

Clarke, Harold and Allan Kornberg. 'The Politics and Economics of Constitutional Choice: Voting in Canada's 1992 National Referendum', *Journal of Politics*, vol. 56, no. 4, 1994.

Clubb, Basil. 'Government and Dail: Constitutional Myth and Political Practice', in Brian Farrell (ed.), *De Valera's Constitution and Ours* (Dublin: Gill & Macmillan, 1988).

Coakley, J., M. Holmes and N. Rees. 'The Irish Response to European Integration: Explaining the Persistence of Opposition', in A. W. Cafruny and C. Laukowski (eds), *Eurupe's Ambiguous Unity: Conflict and Consensus in Post-Maastrict Europe* (Boulder, CO: Reinner, 1997).

Collinge, John. 'Party-Perspectives: National', in John Vowles and Peter Aimer (eds), *Double Decision: The 1993 Referendum in New Zealand*, Occasional Paper, University of Wellington, 1994.

Collini, Steffan. *Public Intellectuals: Political Thought and Intellectual Life in Britain 1850–1930* (Cambridge: Cambridge University Press, 1991).

Collini, Steffan, Donald Winch and John Burrow. *That Noble Science of Politics: A Study in Nineteenth-Century Intellectual History* (Cambridge: Cambridge University Press, 1983).

Commager, Henry Steele. *Majority Rule and Minority Rights* (Gloucester: Peter Smith, 1958).

Conservative Research Department, *The Referendum and the Constitution* (London: Conservative Publication Centre, 1978).

Constitution Unit. *Report of the Commission on the Conduct of Referendums* (London: Constitution Unit, 1996).

Coper, Michael. *Encounters with the Australian Constitution* (North Ryde, NSW: CCH Ltd, 1987).

Corbetta, Piergiorgio and Arturo Parisi. 'The Referendum on Electoral Reform of the Senate: Another Momentous April', *Italian Politics: A Review*, vol. 4, 1994.

Cosgrove, Richard A. *Albert Venn Dicey: Victorian Jurist* (London: Macmillan, 1981).

Coughlin, C. C. 'Domestic Content Legislation', *Economic Inquiry*, July 1985.

Cree, Nathan. *Direct Legislation by the People* (Chicago, IL: A. C. McClurg, 1892).

Crewe, Ivor. 'Electoral Participation', in Butler, Penniman and Ranney (eds), *Democracy at the Polls* (1981).

Crisp, L. F. *Australian National Government*, 4th edn (Chesire: Longman, 1978).

Cronin, Thomas. *Direct Democracy: The Politics of Initiative, Referendum and Recall* (Cambridge, MA: Harvard University Press, 1989).

Curzon, Lord. 'The Referendum', *National Review*, vol. 23, 1894.

Dahl, Robert A. *A Preface to Democratic Theory* (Chicago, IL: Chicago University Press, 1956).

Dahl, Robert A. *Dilemmas of Pluralist Democracy: Autonomy vs. Control* (New Haven, CT: Yale University Press, 1982).

Dahl, Robert A. *Democracy and its Critics* (New Haven, CT: Yale University Press, 1989).

Deacon, Robert and Perry Shapiro. 'Private Preference for Collective Goods Revealed Through Voting on Referenda', *American Economic Review*, vol. 65, no. 5, 1975.

DeDuc, Larry. *The Politics of Direct Democracy: Referendums in Global Perspective* (Peterborough, ON: Broadview Press, 2003).

Denver, David, James Mitchell, Charles Pattie and Hugh Bochel. *Scotland Decides: The Devolution Issue and the Scottish Referendum* (London: Frank Cass, 2000).

Dicey, A. V. 'Can the English Constitution be Americanised?' *The Nation*, vol. 42. 1886.

Dicey, A. V. 'Ought the Referendum to Be Introduced into England?' *Contemporary Review*, vol. 57, April 1890.

Dicey, A. V. 'Alexis de Tocqueville', *National Review*, vol. 21, August 1893.

Dicey, A. V. 'The Referendum', *National Review*, vol. 23, March 1894.

Dicey, A. V. 'The Unionists and the House of Lords', *National Review*, vol. 24, 1895.

Dicey, A. V. 'Will the Form of Parliamentary Government be Permenant?' *Harvard Law Review*, vol. 13, 1899–1900.

Dicey, A. V. 'Representative Government', The Comparative Study of Constitutions, unpublished manuscript, Codrington Library, All Souls' College, Oxford, 1900.

Dicey, A. V. 'Mill: On Liberty', *Working Men's College Journal*, vol. 7, March 1901.

Dicey, A. V. 'The Paralysis of the Constitution', *Contemporary Review*, vol. 88, September 1905.

Dicey, A. V. *Lectures on the Relation Between Law and Public Opinion during the Nineteenth Century* (London: Macmillan, 1905).

Dicey, A. V. 'The Referendum and its Critics', *Quarterly Review*, vol. 212, 1910.

Dicey, A. V. *A Leap in the Dark*, 2nd edn (London: John Murray, 1911).

Dicey, A. V. 'The Parliamentary Act 1911 and the Destruction of All Constitutional Safeguards', in *The Rights of Citizenship: A Survey of Safeguards for the People* (London: Frederick Warne & Co., 1912).

Dicey, A. V. *An Introduction to the Study of the Law of the Constitution* (Indianapolis: Liberty Fund Inc., 1982).

Donovan, Mark. 'The 1997 Referendums: Failure Due to Abuse', unpublished paper.

Downs, Anthony. *An Economic Theory of Democracy* (New York: Harper & Row, 1957).

Drysek, Richard. 'Australian Discourses of Democracy', *Australian Journal of Political Science*, vol. 29, no. 2, 1994.

Dubois, Philip L. and Floyd Feeney. *Improving the Californian Initiative Process: Options for Change*, California Policy Seminar Research Brief and Report (Los Angeles: University of California, 1992).

Eigaard, Soren. *Idealer og Politik* (Odense: Odense Universitets Forlag, 1993).

Einhorn, Eric and John Logue, *Modern Welfare States* (New York: Praeger, 1988).

Emden, Cecil. *The People and the Constitution* (Oxford: Oxford University Press, 1962).

Eule, Julian. 'Checking California's Plebiscite', *Hastings Constitutional Law Quarterly*, vol. 17, 1989.

Eule, Julian. 'Judicial Review of Direct Democracy', *Yale Law Journal*, vol. 99, no. 7, May 1990.

Everson, David H. 'The Effects of Initiatives on Voter Turnout: A Comparative State Analysis', *Western Political Quarterly*, vol. 34, 1981.

Fair Political Practices Committee (FPPC). *Campaign Contribution and Spending Report of the November 7th 1978 General Election* (Sacramento, CA: FPPC, 1978).

Fedele, Marcello. *Democrazia Referendaria* (Rome: Donzelli, 1994).

Feld, Lars P. and Gebhart Kirchgässer. 'Direct Democracy, Political Culture and the Outcome of Economic Policy: A Report on the Swiss Experience', *European Journal of Political Economy*, vol. 16, no. 2, 2000.

Field Institute. *California Opinion Index*, vol. 1, February 1983.

Finer, S. E. *The Changing British Party System 1945–1979* (Washington, DC: American Enterprise Institute, 1980).

Fitzgerald, Maureen. 'Computer Democracy', *California Journal*, vol. 11, June 1980.

Fonsmark, Henning. 'Om Folkeafstemninger i det Representative Demokrati', in Niels Helveg Pedersen (ed.), *Paa Sporet af den Nye Grundlov* (Copenhagen: Gyldendal, 1992).

Ford, Trowbridge. 'Dicey as a Political Journalist', *Political Studies*, vol. 17, no. 2, 1970.

Forfatningskommissionen Årbog 1937–1938 (Copenhagen: Schultz, 1937).

Franklin, Mark, Cees van er Eijk and Michael Marsh, 'Referendum Outcomes and Trust in Government: Public Support for Europe in the Wake of Maastricht', *West European Politics*, vol. 18, no. 3, 1995.

Friedrich, Carl J. *Constitutional Government and Democracy: Theory and Practice in Europe and America* (Boston, MA: Ginn, 1950).

Furlong, Paul. *Modern Italy: Representation and Reform* (London: Routledge, 1994).

Gallagher, Michael. 'Ireland: The Referendum as a Conservative Device', in Gallagher and Uleri (eds), *The Referendum Experience in Europe* (1996).

Gallagher, Michael and Pier Vincenzo Uleri (eds). *The Referendum Experience in Europe* (London: Macmillan, 1996).

Gerber, Elisabeth R. 'Legislative Response to the Threat of Initiatives', *American Journal of Political Science*, vol. 40, no. 1, February 1996.

Gerber, Elizabeth R. *The Populist Paradox* (Princeton, NJ: Princeton University Press, 1999).

Giacomo, Fabio di. 'La Decision des abstensionristes', in Hans-Peter Kriesi (ed.), *Citoyenneté et démocratie directe: compétence, participation et décision des citoyens suisses* (Zurich: Seismo, 1993).

Gilhuis, Piet. *Het Referendum: Een rechtvergelijkende studie* (Hague, Alphen aan den Rijn, 1981).

Gillespie, Charles Guy and Luis E. González. 'Uruguay: Survival of Old and Autonomous Institutions', in Larry Diamond, Juan J. Linz and Seymour M.

Lipset (eds), *Democracy in Developing Countries*, vol. 4: *Latin America* (Boulder, CO: Lynne Rienner Publishers, 1992).

Gilligan, Brian. 'The 1988 Referendums and Australia's Record on Constitutional Change', *Parliamentary Affairs*, vol. 43, no. 4, 1990.

Girvin, Brian. 'Social Change and Moral Politics: The Irish Constitutional Referendum 1983', *Political Studies*, vol. 34, no. 1, 1986.

Girvin, Brian. 'The Divorce Referendum in the Republic, June 1986', *Irish Political Studies* vol. 2, no. 1, 1987.

Gobbi, Mark. 'The Sovereign', in Allan McCartney (ed.), *The Referendum: Constitutional and Political Perspectives* (Edinburgh: Centre for the Study of Scottish Politics, 1989).

Goodhart, Philip. *The Referendum* (London: Tom Stacey Ltd, 1971).

Grimond, J. and B. Neve. *The Referendum* (London: Rex Collin, 1975).

Grundlovsforslaget 1938–1939 (Copenhagen: Schultz, 1939).

Hadwiger, David. 'Money, Turnout, and Ballot Measure Success in Californian Cities', *Western Political Quarterly*, vol. 45, 1992.

Hardy, Melissa A. 'Regression with Dummy-Variables', in Lewis-Beck (ed.), *Regression Analysis*, vol. 2 (1993).

Hague, Rod and Martin Harrop. *Comparative Government and Politics*, 2nd edn (London: Macmillan, 1990).

Hahn, Gilbert and Stephen C. Morton. 'Initiative and Referendum – Do They Encourage or Impair Better State Government?', *Florida State University Law Review*, vol. 5, no. 4, 1977.

Hailsham, Lord. *Elective Dictatorship* (London: BBC Publications, 1976).

Hamilton, Howard. 'Direct Legislation: Some Implications of Open Housing Referendums', *American Political Science Review*, vol. 64, no. 1, 1970.

Hanning, James. 'The Italian Radical Party and the "New" Politics', *West European Politics*, vol. 4, no. 4, 1981.

Hart, Gary and William Shore. 'Corporate Spending on State and Local Referendums: First National Bank v. Bellotti', *Case Western Law Review*, vol. 29, no. 4, 1979.

Hayek, Friedrich August von. *New Studies in Philosophy, Politics, Economics and the History of the Ideas* (London: Routledge, 1978).

Hayek, Friedrich August von. *Law, Legislation and Liberty*, vol. 3: *The Political Order of a Free People* (London: Routledge, 1979).

Heard, Alexander. *The Costs of Democracy* (Chapel Hill: University of North Carolina Press, 1960).

Hertig, Hans Peter. 'Sind Abstimmungserfolg käuflich? Elemente der Meinungsbildung bei eidgenössischen Abstimmungen', in *Schweizerisches Jahrbuch für Politische Wissenschaft*, vol. 22, 1982.

Hertig, Hans Peter and Erich Gruner, *Der Stimmbürger und die 'neue' Politik* (Bern: Verlag Paul, 1983).

Hibbs, Douglas. *Solidarity and Egoism? The Economics of Sociotropic and Egocentric Influences on Political Behaviour* (Århus Århus University Press, 1993).

Hine, David. *Governing Italy: The Politics of Bargained Pluralism* (Oxford: Clarendon Press, 1993).

Hirschman, Albert O. *Exit, Voice, and Loyalty: Responses to Decline in Firms, Organisations, and States* (Cambridge, MA: Harvard University Press, 1970).

Hirst, Paul. *Representative Democracy and its Limits* (Cambridge: Polity Press, 1990).

Hobhouse, L. T. *Liberalism* (Cambridge: Cambridge University Press, 1994 [1911]).

Hobson, J. A. *The Crisis of Liberalism* (London: P. S. King & Son, 1909).

Hoffmann, Erich. 'Folkeafstemning og Demokrati', *Vandkunsten*, vol. 7–8, 1992.

Højlund, Niels. *Folkeafstemninger en trussel mod demokratiet* (Copenhagen: Gyldendal, 1993).

Holman, J. 'The Unfavourable Results of Direct Legislation in Oregon', in Munro (ed.), *The Initiative, Referendum and Recall* (1912).

Holmberg, Sören and Kent Asp. *Kampen om Kärnkraften: En Bok om väjare, massmedier och folkomröstninger* (Stockholm: Publica, 1984).

Horowitz, Donald. *A Democratic South Africa: Constitutional Engineering in a Divided Society* (Berkeley: University of California Press).

House of Representatives (New Zealand). *Report of the Committee of Inquiry into the Administration of the Electoral Act* (Wellington, NZ: House of Representatives, August, 1979).

House of Representatives (New Zealand). *Report of the Electoral Referendum Panel* (Wellington, NZ: House of Representatives, 1993).

Howarth, David. 'The Compromise on Denmark and the Treaty on Edinburgh in December 1992', *Common Market Law Review*, vol. 31, no. 4, August 1994.

Hyink, B., S. Brown and E. Thacker, *Politics and Government in California* (Los Angeles: University of California Press, 1975).

Jacobsen, G. C. 'Money and Votes Reconsidered: Congressional Elections', *Public Choice*, vol. 47, no. 1, 1983.

Jarvis, Anthony. 'The Australian Constitutional Referendum 1988', *Electoral Studies*, vol. 8, no. 1, 1989.

Jeansch, Dean. *The Politics of Australia* (Melbourne: Macmillan, 1992).

Jeansch, Dean and Max Teichmann, *The Macmillan Dictionary of Australian Politics*, 4th edn (Melbourne: Macmillan, 1992).

Jones, Rick and Rick Wilford. 'Further Considerations on the Referendum: The Evidence of the Welsh Vote on Devolution', *Political Studies*, vol. 30, no. 1, 1982.

Joseph, Philip. 'Constitutional Entrenchment and the MPP Referendum', *New Zealand Universities Law Review*, vol. 16, no. 1, 1994–95.

Joseph, Philip. *Constitutional and Administrative Law in New Zealand* (Auckland: Law Book Company Ltd, 1996).

Karp, Jeffrey. 'The Influence of Elite-Endorsements in Initiative Campaigns', in Shaun Bowler, Todd Donovan and Caroline Tolbert (eds), *Citizens as Lawmakers* (Columbia: Ohio State University Press, 1998).

Katz, Richard. 'The 1993 Parliamentary Electoral Reform', in Carol Mershon and Gianfranco Pasquino (eds), *Ending the First Republic* (Boulder, CO: Westview Press, 1995).

Katz, Richard. *Democracy and Elections* (Oxford: Oxford University Press, 1997).

Kaufmann, Bruno (ed.). *Initiative and Referendum Monitor 2004–5* (Amsterdam: Initiative and Referendum Institute, 2004).

Kauffeldt, Carl. 'Folkeafstemningsinstituttets Udvikling i Danmark', *Økonomi og Politik*, vol. 53, no. 4, 1972.

Kautsky, Karl. 'Der Entwurf des neuen Partieprograms', *Die Neue Zeit*, vol. 9, 1890–91.

Kautsky, Karl. *Parliamentarismus und Demokratie* (Stuttgart: J. H. W. Dietz, 1911).

Kavanagh, Dennis. *Election Campaigning: The New Marketing of Politics* (Oxford: Blackwell, 1995).

Kavanagh, Dennis. *British Politics: Continuities and Change* (Oxford: Oxford University Press, 1996).

Key, V. O. *The Responsible Electorate* (New York: Vintage, 1966).

Key, V. O. and Winston W. Crouch. *The Initiative and the Referendum in California* (Berkeley: University of California Press, 1939).

King, Anthony. *The 1975 Referendum on the Common Market* (Washington, DC: American Enterprise Institute, 1977).

Kissinger, Henry. *Diplomacy* (New York: Alfred Knopf, 1994).

Kobach, Kris. 'Recent Developments in Swiss Direct Democracy', *Electoral Studies*, vol. 12, no. 4, 1993.

Kobach, Kris. *The Referendum: Direct Democracy in Switzerland* (Dartmouth: Aldershot, 1993).

Kobach, Kris. 'Switzerland', in Butler and Ranney (eds), *Referendums Around the World* (1994).

Kobach, Kris. 'Direct Democracy and Swiss Isolationism', *West European Politics*, vol. 20, no. 3, July 1997.

Koch, Hal. *Hvad Er Demokrati?* (Copenhagen: Gyldendal, 1992).

Kramer, Gerald. 'The Ecological Fallacy Revisited', *American Political Science Review*, vol. 77, no. 1, 1983.

Kuhn, Thomas. *The Structure of Scientific Revolutions* (Chicago, IL: Chicago University Press, 1962).

Lane, Jan-Erik. *Constitutions and Political Theory* (Manchester: Manchester University Press, 1996).

Lane, Jan-Erik and Svante Erson, *Politics and Society in Western Europe* (Sage: London, 1992).

Lange, Peter. 'The End of an Era: The Wage Indexation Referendum of 1985', *Italian Politics: A Review*, vol. 1, 1986.

LaPalombara, Joseph. *Democracy Italian Style* (New Haven, CT: Yale University Press, 1987).

Lasch, Christopher, *The Revolt of the Elites and the Betrayal of Democracy* (New York: Norton, 1996).

Laurence, J. and S. Elliott. *The Northern Ireland Border Poll* (London: HMSO, 1975).

Lecky, William E. H. *Democracy and Liberty*, vol. 1 (London: Longman, Green & Co., 1899).

Leduc, Lawrence. 'Canada's Constitutional Referendum of 1992: A Great Big "No"', *Electoral Studies*, vol. 12, no. 3, 1993.

Leduc, Lawrence, 'Referendums and Initiatives: The Politics of Direct Democracy', in Lawrence Leduc, Richard G. Niemi and Pipa Norris, *Comparing Democracies*, vol. 2: *New Challenges in the Study of Elections and Voting* (London: Sage), 2002.

Lee, Eugene. 'California', in Butler and Ranney (eds), *Referendums: A Comparative Study of Practice and Theory* (1978).

Lee, Eugene. 'Can the Voters Be Trusted? The Local Referendum and Tax Reform', *Public Administration*, vol. 66, summer 1986.

Lee, Eugene. 'Representative Democracy and the Initiative Process', in John Kirlin and Donald Winkler (eds), *California Policy Choices*, vol. 6 (Los Angeles: USC, School of Public Administration, 1990).

Lesage, Michel (ed.). *Constitutions d'europe centrale, orientale et balte* (Paris: Documentation Française, 1995).

Levellen, Ted. *Political Anthropology* (South Hadley: Bergin & Garvey, 1983).

Levine, Stephen and Nigel S. Roberts. 'The New Zealand Electoral Referendum of 1992', *Electoral Studies*, vol. 12, no. 2, 1993.

Lewin, Leif. *Self-Interest and Public Interest in Western Politics* (Oxford: Oxford University Press, 1991).

Lewin, Leif. 'Economic Man, Political Man', *Politica: Tidsskrift for Politisk Videnskab*, vol. 25, no. 2, 1993.

Lewis-Beck, Michael S. (ed.). *Regression Analysis: International Handbook of Quantitative Applications in the Social Sciences*, vol. 2 (London: Sage, 1993).

Lewis-Beck, Michael S. and Tom Rice, *Forecasting Elections* (Washington, DC: Congressional Quarterly, 1992).

Lijphart, Arend. *Democracy in Plural Societies: A Comparative Exploration* (New Haven, CT: Yale University Press, 1977).

Lijphart, Arend. *Democracies: Patterns of Majoritarian and Consensus Government in Twenty-One Countries* (New Haven, CT: Yale University Press, 1984)

Linder, Wolf. *Swiss Democracy: Possible Solutions to Conflict in Multicultural Societies* (London: Macmillan, 1998).

Lipset, Seymour M. *Political Man* (New York: Doubleday, 1960).

Lipset, Seymour M. and Stein Rokkan. 'Cleavage Structures, Party Systems, and Voter Alignments: An Introduction', in S. M. Lipset and S. Rokkan (eds), *Party Systems and Voter Alignments* (New York: Free Press, 1967).

Listhaug, Ola. *Citizens, Parties and Norwegian Electoral Politics 1957–1985* (Tronheim: Tapir, 1989).

Lloyd, Henry D. *A Sovereign People* (London, 1906).

Locke, John. *Two Treatises of Government* (Cambridge: Cambridge University Press, 1988).

Logue, John and Erich Einhorn. *Modern Welfare States: Politics and Society in Social Democratic Scandinavia* (New York: Praeger, 1989).

Londregan, John and James Snyder. 'Comparing Committee and Floor Preferences', *Legislative Studies Quarterly*, vol. 19, no. 2. 1994.

Lowell, A. Lawrence. *Public Opinion and Popular Government* (New York: Longman, Green & Co., 1913).

Lowenstein, Daniel. 'Campaign Spending and Ballot Propositions: Recent Experience, Public Choice Theory and the First Amendment', *UCLA Law Review*, vol. 29, February 1982.

Lucas, John R. *Democracy and Political Participation* (London: Penguin, 1976).

Lupia, Arthur. 'Short-Cuts Versus Encyclopaedias: Information and Voting Behaviour in California's Insurance Reform Elections', *American Political Science Review*, vol. 88, 1994.

Luthardt, Wolfgang. *Direkte Demokratie: Ein Vergleich in Westeuropa* (Baden-Baden: Nomos Verlagsgesellschaft, 1994).

McAllister, Laura. 'The Welsh Devolution Referendum: Definitely, Maybe?' *Parliamentary Affairs*, vol. 51, no. 2, 1998.

Mclean, Iain. *Democracy and New Technology* (Cambridge: Polity Press, 1989).

McCartney, Patrick. 'The Referendum of 9 June', *Italian Politics: A Review*, vol. 7, 1992.

McClelland, J. S. *A History of Western Political Thought* (London: Routledge, 1996).

Macmillan, Gretchen. 'The Referendum, the Courts and Representative Democracy in Ireland', *Political Studies*, vol. 40, no. 1, 1992.

Madgwick, Peter and Diane Woodhouse. *The Law and Politics of the Constitution of the United Kingdom* (London: Harvester Wheatsheaf, 1995).

Madison, James, Alexander Hamilton and John Jay. *The Federalist Papers* (London: Penguin Classics, 1987).

Magleby, David B. *Direct Legislation: Voting on Ballot Propositions in the United States* (Baltimore, MD: Johns Hopkins University Press, 1984).

Magleby, David. 'Taking the Initiative: Direct Legislation and Direct Democracy in the 1980s', *Political Science and Politics*, vol. 21, no. 3, 1988.

Magleby, David. 'Direct Legislation in the United States', in Butler and Ranney (eds), *Referendums Around the World* (1994).

Maine, Henry Sumner. *Popular Government* (Indianapolis, IN: Liberty Fund, 1976).

Mainwaring, Scott. 'Democracy in Brazil and the Southern Cone', *Journal of Interamerican Studies and World Affairs*, vol. 37, no. 1, 1995.

Malberg, Raymond Carré de. 'Considerations theoretique sur la question de la combination du référendum avec la parlementarisme', *Revue du droit public et la science politique*, vol. 8, no. 4, 1931.

Manning, Maurice. 'Ireland', in Butler and Ranney (eds), *Referendums: A Comparative Study of Practice and Theory* (1978).

March, James and Johan P. Olsen. 'The New Institutionalism: Organizational Factors in Political Life', *American Political Science Review*, vol. 78, no. 3, 1984.

March, James and Johan P. Olsen. *Rediscovering Institutions* (New York: Free Press, 1989).

March, James and Johan P. Olsen. *Democratic Governance* (New York: Free Press, 1995).

Marques, Alvardo and Thomas B. Smith. 'Referendums in the Third World', *Electoral Studies*, vol. 3, no. 1, 1984.

Marradi, Alberto. 'Italy's Referendum on Divorce: Survey and Ecological Data', *European Journal of Political Research*, vol. 4, no. 1, 1976.

Matsusaka, John. 'The Economics of Direct Legislation', *Quarterly Journal of Economics*, vol. 107, no. 2, 1992.

Meadowcroft, J. and M. W. Taylor. 'Liberalism and the Referendum in British Political Thought 1890–1914', *Twentieth-Century British History*, vol. 1, no. 1, 1990.

Mendelsohn, Matthew and Andrew Parkin (eds). *Referendum Democracy: Citizens, Elites and Deliberation in Referendum Campaigns* (London: Palgrave, 2001).

Meny, Yves with Andrew Knapp. *Government and Politics in Western Europe: Britain, France, Italy and Germany* (Oxford: Oxford University Press, 1993).

Michels, Robert. *Political Parties: A Sociological Study of Oligarchical Tendencies of Modern Democracy* (New York: Dover Publications, 1959).

Miles, Richard. 'Australia's Constitutional Referendum', *Representation*, vol. 22, no. 4, 1998.

Mill, J. S. *The Letters of John Stuart Mill*, ed. Hugh S. R. Elliot, vols 1–2 (London: Longman, Green & Co., 1910).

Mill, John Stuart. 'A System of Logic', *The Collected Works of John Stuart Mill*, ed. R. M. Robson, vol. 7 (Toronto: University of Toronto Press, 1973).

Mill, John Stuart. 'Considerations on Representative Government', *John Stuart Mill: On Liberty and Other Writings*, ed. John Gray (Oxford: Oxford University Press, 1991).

Miller, Kenneth. 'Policy-Making by Referendum: The Danish Experience', *West European Politics*, vol. 5, no. 1, 1982.

Miller, Kenneth. 'The Role of the Courts in the Initiative Process – A Search for Standards', paper presented at the Annual Meeting of the American Political Science Association, 2–5 September 1999.

Mitchell, James. 'The Multi-Option Referendum: A Comparative Perspective', in

Allan Macartney (ed.), *Asking the People: The Referendum and Constitutional Change* (Edinburgh: Centre for the Study of Scottish Politics, 1992).

Mitchell, J., D. Denver, C. Pattie and H. Bochel. 'The Scottish Devolution Referendum', *Parliamentary Affairs*, vol. 51, no. 2, April 1998.

Mitteilungen und Bekanntmachen des Landwahlleitersd des Freistaates Bayern (Munich: Beyerisches Landesamt für Statistik, 1998).

Möckli, Silvano. *Direkte Demokratie: Fin Internationaler Vergleich* (Bern: Haubt, 1994).

Montesqieu, Baron de. *The Spirit of the Laws* (New York: Hafner Editions, 1949).

Morel, Laurence. 'Le Referendum: État des recherches', *Revue française de science politique*, vol. 42, no. 5, 1992a.

Morel, Laurence. 'Party Attitudes towards Referendums in Western Europe', *West European Politics*, vol. 16, no. 3, 1992b.

Morel, Laurence. 'France: Towards a Less Controversial Use of the Referendum', in Gallagher and Uleri (eds), *The Referendum Experience in Europe* (1996).

Morel, Laurence. 'The Rise of Government-Initiated Referendums in Consolidated Democracies', in M. Mendelsohn and A. Parkin (eds), *Referendum Democracy: Citizens Elites and Deliberations in Referendum Campaigns* (London: Palgrave, 2001).

Mueller, Dennis. *Public Choice 2* (Cambridge: Cambridge University Press, 1989).

Mulgan, Richard. *Politics in New Zealand*, 2nd edn (Auckland: Auckland University Press, 1990).

Munro, Willam (ed.). *The Initiative, Referendum and Recall* (New York: D. Appleton, 1912).

Mursweik, Dietrich. *Die Vervassungsgebende Gewalt nach der Grundgesetz für die Bundesrepublik Deutschland* (Berlin: Dunker & Humbolt, 1978).

Nairne, Patrick. 'The Conduct of Referendums', unpublished paper (1998).

Neidhart, Leonard. *Plebiszit und pluralitäre Demokratie: Eine Analyse der Funktion des schweizerischen Demokra tie* (Bern: Haupt, 1970).

Newton, Mike. 'The Peoples and the Regions of Spain', in David Bell (ed.), *Spanish Politics After Franco* (New York: St. Martin's, 1983).

Nidegger, Marie-Claude. 'La Participation en fonction des caractéritiques du scrutin et la compétence des citoyens', in Hans-Peter Kriesi (ed.), *Citoyenneté démocratie directe: compétence, participation et décision des citoyens suisses* (Zurich: Seismo, 1993).

Nielsen, Hans Jørgen. 'Voting Age of Eighteen Years Adopted by the Danish Folketing, Rejected by Popular Referendum', *Scandinavian Political Studies*, vol. 3, no. 3, 1979.

Nielsen, Hans Jørgen. *EF paa Valg* (Copenhagen: Columbus, 1992).

Nilson, Sten Sperre. 'Scandinavia', in Butler and Ranney (eds), *Referendums: A Comparative Study of Practice and Theory* (1978).

Nissen, Henrik S. 'Landet blev by', in Olaf Olsen (ed.), *Danmarkshistorien* (Copenhagen: Gyldendal & Politiken, 1991).

Nohlen, Dieter. 'Plebizitäre Demokratie', in Dieter Nohlen and Rainer-Olaf Schultze (eds), *Politikwissenchaft* (Munich: Nomos, 1985).

Nohlen, Dieter. 'Vergleichende Metode', in Dieter Nohlen and Rainer-Olaf Schultze (eds), *Politikwissenchaft* (1985).

Norton, Philip. *The Constitution in Flux* (Oxford: Oxford University Press, 1982).

Oakeshott, Michael. *Rationalism in Politics and Other Essays* (Indianapolis: Liberty Fund, 1991).

Oberholtzer, Elias. *The Referendum in America* (Philadelphia: University of Philadelphia Press, 1893).

O'Leary, Brendan. *The Good Friday Peace-Agreement: Power Sharing Plus* (London: Constitution Unit, 1998).

O'Mahony, Jane. 'The Irish Referendum Experience', *Representation*, vol. 35, no. 4, 1998.

Oliver, Quintin. *Working for Yes* (Belfast: Referendum Company 1998).

Olsen, Erling. 'Folkestyre og Demokrati', in Søren Bald (ed.), *Demokrati* (Krogerup: Forlaget Krogerup, 1996).

Olsen, David. 'Term-Limits Fail in Washington: The 1991 Battleground', in G. Benjamin and M. Malbin (eds), *Limiting Legislative Terms* (Washington, DC: Congressional Quarterly Press, 1992).

Olson, Mancur. *The Logic of Collective Action: Public Goods and the Theory of Groups* (Cambridge, MA: Harvard University Press, 1965).

Ostrogorsky, Morsei. *Democracy and the Organisation of Political Parties* (London: Macmillan, 1902).

Palmer, Jeffrey. *Unabridged Power: An Interpretation of New Zealand's Constitution and Government* (Oxford: Oxford University Press, 1987).

Papadopoulos, Yannis. 'Problematique de colloque: le point sur la démocracie directe', in Yannis Papadoupolos (ed.), *Présent et avenir de la démocratie directe: acte du colloque de l'Université de Lausanne* (Geneva: Georg Editeur SA, 1994).

Pappi, Franz Urban. 'Political Behaviour: Reasoning Voters and Multi-Party Systems', in Robert Goodin and Hans-Dieter Klingemann (eds), *The New Handbook of Political Science* (Oxford: Oxford University Press, 1996).

Pasquino, Gianfranco. 'The Electoral Reform Referendums', in Robert Leonardi and Fausto Anderlini (eds), *Italian Politics: A Review*, vol. 6 (London: Pinter Publishers, 1992).

Pateman, Carole. *Participation and Democratic Theory* (Cambridge: Cambridge University Press, 1970).

Peirce, Neal. 'The Indirect Way for Americans to Take the Initiative', *Sacramento Bee*, 12 February 1979.

Pelinka, Anton and Sylvia Greiderer. 'Austria: The Referendum as an Instrument of Internationalisation', in Gallagher and Uleri (eds), *The Referendum Experience in Europe* (1996).

Peters, B. Guy. *Comparative Politics: Theory and Methods* (Palgrave: London, 1998).

Pierce, Roy Henry Valen and Ola Listhaug. 'Referendum Voting Behaviour: The Norwegian and British Referenda on Membership of the European Community', *American Journal of Political Science*, vol. 27, no. 1, 1983.

Polsby Nelson W. and Aaron Wildavsky. *Presidential Elections: Strategies of American Electoral Politics* (New York: Charles Scribner's Sons, 1984).

Pommerhane, W. W. and F. Schneider. 'Does Government in a Representative Democracy Follow the Majority of the Voters?', in Horst Hanusch (ed.), *Anatomy of Government Deficiencies* (Berlin: Springer, 1983).

Popkin, S. L. *The Reasoning Voter* (Chicago, IL: Chicago University Press, 1991).

Popper, Karl. *The Poverty of Historicism* (London: Routledge & Kegan Paul, 1957).

Popper, Karl. *Conjectures and Refutations: The Growth of Scientific Knowledge* (London: Routledge & Kegan Paul, 1963).

Powell, G. Bingham. 'Voting Turnout in Thirty Democracies', in Richard Rose (ed.), *Electoral Participation: A Comparative Analysis* (London: Sage, 1980).

Powell, G. Bingham. *Contemporary Democracies. Participation, Stability and Violence* (Cambridge, MA: Harvard University Press, 1982).

Price, Charles M. 'Signing for Fun and Profit: The Business of Gathering Petition Signatures', *California Journal*, vol. 22, no. 4, 1992.

Przeworski, Adam and Henry Teune. *The Logic of Comparative Social Inquiry* (New York: Wiley Interscience, 1970).

Putnam, Robert. *Making Democracy Work: Civic Traditions in Modern Italy* (Princeton, NJ: Princeton University Press, 1991).

Qvortrup, Mads. 'Uruguay's Constitutional Referendum 8 December 1996', *Electoral Studies*, vol. 16, no. 4, 1997.

Qvortrup, Mads. 'Voter Knowledge and Participation', *Representation: Journal of Representative Democracy*, vol. 35, no. 4, 1998.

Qvortrup, Mads. 'Constitutional Implications of the Use of the Referendum', doctoral thesis, Oxford University, 1998.

Qvortrup, Mads. 'Checks and Balances in a Unicameral Parliament: The Case of the Danish Minority Referendum', *Journal of Legislative Studies*, vol. 6, no. 3, 2000.

Qvortrup, Mads. 'Denmark September 2000: The Campaign', in Mark Leonard and Tom Arbuthnott (eds), *Winning the Euro Referendum* (London: Foreign Policy Centre, 2001).

Qvortrup, Mads. 'The Danish Euro-Referendum in Comparative Perspective', in *Representation: Journal of Representative Democracy*, vol.38, no. 1 (2001).

Qvortrup, Mads. *The Political Philosophy of Jean-Jacques Rousseau: The Impossibility of Reason* (Manchester: Manchester University Press, 2003).

Qvortrup, Mads. 'In Search of Lost Time', *European Journal of Political Research*, vol. 30, no. 1, 2004.

Rait, R. S. *Memorials of A. V. Dicey* (London: Macmillan, 1925).

Rawls, John. *A Theory of Justice* (Oxford: Oxford University Press, 1973).

Rawls, John. *Political Liberalism* (New York: Columbia University Press, 1993).

Ranney Austin (ed.). *The Referendum Device* (Washington, DC: American Enterprise Institute, 1981).

Ranney, Austin. 'Regulating the Referendum', in Austin Ranney (ed.), *The Referendum Device* (1981).

Ranney, Austin. 'Non-Voting Is Not a Social Disease', *Public Opinion*, vol. 11, 1989.

Reit, Karlheinz and Anna Melich. *Eurobarometer 39*, March–April 1993.

Rentoul, John. *Tony Blair* (London: Warner Books, 1996).

Riker, William. *Liberalism Against Populism: A Confrontation between the Theory of Democracy and the Theory of Social Choice* (Prospect Heights, IL: Waveland Press, 1982).

Rouke, John T., Richard P. Hiskes and Cyrus Ernesto Ziràkzadeh. *Direct Democracy and International Politics: Deciding International Issues through Referendums* (Boulder, CO: Rienner, 1992).

Rousseau, Jean-Jacques. *A Discourse on the Origin of Inequality*, in Jean-Jacques Rousseau, *The Social Contract and the Discourses*, trans G. D. H. Cole (London: Everyman, 1993).

Rousseau, Jean-Jacques. *The Social Contract*, in Jean Jacques Rousseau, *The Social Contract and the Discourses* (1993).

Ruin, Olaf. *Folkomröstning om medlemskab in EG – ett diskussionsunterlag* (Stockholm: Justitiedepartementet, 1992).

Ruin, Olaf. 'Sweden: The Referendum as an Instrument for Defusing Political Issues', in Gallagher and Uleri, *The Referendum Experience in Europe* (1996).

Santerre, R. E. 'Representative versus Direct Democracy: A Tiebaut Test of Relative Performance', *Public Choice*, vol. 48, no. 1, 1986.

Särlvik, Bo. *Opinionsbilningen vid folkomröstningen 1957* (Stockholm: Justitie-departamentet, 1959).

Sartori, Giovanni. *Parties and Party Systems* (Cambridge: Cambridge University Press, 1976).

Sartori, Giovanni. *The Theory of Democracy Revisited* (Chatham: Chatham House, 1987)

Sartori, Giovanni. *Comparative Constitutional Engineering* (London: Macmillan, 1989).

Schmidt, David. 'United States' Direct Democracy in Perspective', paper presented at the annual meeting of the Direct Democracy Research Group, American Political Science Association, Washington, DC, August 1980.

Schmidt, David. *Citizen Lawmakers: The Ballot Initiative Revolution* (Temple: Temple University Press, 1989).

Schumpeter, Joseph. *Capitalism, Socialism and Democracy* (London: Allen & Unwin, 1976).

Seldon, Anthony. 'Conservative Century', in Anthony Seldon and Stuart Ball (eds), *Conservative Century: The Conservative Party since 1990* (Oxford: Oxford University Press, 1994).

Seyd, Ben. *The Electoral Reform Referendums in New Zealand: Lessons for the UK* (London: Constitution Unit, 1998).

Sharlet, Robert. 'Transitional Constitutionalism', *Wisconsin International Law Journal*, vol. 14, no. 3, 1996.

Sharp, Clifford. *The Case Against the Referendum*, Fabian Tract 151 (London: Fabian Society, 1911).

Shockley, John. 'Direct Democracy Campaign Finance and the Courts: Can Corruption, Undue Influence and Voter Confidence Be Found?' *University of Miami Law Review*, vol. 39, no. 2, 1985.

Sidgewick, Henry. *Elements of Politics* (London: Macmillan, 1891).

Sinott, Richard. *Irish Voters Decide* (Manchester: Manchester University Press, 1995).

Siune, Karen. 'Mass Media and Their Agenda Setting Function', in Karen Siune and Peter Gundelach (eds), *From Voters to Participants* (Århus: Politica, 1992a).

Siune, Karen. *EF paa Dagsordenen* (Århus: Politica: 1992b).

Slater, Wendy. 'Russia's Plebiscite on a New Constitution', *Radio Free Europe–Radio Liberty*, vol. 3, no. 3, 1996.

Smith, Gordon. 'The Referendum and Political Change', *Government and Opposition*, summer, 1975.

Smith, Gordon. 'The Functional Properties of the Referendum', *European Journal of Political Research*, vol. 4, no.1, 1976.

Sniderman, R., T. Brody and P. E. Tetlock. *Reasoning and Choice* (New York: Cambridge University Press, 1991).

Sørensen, Max. *Elementær Statsforfatningsret* (Copenhagen: Gyldendal, 1973).

Spotts, F. and T. Weiser. *Italy: A Difficult Democracy. A Survey of Italian Politics* (Cambridge: Cambridge University Press, 1986).

Standing Committee on Legal and Constitutional Affairs. *Constitutional Change* (Canberra, Australia: House of Representatives, 1997).

Stepan, A. C. and J. J. Linz. *Problems of Democratic Transition and Consolidation* (Baltimore, MD: Johns Hopkins University Press, 1996).

Stepan, Alfred and Cindy Skach. 'Presidentialism and Parliamentarianism in Comparative Perspective', in Juan J. Linz and Arthuro Valenzuala (eds), *The Failure of Presidential Democracy: Comparative Perspectives*, vol. 1 (Baltimore, MD: Johns Hopkins University Press, 1994).

Stockwin, J. A. *Japan: Divided Politics in a Growth Economy*, 2nd edn (London: Norton, 1982).

Strachey, J. St Loe. 'An Appeal to the Lords', *National Review*, vol. 22, 1893–94.

Strachey, J. St Loe. *The Referendum: A Handbook to the Poll of the People, the Referendum, and Democratic Right of Veto on Legislation* (London: Fischer Unwin Ltd, 1924).

Suksi, Markku. *Bringing in the People: A Comparison of the Constitutional Forms and Practices of the Referendum* (Dortrecht: Martinus Nijhoff, 1993).

Sullivan, J. W. *Direct Legislation by the Citizenship through Initiatives and Referendums* (New York: True Nationalist Publishing, 1893).

Sunstein, J. 'Special Interest Groups in American Public Law', *Stanford Law Review*, vol. 29, 1985.

Svenson, Palle. 'Denmark: The Referendum as Minority Protection', in M. Gallagher and Pier Vincenzo Uleri (eds), *The Referendum Experience in Europe* (London: Macmillan, 1996).

Szporluk, Roman. *The Political Thought of Thomas G. Masaryk* (New York: Columbia University Press, 1981).

Talliran, Laura. *Direct Democracy* (Los Angeles, CA: People's Lobby, 1977).

Thatcher, Margaret. *Path to Power* (London: Harper Collins 1995).

Thompson, Dennis. *John Stuart Mill and Representative Government* (Princeton, NJ: Princeton University Press, 1976).

Thucydides. *The Peleponesian War* (Penguin: London, 1954).

Tocqueville, Alexis de. *Democracy in America*, trans. George Lawrence (New York: HarperPerennial, 1988).

Tonsgaard, Ole. 'A Theoretical Model of Referendum Behaviour', in Siune and Gundelach (eds), *From Voters to Participants* (1992.

Tossini, T. C. and E. Tower. 'The Textile Bill of 1985: Determinants of Congressional Voting Patterns', *Public Choice*, vol. 54, no. 1, 1988.

Treschel, Alexander and Hans-Peter Kriesi. 'Switzerland: The Referendum as Centrepiece of the Political System', in Gallagher and Uleri (eds), *The Referendum Experience in Europe* (1996).

Troitzsch, Kalus. 'Volksbegehren und Volksentscheid: Eine vergliechende Analyse directdemokratischer Verfassungsinstitutionen unter besonderer Berück-sichtung der Bundesrepublik und der Schweiz', unpublished PhD thesis, Meisenheim am Glan, 1979.

Tullock, Gordon. *Towards a Mathematics of Politics* (Ann Arbor: Michigan University Press, 1967).

Tvevad, J. 'Danske Vaelgeres Vetoret', *Statsvetenskablig Tidsskrift*, vol. 8, no.2, 1964.

Uleri, P. V. 'The Deliberative Referendum of June 1985 in Italy', *Electoral Studies*, vol. 4, no. 3, 1985.

Uleri, P. V. 'Italy: Referendums and Initiatives: From Origins to the Crisis of the Republic', in Gallagher and Uleri (eds), *The Referendum Experience in Europe* (1996).

Uleri, P. V. 'Introduction', in Gallagher and Uleri (eds), *The Referendum Experience in Europe* (1996).

Updike, John. *Memories of the Ford Administration* (New York: Alfred Knopf, 1992).

Vanhanen, Tatu. *Prospects for Democracy* (London: Routledge, 1997).

Walker, Geoffrey de Q. *The Initiative and Referendum: The People's Law* (Sydney: Centre for Independent Study, 1987).

Wamburgh, Sarah. *Plebiscites Since the War* (Washington, DC: Carnegie Endowment for International Peace, 1993).

Ware Alan. *Political Parties and Party Systems* (Oxford, Oxford University Press, 1996).

Warren, Preston. *Masaryk's Democracy* (London: Allen & Unwin, 1941).

Weaver, D. 'Media Agenda-Setting and Elections: Voter Involvement or Alienation?', *Political Communication*, vol. 11, no. 4, 1994.

Welsh, W. P. 'The Effectiveness of Expenditures in State Legislative Races', *American Politics Quarterly*, vol. 4, 1976.

Whitehead, Laurence. 'Democratization Studies', in Robert Goodin and Hansdieter Klingemann (eds), *A New Handbook of Political Science* (Oxford: Oxford University Press, 1996).

Wilcox, Delos F. *Government by All the People: Or the Initiative, the Referendum, the Recall as Instruments of Democracy* (New York, Macmillan, 1912).

Williams, R. J. and J. R. Greenaway. 'The Referendum in British Politics: A Dissenting View', *Parliamentary Affairs*, vol. 26, no. 2, 1975.

Wood, Roger. *The Death Penalty* (Oxford: Clarendon Press, 1996).

Worre, Torben. *Dansk Vælgeradfærd* (Copenhagen: Akademisk Forlag, 1987).

Worre, Torben. 'Danish Voters at the Cross-Roads: The Danish Referendum of February 1986 on the EC Reform Package', *Journal of Common Market Studies*, vol. 26, no. 4, 1988.

Wright, Tony. *Citizens and Subjects: An Essay on British Politics* (London: Routledge, 1994).

Wright, Tony (ed.). *The British Political Process* (London: Routledge, 2000).

Wright, Vincent. 'France', in Butler and Ranney (eds), *Referendums. A Comparative Study of Practice and Theory* (1978).

Wright, Vincent. *The Government and Politics of France*, 3rd edn (London: Unwin, 1989)

Wyller, Thomas Chr. *Skal Folket Bestemme?* (Oslo: Universitets Forlaget, 1992).

Wyller, Thomas Chr. 'Norway: Six Exceptions to the Rule', in Gallagher and Uleri (eds), *The Referendum Experience in Europe* (1996).

Zahle, Henrik. *Dansk Statsforfatningsret*, vol. 2: *Regering, Forvaltning og Dom* (Copenhagen: Christian Ejlers, Forlag, 1989).

Zimmerman, Joseph E. *Participatory Democracy: Populism Revisited* (New York: Praeger, 1986).

Zisk, Betty. *Money, Media, and Grass Roots: State Ballot Issues and the Electoral Process* (Newbury Park, CA: Sage, 1987).

Zucher, Arnold J. 'The Hitler Referenda', *American Political Science Review*, vol. 29, no. 2, 1935.

Index

Churchill, Winston, 95–6, 102
Cicero, 103
citizen-initiated votes *see* initiatives
Citizens Against Rent Control v. *City of
    Berkeley*, 141
Citizens for Congressional Reform,
    161
'civic reserve' theory, 28–31, 133
civil liberties, 18
Coca-Cola (company), 154
Colorado, 18
Commager, Henry Steele, 17
Communist Party, 17, 19, 97, 127
comparative politics, 3, 25, 165
compromise, political, 10, 13–15, 20,
    129
Condorcet, Marie-Jean de, 125
consensus, political, 12, 16, 23, 81, 123,
    125
consequentiality, logic of, 98
conservatism of voters, 4, 77–84, 137
Conservative Party, 108–11
constitutional change, 47–8, 73–6,
    83–8, 94–5, 107, 113–14
constitutional safeguards, refer-
    endums as, 90–1, 94–5, 98–9,
    115–18
constitutions, written and un-written,
    58
Cook, Robin, 109–10
corporatism, 160
corruption, 142
Coughlin, C. C., 145
Cowen, Brian, 66
Craxi, Benito, 81
Cree, Nathan, 13, 46, 55
Crisp, L. F., 74
Cronin, Thomas, 153
cross-cutting cleavages, 21
Cunningham, George, 106, 168
Currie, Edwina, 109–10
Curzon, Lord, 59

Dahl, Robert, 2, 140
Dalgaard, Bertel, 121
Davis, Quentin, 109–10
de Valera, Eamon, 64, 76, 94
de Valera, Sile, 71
deadlocks, political, 85–8
death penalty, 63, 80

decision-making referendums,
    104, 111
democracy, definitions of, 9–10, 22,
    137, 164–5; *see also* representative
    democracy
democratic institutions, criteria
    needing to be met by, 2–4
Denmark, 2, 15–16, 20–1, 30–4, 37–9,
    41, 64–5, 73, 80–1, 95–101, 104–7,
    112, 117–25, 131–2, 153, 157,
    165–70
Denver, David, 114
devolution, 20, 64, 102, 105–14, 137,
    157–8, 164, 168
Dicey, A. V., 4, 12, 46–61, 77, 89–91,
    94–5, 98–101, 115–16, 122, 126, 131,
    136
Dion, Stephane, 166
direct democracy, 6–14, 17–18, 24–6,
    40, 44–6, 51–2, 55–7, 126, 135, 140,
    143, 145, 162–3
disclosure laws, 161, 163
discussion, democracy as, 10, 14, 42
divorce, 77–80, 97, 127–31, 165, 170
Donovan, Todd, 17, 21, 42–3, 142–4,
    149, 154
'double majority' requirement, 18–19,
    73, 167, 172
Downs, Anthony, 42, 150

East Timor, 170, 173
economic issues, referendums on,
    80–2
Economist, The, 9, 108, 110, 139
education, political, 54–5
eligible majority requirements, 168–72
elites and elitism, 11, 20, 22–3, 32, 35,
    39, 41, 43, 50, 77, 80, 90–1, 95, 131,
    133, 136, 174
emotive issues in politics, 20–3
entrenchment, 58
environmental issues, 144, 146, 160
Eriksen, Erik, 122
Erlander, Tage, 81, 128
ethnic divisions, 22, 42, 165, 167, 170,
    173
Euro currency, 109–12
Eurobarometer surveys, 38, 67
European integration process,
    65–6, 73, 88, 162